Shakespeare the Director

PLATE III

JOHANNES DE WITT: *Observations on London, c. 1596*

(*see Plate IV A*)

Shakespeare the Director

tectum

poeticus

sedilia

orchestra

mimorum
ædes

ingressus

proscenium

planities sive arena

JOHANNES DE WITT: *Observations on London, c. 1596*
(Bibliotheek der Rijksuniversiteit, Utrecht, MS. 842)

Shakespeare
the Director

Ann Pasternak Slater

Fellow of St Anne's College, Oxford

THE HARVESTER PRESS · SUSSEX

BARNES & NOBLE BOOKS · NEW JERSEY

First published in Great Britain in 1982 by
THE HARVESTER PRESS LIMITED
Publisher: John Spiers
16 Ship Street, Brighton, Sussex
and in the USA by
BARNES & NOBLE BOOKS
81 Adams Drive, Totowa, New Jersey 07512

© Ann Pasternak Slater, 1982

British Library Cataloguing in Publication Data
Slater, Ann Pasternak
   Shakespeare the director.
    1. Shakespeare – William – Dramatic production
    I. Title
    822.3'3   PR3091

   ISBN 0-7108-0446-6

Library of Congress Cataloging in Publication Data
Slater, Ann.
   Shakespeare, the director.

   Includes bibliographical references.
    1. Shakespeare, William, 1564–1616—Technique.
  2. Shakespeare, William, 1564–1616—Dramatic production.
  3. Theater—Production and direction.   I. Title.
  PR2997.G4S57   1982   822.3'3   82-6704
  ISBN 0-389-20304-1   AACR2

Typeset in 10/11½ pt Bembo by
Rowland Phototypesetting Ltd
Bury St Edmunds, Suffolk
Printed in Great Britain by
Mansell Ltd, Witham, Essex

Дорогой моей Маме

These little things in Shakespeare are not accidents.
A. C. Bradley: *Shakespearean Tragedy*

Contents

A note on the texts

Quotations from Shakespeare's works are taken from Charlton Hinman's Norton Facsimile of *The First Folio of Shakespeare* (New York 1968); the Shakespeare Quarto Facsimiles, prepared by W. W. Greg and C. Hinman (Oxford and London, 1939–75), and, where necessary, the Shakspere-Quarto Facsimiles, prepared by C. Praetorius and W. Griggs (1880–91). The choice of text for each play is based on the conclusions of W. W. Greg: *The Shakespeare First Folio* (Oxford 1969); my sole criterion in each case is to use the text supposedly closest to the author's manuscript. The texts chosen are listed below.

References for quotations from Shakespeare's plays give act and scene numbers, followed, as appropriate, either by the Folio Total Line Number, or, in the case of the Quartos, by Q (or Q2, if the second Quarto is quoted) and the page signature. References to the Bad Quartos give Q (or Q1, if the second Quarto provides the authoritative text), or O (in the case of *The True Tragedy*), and the signature only, when their act and scene divisions are erratic. In the notes, references without accompanying quotations are made, when possible, to the First Folio, which I have assumed to be the more readily available, and in which the line in question can be identified. This was not, of course, possible in those cases where the passage referred to stands in the Quarto alone.

Literals and punctuation are silently emended when necessary; abbreviations are silently expanded; all stage directions are centred and italicised; faulty signatures in the Quartos are silently corrected. Lineation is not altered, but the initial letters of verse lines are silently capitalised. Speech headings are not normalised, since they can be authorial and of interest. However, for the sake of clarity, their spellings are modernised and abbreviations expanded. All textual emendations are enclosed in square brackets, and these are only introduced between Quarto and Folio variants (references to both are given), or if they are generally accepted.

Shakespeare's sources are quoted from G. Bullough: *Narrative and Dramatic Sources of Shakespeare*, I–VIII (1957–75). The plays' chronology has been assumed to be that proposed by E. K. Chambers: *William Shakespeare* (Oxford 1930), I.270–1. For details of all other works referred to, see the Bibliography (p. 231). In all references, the place of publication is London, unless otherwise stated.

Texts used

Two Gentlemen of Verona	F
Venus and Adonis	Q (1593)
The Winter's Tale	F

Acknowledgements

I could not have begun this book without a Junior Research Fellowship from Lady Margaret Hall, Oxford. I could not have finished it without a term's maternity leave from St Anne's College, which I spent surreptitiously hatching the final chapters. I am most grateful to Emrys Jones and Richard Proudfoot for correction and advice in the early stages, and to Professor Harold Jenkins for generously criticising the finished work with great shrewdness and good humour. Above all, I shall always be indebted to Miss K. M. Lea, who first introduced me to the English Renaissance, and whose truly Elizabethan courtesy and gentleness have remained a permanent example to me.

Abbreviations

Bullough	G. Bullough, ed.: *Narrative and Dramatic Sources of Shakespeare* I–VIII (1957–75)
ELH	*Journal of English Literary History*
E & S	*Essays and Studies*
F	*The First Folio of Shakespeare*, The Norton Facsimile, prepared by Charlton Hinman (New York 1968).
MLR	*Modern Language Review*
M. Phil.	*Modern Philology*
OED	*Oxford English Dictionary*
PMLA	*Publications of the Modern Language Association of America*
Q or Q1	The first Quarto of a given play
Q2	The second Quarto of a given play
Ren. Dr.	*Renaissance Drama*
RES	*Review of English Studies*
RORD	*Research Opportunities in Renaissance Drama*
SD	Stage Direction
SFF	W. W. Greg: *The Shakespeare First Folio* (Oxford, 1969)
SH	Speech Heading
Shk. Studies	*Shakespeare Studies*
S. Phil.	*Studies in Philology*
SQ	*The Shakespeare Quarterly*
SRO	*Shakespearean Research and Opportunities*
SS	*Shakespeare Survey*
TES	*Times Educational Supplement*
Tilley	M. P. Tilley: *A Dictionary of Proverbs in England in the Sixteenth and Seventeenth Centuries* (Michigan 1950)
TLS	*Times Literary Supplement*
W. Shk.	E. K. Chambers: *William Shakespeare* I–II (Oxford, 1930)

Introduction

This book is a study of Shakespeare's direction of his plays, analysing the implications of theatrical effects specifically engineered by him.

Its origins lie in Sir W. W. Greg's classic work, *The Shakespeare First Folio*, which first brought home to me how many of Shakespeare's own stage directions can be identified, and distinguished from those of the original playhouse book-keepers and the actor-reporters. My sense of revelation was intense. Apparently insignificant details of staging suddenly hummed with Shakespeare's unobtrusive authority. Enobarbus may tell us that Cleopatra is a gypsy as well as a queen, that he has seen her hop forty paces through the public street, but this remains mere poetic reminiscence, an idea of character as drowsily pictorial as Yeats's Helen of Troy, whose feet 'Practise a tinker shuffle / Picked up on a street'. The violence of Shakespeare's vision of Cleopatra becomes clear only with his own stage directions to her first scene with the Messenger, from *Strikes him downe* to *Draw a knife*. This harridan Queen is to be no poetic hyperbole, but palpable stage fact.

Further, less spectacular insights are afforded by the non-authorial stage directions of the original Quartos and the First Folio. Folio texts based on prompt-annotated copy afford minor insights into stage practice; more illuminating are the Bad Quartos of the actor-reporters. Although their dialogue is garbled, their directions contain fascinating glimpses of Elizabethan stage practice. On their evidence, for instance, we can infer that the actors embodied the acts mooted in their words, occasionally added the stage symbol that concretised a verbal metaphor, and, in the history plays, added accurate historical details Shakespeare had ignored. The long-stagnating debate on the formalism versus naturalism of the Elizabethan actor can be partially resolved by a study of the Bad Quartos, and of their stage directions in particular.

Richly suggestive as the original stage directions proved to be, they are far outshadowed by the even richer mass of Shakespeare's indirect stage directions – the oblique imperatives of the dialogue.

Here again the authorial control is ubiquitous and absolute, if only
the actor is to carry out the implicit instructions of his words:

Old Countess	You know Hellen I am a mother to you.
Helen	Mine honorable Mistris.
Old Countess	Nay a mother, why not a mother? when I sed a mother
	Me thought you saw a serpent, what's in mother,
	That you start at it?
	(*All's Well* I.iii.461ff)

However, it is curiously difficult to sustain the imaginative effort of
visualising all the actions the plays demand. From school onwards
our training is still to read Shakespeare primarily as poetry rather
than drama, and details of staging are habitually ignored. And yet,
by focusing on these, the plays jump to life again, with even more
vitality than the specific stage directions require. New insights of
every kind arise. Nor are they limited to details of characterisation,
or the mere trivia of stage presentation. A number of unifying
themes and patterns emerge.

Of basic importance is the theme of seeming. Shakespeare's contemporaries conventionally dismissed all aspects of deceptive outer
show; with greater logic and originality, Shakespeare extended the
cliché to all the theatre's necessarily external means of communication. Drama depends on show, the heard and the seen, but speech,
costume and gesture can all be used to lie. Hence the Shakespearean
moral elevation of the theatrical ciphers of silence and nakedness.
Seeming is the single dominant theme underlying much of
Shakespeare's stage practice, and its rationale recurs throughout this
book. It, for instance, lies behind Shakespeare's curious self-
limitation in the early Lavinia of *Titus Andronicus*, who is robbed of
the actor's two main means of communication, being virtually
incapable of gesture (she has no hands), and quite incapable of speech
(she has no tongue). Lavinia is a typically flamboyant piece of early
theatrical experimentation, original even to absurdity. Shakespeare's discretion refined with age, and Lavinia's virtues are later
reincarnated in the low-voiced Cordelia, whose loving silence has
more power to move, if less to startle and repel.
    Such examples of Shakespeare's technical development are a
further unifying theme. The more obvious elements of theatrical
technique show his swift progress from experimentation in the
earliest plays to controlled expertise in the polished successes of the
middle period. It is curious, however, that this upward graph of

technical accomplishment is not maintained thereafter. In the vaster conceptions and more esoteric experimentation of the later plays, standard dramaturgical skills are ignored or clumsily dispatched in a manner that contrasts poorly with Shakespeare's earlier work.

This decline is most evident in the conventional techniques shared with his contemporaries, while in the more idiosyncratic details of his art Shakespeare continues to learn from himself, constantly reapplying and refining the lessons of the past. To take only a small, largely linguistic example: in *Julius Caesar*, Antony undermines his praise of the conspirators by his ironic over-repetition of 'honourable men'. In *Othello*, Shakespeare appropriates Antony's trick, and many of the cast refer repeatedly to 'honest Iago', with no consciousness of irony. The device is now that of the author, not one of his characters, the irony one that takes a full play to emerge. What was originally a mere rhetorical trope has been extended into a theatrical technique.

Such a commerce between the rhetorical and theatrical raises what is undoubtedly the most important single theme to emerge from this study – the emblematic significance of much of Shakespeare's stage action, and its crucial relationship to his verbal imagery.

It is obvious enough that Shakespeare shared with his contemporaries a certain range of symbolic actions, which could stage abstract ideas in a concrete, visually striking way. A simple example would be the traditional use of the different stage levels, elevation in the gallery carrying connotations of the ticklish glory of the top of Fortune's wheel, while the trap was naturally associated with earth, the grave, and all hell below. Such traditional symbols are generally accepted and exploited only in Shakespeare's earliest work, his tendency thereafter being to modify and invert the stage cliché. To understand such later sophisticated reversals properly, their earlier, conventional forms must also be analysed.

Shakespeare did not only exploit traditional stage symbols; he also evolved a rich stage language of his own. He rarely demands some detail of stage presentation that has no significance, although this ranges from the naturalistic to the emblematic. From the very earliest stages of this study, the mere tabulation of all Shakespeare's stage directions, whether explicit or oblique, my curiosity was continually teased by the problem of rationale. *Why* should Shakespeare make old Hamlet's Ghost stalk off, 'offended'? *Why* should he choose to make Lucio unmuffle the Duke at the end of *Measure for Measure*? *Why* should he engineer the absurd scene in

Cymbeline, where Imogen mistakes the headless Cloten for her husband? Answers offered themselves in a variety of ways and I have tried to be equally flexible in my approach. Some visual images are common to Shakespeare's contemporaries, with whom fruitful comparison can be made. Sometimes the stage symbol is peculiar to its play, and needs to be interpreted in terms of its immediate dramatic setting. Most often it has a broad significance that remains approximately constant throughout the canon, and its implications are best explored by comparison with its use elsewhere in Shakespeare. Hence the structure of this book, which moves from one general chapter basic to the rest, on the direction of action through speech, to specific studies of the essential stuff of staging – recurrent actions like handshakes, kissing and kneeling, and the stage equipment of properties, costumes, and different stage levels. (Much as I would have liked it, the inclusion of two completed chapters on the use of sound effects and lights would have swollen the book beyond all reasonable compass.)

Furthermore, this teeming symbolic language recurs in both a verbal and a visual form. The implications of a stage image are often expanded in the accompanying dialogue: so, for instance, all the fleeting visual suggestions of Othello's entry, candle in hand, to Desdemona, are made explicit in his meditation, 'Put out the light, and then put out the light . . .' A visual image can moreover draw together a whole sequence of precedent linguistic images. So, to take another obvious example, Richard II's descent from Flint Castle walls into Bolingbroke's custody is not only given its immediate poetic gloss in his self-comparison to Phaeton, but stage image and poetic commentary together mark the culmination of all the images of sun and decline running through the rest of the play. There is nothing random or accidental about this exercise of dramaturgical art.

Such an impression of conscious control is further confirmed by a study of Shakespeare's sources, most of which were prose or verse narratives, rather than plays. Shakespeare shows a striking, consistent tendency to modify his source, or to invent, in order to introduce stage business which can crystallise the play's themes in visual terms. This, even more than the simplification of narrative or compression of time, is the essential skill of the dramatic translator. Nowadays the intentional fallacy has become a familiar critical trap, which the wary commentator retreats from all too readily, reverting instead to a glib confidence that no authorial intentions can be identified, leaving producer and critic equally free. So Jonathan

Miller, in interview: 'the author's intentions are beyond guess. There is no way of finding out what he intended . . .'[1] But this too is a palpable error. Not only do we have the incontrovertible imperatives of Shakespeare's stage directions; we have too the secondary evidence of the sources. How did Shakespeare 'intend' Coriolanus to die? His stage direction tells us that he required a death of unparalleled indignity for a martial Roman: *Draw both the Conspirators, and kils Martius, who falles, Auffidius stands on him.* Nor was this death just a historical accident, for Shakespeare has specifically altered his source to introduce it. Plutarch merely tells us that 'they all fell upon him, and killed him in the market place, none of the people once offering to rescue him.' In so far as stage action is concerned, the author's intentions are clear enough, though their further interpretation is another matter. I have, therefore, habitually compared stage action in the plays with the sources, in order to identify the telling Shakespearean alterations, prior to interpretation.

However, there is also a strong *sub*conscious element in Shakespeare's use of both verbal and visual imagery. The same images can recur from play to play, now in a linguistic, now an enacted form. So, to take another straightforward example, in *Hamlet* Claudius tries to comfort himself with a mere poetic image:

> . . . what if this cursed hand
> Were thicker then it selfe with brothers blood,
> Is there not raine enough in the sweete Heauens
> To wash it white as snowe?
> (*Hamlet* III.iii. Q2:I)

But his optimistic fallacy is later *staged* in the pathetic action of Lady Macbeth's sleep-walking scene ('Looke how she rubbes her hands . . .'). Furthermore, the stage image of this scene has been verbally prepared for in her exchange with Macbeth at the time of the murder, with all its sad irony: 'A little Water cleares vs of this deed. / How easie is it then?' One echo is conscious and organised; the other, presumably not.

There are no easy rules for this intercourse between the spoken and the staged. Shakespeare does not show a convenient progression from crude stage symbols to their subtler evocation in a poetic form, nor from dogmatic verbal images to their more subtly suggested visual equivalents. He appears rather to have drawn on a stock of images, to which he would return in play after play in whatever form. Nor are these confined to clear single images, like the futile hand-washing of guilt, which has its obvious biblical original. The

associative Shakespearean image-cluster was first illustrated by
Walter Whiter in 1794, and only thoroughly analysed by Caroline
Spurgeon and her successors in the twentieth century. It is clear,
however, that such clusters span the verbal-visual range. I have
found several examples of idiosyncratic image-clusters that occur in
a verbal form in one play, in a staged form in another, while *disiecta
membra* of the same cluster reappear still elsewhere in a partial form,
sometimes spoken, sometimes staged. The inference is clear:
Shakespeare thinks in images, but their form depends on the moment.

Who can tell the dancer from the dance? Drama is composed of
both the spoken and the seen. Inevitably, then, this study has
combined a theatrical with a linguistic approach, for the two can
hardly be separated. Johnson's partisan definition, 'A dramatick
exhibition is a book recited with concomitants that encrease or
diminish its effect',[2] divorces the two elements of drama that are
indissolubly one.

The need for stage-orientated study of Shakespeare's imagery has
become something of a critical cliché in the past three decades. First
canvassed by R. A. Foakes in 1952, such an approach reached early
fruition in M. Charney's *Shakespeare's Roman Plays* (1960), perhaps
the best extended critical work to combine theatrical with linguistic
perception, albeit in the specialised area of a single group of plays and
with a preponderantly linguistic bias. However, after a flurry of
critical excitement, and a number of manifestos theoretically extol-
ling the validity of such an approach, it appears to be dying a lingering
and undeserved death. By the mid-1970s, its most enthusiastic
propagandists had turned to the attack, leaving what should have
been a crucial way of reading Shakespeare with a number of articles,
and a few books to its name.[3]

Perhaps this decline can be attributed to one cause in particular.
Most approaches to Shakespeare are necessarily specialised, with
inevitable limitations. Studies of the Elizabethan stage tend to be
concerned with its historical reconstruction, while interpretation of
its emblematic use lies outside the historian's brief. Theatrical history is concerned with post-Elizabethan staging of Shakespeare,
where the interest naturally lies in the variations in staging from age
to age, rather than a pedantic evaluation of the producers' fidelity to
Shakespeare's minutest demands. Analysis of Shakespeare's stage
directions and speech headings has remained almost exclusively
bibliographical, while the literary critic refers to a few old favourites

(*Enter . . . Hamlet, Cum Alijs* or Coriolanus's *Holds her by the hand silent*), and is generally uninformed about their textual status. Work on the sources is usually concerned with the identification of new sources and verbal parallels, while their translation into theatrical terms, and the insights this can afford into Shakespeare's theatrical techniques, go unregarded. Studies of Shakespeare's stage symbolism tend to take isolated moments, single plays or groups of plays, and are undermined by a consequent weakness: an ignorance of Shakespeare's standard vocabulary of stage action, and its meaning as evident from recurrent usages throughout the canon.[4]

Shakespearean criticism is not only bedevilled by its proliferation into a number of specialised fields, but by the learning of each discipline. It is a daunting task for the literary critic to familiarise himself with the mass of unresolved scholarship surrounding textual, bibliographical and historical questions. Yet this learning can also betray its own proponents. The iconographic approach is one of the most stimulating to have emerged in recent years: at its best, it can identify and elucidate visual effects with an authority and brilliance denied to the artistically unlettered critic. But a lot of learning is a dangerous thing, as Dieter Mehl points out:

It has become rather fashionable in recent years to point out the emblematic or iconographic aspects of Elizabethan staging. This approach was in many ways a necessary reaction against a merely literary interpretation of the plays, but it is in itself not free from a certain bookishness and some of its general results seem to me more relevant to the study than to the stage although often the opposite is claimed . . . Many of the iconographic associations pointed out by scholars in recent years would probably be no more evident to the average Elizabethan spectator than image-clusters or verbal ambiguities brought to light by literary critics.

Mehl's reservations are echoed by J. M. Steadman.[5] Both stress the other recurrent error of the iconographic school – its identification of icons not specifically suggested by the author, or evoked by him in a verbal but not enacted form. Steadman and Mehl were the best original proponents of the iconographic approach and write with the authority of the disillusioned intimate.

In this book I have tried to avoid the dangers of over-specialisation by drawing freely on established scholarship for information on the texts, the sources, and the Elizabethan and Jacobean stage. Above all, I have tried to take Shakespeare as my guide, using the glosses he provides for the actions he has required. It would be gratifying if some of the suggestions made here were of interest to the Shakespearean producer. But the theatre cannot, and should not, stand still: it is not its function to propagate historically accurate, academic reproductions of Shakespeare's plays. My prime aim has been to awaken the reader to Shakespeare's manipulation of theatrical effects, and to bring him to an understanding and appreciation of them.

CHAPTER 1

Action and expression

Theory

What doe we with our hands? . . . And with our head? . . . What doe we with our eye-lids? and with our shoulders? . . . there is no motion, nor jesture that doth not speake, and speakes in a language very easie, and without any teaching to be understood.

(Montaigne: *An Apologie of Raymond Sebond*)

'Words move . . .' – and after words, deeds: gesture is the dramatist's second means of communication. Shakespeare, of course, was well aware of the theoretical power of action, and makes frequent reference to it from his earliest work. In Lucrece's picture of Troy, Nestor holds his audience by 'Making such sober action with his hand, / That it beguild attention, charm'd the sight.'[1] Later the same point is embellished with a wincing pun, when Volumnia urges Coriolanus to go to the people, cap in hand, 'Thy Knee bussing the stones: for in such businesse / Action is eloquence, and the eyes of th'ignorant / More learned then the eares.'[2] The assumption is so basic, that it recurs in incidental images and parallels: 'The head is not more natiue to the hart / *The hand more instrumentall to the mouth* / Then is the throne of Denmarke to thy father'; 'There was speech in their dumbnesse, Language in their very gesture'; even the Roman assassin's 'Speake hands for me'![3] Nor does Shakespeare intend the stylised gesture of classic actor and orator. Hamlet is quite explicit in his stress on tempered realism: 'doe not saw the ayre too much with your hand thus, but vse all gently . . . Be not too tame neither . . . sute the action to the word, the word to the action, with this speciall obseruance, that you ore-steppe not the modestie of nature: For any thing so ore-doone, is from the purpose of playing.' His shocked account of the Player's performance demonstrates how effective an actor's good use of gesture and expression can be: 'Teares in his eyes, distraction in his aspect, / A broken voyce, an[d] his whole function suting / With formes to his conceit.'[4] Both action and expression are demanded of the actor, and it is they that give added force to his words.

However, Hamlet's speech is the centre of a protracted critical debate about the realism or stylisation of Elizabethan acting. The most trampled ground is the external evidence – the comments of playwrights and outside observers.[5] To the uncommitted bystander, this would clearly seem to favour an informal naturalism. Hamlet's recommendations are seconded by Heywood's:

. . . without a comely and elegant gesture, a gratious and bewitching kinde of action, a naturall and familiar motion of the head, the hand, the body, . . . I hold all the rest as nothing . . . And this is the action behoovefull in any that professe this quality [i.e. that of the actor], not to use any impudent or forced motion in any part of the body, nor rough or other violent gesture; nor on the contrary to stand like a stiffe starcht man, but to qualifie every thing according to the nature of the person personated.

(*Apology for Actors*, 1612)[6]

Such positive witness is corroborated by its more prolific negative – the innumerable attacks on the strutting player who 'does ouer-act prodigiously in beaten satten' (Ben Jonson),[7] 'whose conceit / Lyes in his ham-string, and doth thinke it rich / To heere the woodden dialogue and sound, / Twixt his stretcht footing and the scoaffollage' (Shakespeare).[8] The external evidence suggests a naturalistic style that was imperfectly achieved in practice.

The internal evidence of the plays strongly supports this view. Here the evidence rests on the stage directions proper, *and* the implicit directions of the text. Far from being stylised, Shakespeare's explicit stage directions can be positively prosaic (*They set them downe on two lowe stooles and sowe*), or absurdly flippant, as when England is preparing for civil war: *Enter the prince marching, and Falstalffe meetes him playing vpon his trunchion like a fife.*[9] (Both these stage directions are most probably authorial.) But, it is argued by the formalists, such authorial directions may well have been ignored in practice. Here the neglected evidence of the bad Quartos is crucial.

Generally, the bad Quartos are accepted as representing the actors' memorial reconstructions of plays in which they had performed. Their stage directions are thus particularly important because they give us a unique insight into how the plays were actually staged. It is clear from them that the actors did indeed carry out the stage directions proper, as well as the implicit directions of the text:

Paris	These times of woe affoord no time to wooe,
	Maddam, farwell, commend me to your daughter,
	Paris offers to goe in, and Capolet calles him againe.
Capulet	Sir Paris? Ile make a desperate tender of my child.

> I think she will be rulde in all respectes by mee.
> (*Romeo and Juliet* III.iv.Q1:G2ᵛ)

Moreover, *extra* business of a realistic kind was introduced:

> *Nurse* . . . I am none of his flurtgills, I am none of his skaines mates.
>   *She turnes to Peter her man.*
>   And thou like a knaue must stand by, and see euerie Iacke
>   vse me at his pleasure.
>   (*Romeo and Juliet* II.iv.Q1:E3)

Such extra business could tellingly underline the implications of the text. At the lovers' betrothal, the actors forget the dialogue, but remember the action that gives it immediate significance:

> *Romeo*   . . . come she will.
> *Friar*   I gesse she will indeed,
>   Youths loue is quicke, swifter than swiftest speed.
> [Replacing   Therefore loue moderately, long loue
> Shakespeare's: doth so,
>   Too swift arriues as tardie as too slowe.]
>   *Enter Iuliet somewhat fast, and embraceth Romeo.*
>   (*Romeo and Juliet* II.vi.Q1:E4, Q2:F2)

As the Friar warned Romeo, 'Wisely and slow, they stumble that run fast'. Juliet's *somewhat fast* entry stresses the prophetic truth of his words, and is one more instance of the dramatic ironies riddling this play.

Finally, just as the actors remembered what they did better than what they said, so they remembered what they said best, when it described what they did. The essence of dialogue requiring action survives, while 'poetic' passages are blown to fractured atoms. Compare this Shakespearean original with its impoverished reminiscence:

> Good Quarto
> *Enter Paris and his Page.*
> *Paris* Giue me thy Torch boy, hence and stand aloofe,
>   Yet put it out, for I would not be seene:
>   Vnder yond young Trees lay thee all along,
>   Holding thy eare close to the hollow ground,
>   So shall no foote vpon the Church-yard tread,
>   Being loose, vnfirme with digging vp of Graues,
>   But thou shalt heare it, whistle then to me
>   As signall that thou hearest some thing approach.
>   Giue me those flowers, do as I bid thee, go.

Page I am almost afraid to stand alone,
       Here in the Church-yard, yet I will aduenture.
Paris Sweet flower, with flowers thy Bridall bed I strew.
       O woe, thy Canapie is dust and stones,
       Which with sweete water nightly I will dewe,
       Or wanting that, with teares distild by mones.
       The obsequies that I for thee will keepe
       Nightly shall be to strew thy graue and weepe.
       Whistle Boy.

                          Bad Quarto
       Enter Countie Paris and his Page with flowers and sweete water.
Paris Put out the torch, and lye thee all along
       Vnder this Ew-tree, keeping thine eare close to the hollow ground.
       And if thou heare one tread within this Churchyard
       Straight giue me notice.
Boy   I will my Lord.
       Paris strewes the Tomb with flowers.
Paris Sweete Flower, with flowers I strew thy Bridale bed:
       Sweete Tombe that in thy circuite dost containe
       The perfect modell of eternitie:
       Faire Iuliet that with Angells dost remaine,
       Accept this latest fauour at my hands,
       That liuing honourd thee, and being dead
       With funerall praises doo adorne thy Tombe.
Boy whistles and calls. My Lord.
            (*Romeo and Juliet* V.iii.Q2:L^v–L2, Q1:14^v)

The implicit directions of the original text become action, recorded
in the stage directions proper, or shrink to précis in the dialogue
(Paris's first speech contracts from 9 lines to 4). Paris's lament,
lamentable though it may have been (the fireworks, perhaps, are
being reserved for Romeo), expires in gibberish and cliché. There
could be no better demonstration of the players' enactment of the
words they forgot. And so Rymer's cynical encomium may well
epitomise the original actors' attitude:

Action is speaking to the Eyes . . . Many, peradventure, of the Tragical
Scenes in *Shakespear*, cry'd vp for the *Action*, might do yet better without
words: Words are a sort of heavy baggage, that were better out of the way, at
the push of Action.

                          (*A Short View of Tragedy*)[10]

Formalists citing the brevity of running time in the Elizabethan
theatre as evidence of minimal stylised action are also contradicted
by such quotations. For while it can certainly be argued that the Bad

Quartos present only distant reminiscences, they say little for the integrity of words in performance, while amply testifying to the preeminence of action. The speed of delivery ('Speake the speech . . . trippingly on the tongue') may well have encouraged garbling.[11]

Curiously, the Bad Quartos, a raffish ace witness, have been loftily ignored, and the more respectable internal directions of the dialogue have also been dismissed after a cursory cross examination. Yet these generally demand action of an overwhelmingly realistic kind – like Leontes, tenderly wiping his son's nose: 'Why that's my Bawcock: what? has't smuch'd thy Nose?'[12] It seems merely perverse that such directions should be used in support of the formalists' position. Their arguments are, basically, two: that life-like descriptive directions evolved of necessity, to compensate for the rigidity of the acting; and that it is in any case absurd to imagine descriptive directions for 'acting', as opposed to 'action', being staged. So Harbage, father of the formalist school, distinguishes between the genuine imperative of the stage direction, *Leaps in the graue*, and the descriptive line, 'The angry spot doth glow on Caesars brow', which cannot represent a practicable instruction to the actor. Are we to suffer future theses on 'Could our Older English Actors Turn Pale?', he mockingly demands.[13] And yet neither argument stands.

The first is continually contradicted by the wording of the internal stage directions, which demand their enactment (a point to be illustrated later), while the Bad Quartos give ample evidence of such demands being fulfilled. The second is false merely by its absoluteness. It is equally ridiculous to insist that none of the internal directions were acted, as to assume that they all were. It is true that invisible details, particularly of expression, are created initially by the dialogue. Lines like 'The angry spot doth glow on Caesars brow' could even be termed 'audience directions', rather than 'actor directions', since primarily they tell the audience what to imagine they see. Yet jesting Harbage must still stay for an answer, even in his partial victory over Shakespeare's novelistic vividness. In *Titus Andronicus*, Marcus finds Lavinia raped, mutilated, and hot with embarrassment:

> Ah now thou turn'st awaie thy face for shame,
> And notwithstanding all this losse of blood . . .
> Yet doe thy cheekes looke red as Titans face,
> Blushing to be encountred with a Clowde.
> (*Titus* II.iv. Q:E2ᵛ)

Our older actors may not have been able to blush or blanche at will, but they could suggest either, by turning aside, as the youthful Shakespeare himself directs. Even the most apparently unstageable 'audience directions' implicated the actor to a certain degree.

Harbage's theories are disproved again and again by the texts. Take his statement that 'The position of Burbage was more nearly that of his ancient fellow in the Greek amphitheatre than of his modern fellow behind a proscenium arch . . . The whimsical smile, the arched brow, the significant sidelong glance would not do. He had to act with his body.'[14] This is flatly denied by Shakespeare's own stage directions: *Exit King, frowning vpon the Cardinall, the Nobles throng after him smiling, and whispering . . . Enter King frowning on them, takes his Seate.*[15] And the Bad Quarto of *Romeo and Juliet*, particularly rich in such directions, shows the actors implementing the suggestions of the text. What is this but a significant sidelong glance?

Nurse	Your Romeo he is banisht, and all the world to nothing
	He neuer dares returne to challendge you.
	Now I thinke good you marry with this County . . .
Juliet	Speakst thou this from thy heart? . . .
	Well, thou hast comforted me wondrous much,
	I pray thee goe thy waies vnto my mother:
	Tell her I am gone hauing displeasde my Father
	To Fryer Laurence Cell to confesse me . . .
Nurse	I will, and this is wisely done.
	She lookes after Nurse.
Juliet	Auncient damnation, O most cursed fiend . . .

(*Romeo and Juliet* III.v.Q1:Hᵛ–H2)

The evidence, then, tilts heavily in favour of a theatre that carried out the directions of the dialogue, and was, therefore, generally realistic. However, this balance must be partially redressed. A series of reservations should be made.

Firstly, stage practice demonstrably fell short of the ideal, just as it does now and must always have done. Our earliest quotations from Jonson and Shakespeare (p. 10) made this clear.

Secondly, the theatre did not stand still. The detailed studies of the following chapters will show Shakespeare's progression from the ritualised and formulaic use of stage action, to the lively realism of the middle plays and the uneven but often sophisticated mannerism of the last plays. One need only think of the emblematic, repetitive kneelings in *Titus*, the endless knightings in the first history trilogy, or the pomps of *Henry VIII*, to admit stylisation of different kinds at different stages. This development is naturally related to that of

Shakespeare's contemporaries, the formal effects of the early plays finding frequent parallels in Kyd and Marlowe, while the later complex union of realistic symbolism is echoed by the best Jacobeans. Thus the substance of Elizabethan and Jacobean action changed.

Thirdly, the *style* of internal directions is of paramount importance. It is an easy, and dangerous error, to assume that stiff writing is evidence of stiff acting. Passages like the following have been quoted in support of a formal theatre:[16]

> *She opens the letters.*
> Ragan   How fares our royall sister?
> Messenger I did leave her at my parting, in good health.
> *She reads the letter, frownes and stamps.*
> See how her colour comes and goes agayne,
> Now red as scarlet, now as pale as ash:
> See how she knits her brow, and bytes her lips,
> And stamps, and makes a dumbe shew of disdayne,
> Mixt with revenge, and violent extreames.
>   (*King Leir*, Bullough VII. 366)

Intrinsically, however, the actions are not at fault; it is the pell-mell presentation that is artificial. The commentary is clumsy ('red as scarlet'), blatantly explanatory ('makes a dumbe shew of disdayne'), and gives Ragan's actress no time to allow her reactions natural development. Shakespeare is generally more tactful, though examples of a similar kind can be found in his poorer work.

Fourthly, a number of gestures commonly described by the Elizabethans are bound to strike us as hopelessly formulaic. The lover's arms are crossed, his hat pulled over his brows in the stock attitude of melancholy: 'Deep in a dump John Forde was alone got / With folded arms and melancholy hat'. The braggart walks on tip-toe: 'A soldier and a braggart he is (thats concluded); he ietteth strouting, dancing on hys toes with his hands vnder his sides'. The elbow is itched in delight: 'my hart hopt and danst, my elbowes itcht, my fingers friskt, I wist not what should become of my feete, nor knewe what I did for ioy.' Fearful suspicion starts at straws: 'vpon the least wagging of a straw to put them in feare where no feare is.'[17] Shakespeare's more inventive style often disguises the standard nature of such actions, as these non-Shakespearean examples have failed to do. He can be humorous: 'your hat penthouse like ore the shop of your eyes, with your armes crost on your thinbellies doblet like a Rabbet on a spit'.[18] He can be wonderfully realistic:

> This day is call'd the Feast of Crispian:
> He that out-liues this day, and comes safe home,
> Will stand a tip-toe when this day is named . . .
> Then will he strip his sleeue, and shew his skarres . . .
>   (*Henry V* IV.iii.2284ff)

He elaborates and re-phrases:

Enobarbus   Where's Anthony?
Eros   He's walking in the garden thus, and spurnes
              The rush that lies before him. Cries Foole Lepidus . . .
                      (*Antony and Cleopatra* III.v.1740ff)

Once again, presentation is the decisive factor: if the style of description is natural, then the action itself appears natural also. It is,
however, worth noting that Shakespeare tends to avoid demanding
such standard gestures; all the Shakespearean equivalents quoted
above occur in novelistic descriptions, rather than internal stage
directions.[19]

A fifth point is our inescapable subjectivity in what we admit as
natural. We too have our common, accepted gestures – the V sign,
the commiserating tap on the forehead. Saying goodbye, a supersti-
tious Italian jabs index and little finger at you, as horns to ward off
the evil eye. When a Portuguese pays you a compliment, he slides a
flattened palm under your chin, to catch the drool of delight. An
impudent Russian will tell you to mind your own business by
waving his hand at you, thumb obscenely protruding between
second and third fingers. Are these gestures stylised or 'formal'?
They are the gestures of the street – commonplace to those who
practice them, quaint and absurd to those who do not; lumbering to
verbalise, a vivid flash in action. In the revised second edition of
Elizabethan Acting, B. L. Joseph rightly stressed that the orator's
gestures on which his book was founded had been culled by John
Bulwer from the market-place.[20] One of Tarlton's Jests will provide
a last illustration of the Elizabethans' familiarity with such so-called
'stylised' gesture:

It chanced that in the midst of a Play, after long expectation for Tarlton . . .
at length hee came forth: where (at his entrance) one in the Gallerie pointed
his finger at him, saying to a friend that had neuer seene him, that is he.
Tarlton to make sport at the least occasion giuen him, and seeing the man
point with the finger, he in loue againe held vp two fingers: the captious
fellow, iealous of his wife (for he was married) and because a Player did it,

tooke the matter more hainously, & asked him why he made the hornes at
him, No (quoth Tarlton) they be fingers:
>   For there is no man, Which in loue to me
>   Lends me one finger, but he shall haue three . . .
This matter grew so, that the more he meddled, the more it was for his
disgrace: wherefore the standers by counselled him to depart, both hee and
his hornes . . . So the poore fellow, plucking his hat ouer his eyes, went his
wayes.

(Tarltons Jests (1638) B2ᵛ)

Johnson professes distaste at Shakespeare's frequent references to the
horns of the cuckold. But for a moving use of the last gesture, see p.
134 below.

Decorum is the final factor. Nashe has an attractive digression to
his actors in *Summer's Last Will and Testament*, warning them against
the habitual improprieties of the actor who has forgotten his lines,
and does not know what to do with his hands:

Actors, you Rogues, come away, cleare your throats, blowe your noses, and
wype your mouthes ere you enter, that you may take no occasion to spit or
to cough, when you are *non plus*. And this I barre, ouer and besides: That
none of you stroake your beardes to make action, play with your cod-piece
poynts, or stand fumbling on your buttons, when you know not how to
bestow your fingers. Serue God, and act cleanly.

(Works III.236)

The actors evidently had recourse to gestures that are natural enough
– another indication of the predominantly realistic theatre. Nashe
objects not to their realism, but their impropriety. His play is a court
entertainment and its use of action is correspondingly stylised. In the
comic scenes, though, Backwinter rolls in the straw covering the
stage. Elizabethan and Jacobean drama exploited both kinds of
action, depending on the type of drama, just as it used colloquial
prose and the heroic line, just as it turned to comedy and tragedy in a
single play. We no longer jib at Shakespeare's skilful fusion of the
comic and tragic. Nor do we have trouble in accepting the
Shakespearean blend that gives us prosaic verse ('Neuer, neuer,
neuer, neuer, neuer'), and rhetorical, highly patterned prose ('What
peece of worke is a man, how noble in reason, how infinit in
faculties, in forme and moouing how expresse and admirable . . .').
Why then can we not accept a theatre that demands lively, realistic
action at one moment, the stately and formal at the next? As in many
debates, the truth is an unexciting compromise.[21] The excitement lies
in the minutiae of Shakespeare's practice.

Practice

> Ther's language in her eye, her cheeke, her lip,
> Nay her foote speakes . . .
> (*Troilus and Cressida* IV.v.Q:I^v)

Let us return then to Shakespeare's observation of movement, since it is from this that his direction will spring. His gleeful eye for gesture is evident in countless novelistic descriptions that do not demand to be staged. They are the notebook jottings of the director-dramatist, the raw materials that he will then put on his stage. Shakespeare's gift for description is passed to his characters. Falstaff's rabble of conscripts 'march wide betwixt the legs as if they had giues on', because, as he admits, he had most of them out of prison. The swollen-headed Ajax 'stalkes vp and downe like a peacock, a stride and a stand: ruminates like an hostisse, that hath no Arithmatique but her braine to set downe her reckoning: bites his lip with a politique regarde, as who should say there were witte in this head and twoo'd out . . .' Antonio's bizarre parting from Bassanio is painstakingly detailed: 'his eye being big with teares, / Turning his face, he put his hand *behind* him, / And with affection wondrous sencible / He wrung Bassanios hand . . .' 'Admirable!' the Poet flatters the Painter, in *Timon*: 'How bigge imagination / Moues in this Lip, to th'dumbnesse of the gesture, / One might interpret'. Shakespeare's own descriptions have this graphic art.[22]

He starts as a painter might, in Lucrece's picture of Troy describing Nestor, silver beard wagging as he speaks, holding a crowd packed close as a crammed Carpaccio – 'Here one mans hand leand on anothers head, / His nose being shadowed by his neighbours eare'.[23] Later, he affects to detail the living world:

> Yong Arthurs death is common in their mouths,
> And when they talke of him, they shake their heads,
> And whisper one another in the eare.
> And he that speakes doth gripe the hearers wrist,
> Whilst he that heares, makes fearefull action
> With wrinkled browes, with nods, with rolling eyes.
> I saw a Smith stand with his hammer (*thus*)
> The whilst his Iron did on the Anuile coole . . .
> (*King John* IV.ii.1912ff. My italics)

The gestures he observes are those the painter portrays. But compare Shakespeare's active and individualised image, with Leonardo's null paradigm:

Of representing a man speaking to a multitude.

. . . the people. These you must represent as silent and attentive, all looking at the orator's face with gestures of admiration; and make some old men, in astonishment at the things they hear, with the corners of their mouths pulled down and drawn in, their cheeks full of furrows, and their eyebrows raised, and wrinkling the forehead where they meet. Again, some sitting with their fingers clasped holding their weary knees. Again, some bent old man, with one knee crossed over the other; on which let him hold his hand with his other elbow resting in it and the hand supporting his bearded chin.

This is the difference between writer and artist. The artist's models are frozen in action, even in the Baconian blur. But an eye for continuous gesture is characteristic of the observant writer, whether dramatist, poet or novelist. Wordsworth catches the French royalist, reading disquieting news: 'while he read, / Or mused, his sword was haunted by his touch / Continually, like an uneasy place / In his own body'. It is one of Sterne's triumphs – 'And pray, brother, quoth my uncle Toby, laying the end of his pipe upon my father's hand in a kindly way of interruption . . .' Falstaff's aperçu, with which we began, is echoed by Kipling: / 'walking wide and stiffly across the strong shadows, the memory of the leg-irons still on him, strode one newly-released from the jail.'[24] But, as Keats wrote to his brother and sister-in-law, these are only descriptions:

Writing has this disadvan[ta]ge of speaking – one cannot write a wink, or a nod, or a grin, or a purse of the Lips, or a *smile* – O law! One can-[not] put ones finger to one's nose, or yerk ye in the ribs, or lay hold of your button in writing – but in all the most lively and titterly parts of my Letter you must not fail to imagine me as the epic poets say – now here, now there, now with one foot pointed at the ceiling, now with another – now with my pen on my ear, now with my elbow in my mouth. O my friends you lose the action – and attitude is every thing . . .

(17–27 September, 1819)

The dramatist has the insuperable advantage of living speech, and the gestures that go with his words. As Keats concluded, 'does not the word mum! go for ones finger beside the nose . . .'[25] Shakespeare forces his instinctive mimicry of gesture on his actors, who must parody one another as irrepressibly as he.

So Hamlet and Leontes both know the gossip's shifty, suggestive evasions, but while Leontes merely *describes* 'The Shrug, the Hum, or Ha, (these Petty-brands / That Calumnie doth vse'), Hamlet, the natural actor, *demonstrates* 'With armes incombred *thus*, or *this* head shake, / Or by pronouncing of some doubtfull phrase, / As well,

well, we knowe . . .' Gratiano, promising sobriety, mocks it even as
he swears to 'Weare prayer bookes in my pocket, looke demurely, /
Nay more, while grace is saying hood mine eyes / *Thus* with my hat,
and sigh and say amen.' Most malicious on Shakespeare's part is
Malvolio's unconscious self-parody, as he daydreams of life as lord of
his lady. He sets the scene with innocent relish: 'Calling my Officers
about me, in my branch'd Veluet gowne: hauing come from a day
bedde, where I haue left Oliuia sleeping . . .' He pictures his little
flourishes of consciously casual grandeur: 'I frowne the while, and
perchance winde vp my watch . . .' He directs the action: 'Toby
approaches; curtsies *there* to me . . .'; and acts as well: 'I extend my
hand to him *thus*: quenching my familiar smile with an austere regard
of controll . . .'[26] And *thus*, time and again, the gesture is forced on
the actor, as the natural flourish for his words. 'There was a Crowne
offer'd him, and being offer'd him, he put it by with the backe of his
hand *thus*.' 'He tooke me by the wrist, and held me hard, / Then goes
he to the length of all his arme, / And with his other hand *thus* ore his
brow / He falls to such perusall of my face . . .' 'I kneel'd before him,
/ 'Twas very faintly he said Rise: dismist me / *Thus* with his
speechlesse hand . . .'[27] Brutus's anger is easily acted as his clenched
fist drives his argument home:

> . . .shall we now
> Contaminate our fingers with base Bribes?
> And sell the mighty space of our large Honors
> For so much trash, as may be grasped *thus*?
> (*Julius Caesar* IV.iii. 1993ff. My italics)

Surely one reason why Shakespeare still dominates our stage is that
he plays direct into his actors' hands.

Gesture is continually called for, not merely by the automatic
demonstratives ('by these pickers and stealers', 'by these gloues'),
but by every form of retrospective description, concurrent description, question, and command. Actions vary with the character and
the moment. They can be painfully histrionic – a characteristic of
Othello, who tells Iago with dreadful vividness, 'looke here Iago, /
All my fond loue, *thus* doe I blow to heauen, – tis gone.' Or they can
be simply comic, like Touchstone, parenthetically rebuking Audrey
for who knows what impropriety: '(beare your bodie more seeming
Audry)'. They can be grimly formal:

Lear   Do you but marke how this becomes the house?
       Deere daughter, I confesse that I am old;

Age is vnnecessary: on my knees I begge,
That you'l vouchsafe me Rayment, Bed, and Food.
(*King Lear* II.iv.1434ff)

Or they can be instinctive, as Marina in *Pericles* shuts her ears to the
Bawd's nauseating sexual menu: 'You shall fare well, you shall haue
the difference of all complexions, what doe you stop your eares?'[28]
The formalist argument concludes that 'There would be compara-
tively little business, and gesture would be formalised. Conventional
movement and heightened delivery would be necessary to carry off
the dramatic illusion.'[29] But Hamlet, surely, speaks with the greater
authority, and we can hardly doubt that his requirements tallied with
those of his creator. The action should be suited to the word, the
word to the action; whether it is formal or otherwise depends on the
dramatic dictates of the moment.

Expression

Expressions are no less subject to direction, although here the
descriptions are aimed as much at the audience as the actor. Yet the
technique is theatrical as well as novelistic. For the intimate reality of
the drama is intensified and substantiated when characters scrutinise
each others' expressions, and react to what they see. 'Shame it selfe, /
Why do you make *such* faces?' Lady Macbeth angrily hisses at her
husband, mesmerised by the ghost. 'I feare you, for you are fatall
then, / When your eyes roule *so*,' Desdemona quavers; 'Alas, why
gnaw you *so* your neather lip? . . . These are portents.' Or Prospero,
praising Miranda as his 'rich guift' to Ferdinand, breaks off, saying,
'O Ferdinand, / Doe not smile at me, that I boast her of . . .'[30]
Perhaps he was forestalling Ferdinand's amusement; perhaps Ferdinand had grinned at his paternal pride; perhaps he was smiling for
sheer joy. Whatever the actor's interpretation, that Ferdinand should
react, and that Prospero should react to his reaction, sharpens the
reality of their exchange. They are not stiffly separate puppets, but
human beings, with all the flickering variability of human response.

The technique is simply good theatre. Take Hamlet's first scene
with Guildenstern and Rosencrantz. He twice catches them out, just
by watching them, first in his demands whether they were sent for or
not ('you were sent for, and there is a kind of confession in your
lookes, which your modesties haue not craft enough to cullour
. . .'), then in his abrupt rounding on them in his great speech of
disillusion. '. . . And yet to me, what is this Quintessence of dust:

man delights not me,' he muses, adding sharply, 'nor women neither, though by your smi[l]ing, you seeme to say so.' Rosencrantz is aggrieved: 'My Lord, there was no such stuffe in my thoughts.' Hamlet: 'Why did yee laugh then, when I sayd man delights not me?' For all their protests, embarrassed asides ('What say you?'), and uncomfortable silences, Hamlet can read them – 'Nay then I haue an eye of you', and a paranoid eye too. The effectiveness of these moments is evident, once again, from the Bad Quarto, whose actor-reporters have remembered little else in their brief butchery of one of the best scenes in the play.[31]

Significance

Yet only too often such internal directions are inexplicably ignored in performance. Has any production of *Romeo and Juliet* obeyed Shakespeare's implicit instructions, and shown a citizen trying to arrest the dead Tybalt, in the confusion after the brawl? The dialogue makes this macabre comedy quite clear (and it is, characteristically, Shakespeare's addition to his source):[32]

	Enter Citizens.
Citizen	Which way ran he that kild Mercutio?
	Tybalt that murtherer, which way ran he?
Benvolio	There lies that Tybalt.
Citizen	Vp sir, go with me:
	I charge thee in the Princes name obey.

(Romeo and Juliet III.i.Q2:F4^v)

It is always worth visualising the action demanded by the dialogue. It can be simply funny. Malvolio's inadvertent bawdy when he stoops to read the decoy letter has long been recognised, partly because Shakespeare draws attention to it through Sir Andrew. But who has realised that his sudden squat at 'thus', to pick the letter up, would give body to another innuendo?

Malvolio	By my life this is my Ladies hand: these bee her very C's, her U's, and her T's, *and thus makes shee her great P's* . . .
Sir Andrew	Her C's, her U's, and her T's: why that?

(Twelfth Night II.v.110ff. My italics)

Implicit action of this kind can make sense of an otherwise obscure exchange. It has been pointed out, for instance, that Doll Tearsheet tries to avoid imprisonment by pretending she is pregnant, and stuffing a cushion down her dress. Hence the Hostess's exclamation, 'I pray God the fruite of her womb miscarry', and the beadle's retort, as the cushion is extracted: 'If it doe, you shall haue a dozzen of cushions againe, you haue but eleuen now . . .'[33]

Moreover, such action can have more than a local significance. Why was the ghost in *Hamlet* 'offended', stalking off when Horatio hailed it? Surely, because his very first words to it were 'What art thou that *vsurpst* this time of night' – an unhappy metaphor most tactlessly ill-suited to the usurped king.[34] Again, it is ironic that Hamlet's first resolve, after meeting his father's ghost, is metaphorically to wipe away all trivial observations from the tables of his memory, and to remember only the ghost's injunction to revenge. Yet his first impulse, following hot on this resolve, is to note down just such an observation: 'My tables, meet it is I set it downe / That one may smile, and smile, and be a villaine . . .' 'At least I am sure it may be so in Denmarke,' he adds with a philosopher's pedantry as he writes; then, putting the 'tables' away, briskly concludes: 'So Vncle, there you are, now to my word'. But his word ('remember thee') has already been broken. 'Yea, from the table of my memory / Ile wipe away all triuiall fond records' remains an unfulfilled metaphor; 'My tables, meet it is I set it downe . . .' is the actuality. The sequence has betrayed his imaginary resolution, and revealed the reality of his philosophical nature; it loses its point when it is not staged. Theoretically, Hamlet is ready to act; in actuality, he is a theoretician, as the rest of the play bears out.[35]

Development, and *Julius Caesar*

Even in his first poems Shakespeare had an eye for action. In *Lucrece* he describes Tarquin thrusting open Lucrece's bedroom door – with his knee; in *Venus and Adonis* his art of direction through obliquely descriptive speech finds early expression. So Adonis whines, 'You hurt my hand with wringing . . . you crush me, let me go', and Venus urges, 'Lye quietly, and heare a litle more, / Nay do not struggle, for thou shalt not rise . . .' No wonder Coleridge believed that 'His Venus and Adonis seem at once the characters themselves, and the whole representation of those characters by the most consummate actors. You seem to be *told* nothing, but to see and hear everything.'[36] Yet in the early plays Shakespeare's implicit stage directions are often clumsy, reminiscent of the cack-handed writing in *King Leir*, that was quoted in support of the formalists' position (see p. 15 above). In *King John*, Shakespeare twitches the actor

playing a Messenger into obedience by Constance's baldly imperative questions:

> What dost thou meane by shaking of thy head?
> Why dost thou looke so sadly on my sonne?
> What meanes that hand vpon that breast of thine?
> Why holdes thine eie that lamentable rhewme . . .
> Be these sad signes confirmers of thy words?
> (*King John* III.i.940ff)

Later, the dialogue ceases to direct so blatantly, appearing rather the
natural *consequence* to less schematised action:

Portia   There are some shrowd contents in yond same paper
> That steales the colour from Bassanios cheeke,
> Some deere friend dead, else nothing in the world
> Could turne so much the constitution
> Of any constant man: what worse and worse? . . .
> (*Merchant of Venice* III.ii.Q:F2^v–3)

In the last plays it is disappointing to find some lapses into the jerky
questions and prodding commentary of *King John*:

Imogen   . . . Pisanio, Man:
> Where is Posthumus? What is in thy mind
> That makes thee stare thus? Wherefore breaks that sigh
> From th'inward of thee? . . .
> Why tender'st thou that Paper to me, with
> A looke vntender?
> (*Cymbeline* III.iv.1673ff)

It is almost as though, in Shakespeare's later works, his interest in the
technique he had mastered withers into automatic competence. But
at the mid-point of his career his gift of indirect direction reaches
perfection. In *Julius Caesar* he excels in the tightness of his control,
and the discretion with which it is exercised.

Plutarch describes Julius Caesar's assassination in meticulous detail:

. . . Then Casca behinde him strake him in the necke with his sword . . .
Caesar did still defende him selfe against the rest, running everie waye with
his bodie: but when he sawe Brutus with his sworde drawen . . . he pulled
his gowne over his heade, and made no more resistaunce, and was driven
. . . against the base whereupon Pompeys image stoode, which ranne all of a
goare bloude, till he was slaine.

(*Life of Caesar*, Bullough V.86)

. . . Then the conspirators thronging one upon an other bicause everie man was desirous to have a cut at him, so many swords and daggers lighting upon one bodie, one of them hurte an other, and among them Brutus caught a blowe on his hande . . . and all the rest also were every man of them bloudied.

(Life of Brutus, Bullough V.102)

At the climax of Shakespeare's play, there is no room for directions in the rush of action:

Casca Speake hands for me.
   They stab Caesar.
Caesar *Et Tu Brutè?* – – Then fall Caesar.
   Dyes.

(Julius Caesar III.i.1286ff)

As the play progresses, however, Shakespeare gradually leaks Plutarch's details, and it becomes clear that the assassination was visualised as a replica of its historical original, accurate in every detail. Brutus is the first. Standing over Caesar's corpse, he significantly hails this scene as the *reality*, no play-acting: 'How many times shall Caesar bleed in sport, / *That now on Pompeyes Basis lye[s] along,* / No worthier then the dust?' In the funeral oration of the next scene, Antony continues to reconstruct the kill as he describes it to the crowd: 'then burst his Mighty heart, / And *in his Mantle, muffling vp his face,* / *Euen at the Base of Pompeyes Statue* / (*Which all the while ran blood) great Caesar fell*'. Returning bitterly to it once more at the end of the play, Antony answers Brutus's accusation of threatening behaviour with 'you did not so, *when your vile daggers* / *Hackt one another in the sides of Caesar:* / You . . . bow'd like Bondmen, kissing Caesars feete; / Whil'st *damned Caska, like a Curre, behinde* / *Strooke Caesar on the necke.*' Now it may well be argued that these descriptions are merely novelistic – a businesslike transcription of Plutarch's account, after the event. This would be true of a bad production of the play, in which the retrospective descriptions had not been given their due physical original. But if these speeches are to have any dramatic force, they must describe the scene as the audience actually saw it: Caesar, stabbed in the neck from behind, struggling to escape, and finally brought up against Brutus, covering his face in surrender (a most pathetic gesture) to fall at the base of Pompey's statue. The statue, too, should be so bespattered with his blood, and that of the conspirators (who wounded one another in the press, as

Plutarch and Shakespeare both point out), that it should seem to spout blood, almost as in Calphurnia's dream.[37]

Yet modern productions can be inexplicably impressionistic about such detail. Conversely, the Elizabethan theatre had a marked penchant for historical accuracy, to which the Bad Quartos once again bear witness. So the actors' memorial version of *3 Henry VI* correctly stages Clifford's death, *wounded, with an arrow in his necke*, as Hall states and as Shakespeare neglects to detail. Elsewhere in the play, the actors' plodding stage directions (*Alarmes to the battell, Yorke flies, then the chambers be discharged. Then enter the king, Cla and Glo . . .*) spell out Shakespeare's enigmatic shorthand (*Alarum, Retreat, Excursions. Exeunt. / Flourish. Enter Edward . . .*), and show it once more to be an accurate dramatisation of Hall. There are other, more complicated instances of this surprising scholarly tendency to historical punctiliousness in the popular theatre.[38] Not surprising, then, that the audience was willing to accept the documentary fiction for the reality, as Nashe asserts in his reference to Talbot, in *1 Henry VI* 'newe embalmed with the teares of ten thousand spectators at least . . . who, in the Tragedian that represents his person, imagine they behold him fresh bleeding . . .' Again, Caesar's story was no less familiar than Henry V's famous victories, which Shakespeare's Chorus assumes some of the audience to have read. Here, significantly, Shakespeare even excuses himself for not presenting things just as they happened:

> Chorus   Vouchsafe to those that haue not read the Story,
>   That I may prompt them: and of such as haue,
>   I humbly pray them to admit th'excuse
>   Of time, of numbers, and due course of things,
>   Which cannot in their huge and proper life
>   Be here presented.
>   (*Henry V* V.i.2851ff)

The assumption is clearly that the presentation *should* be as accurate as possible. There are obvious logistic problems in staging battles and Channel crossings. But there are no such difficulties in the telling details of Caesar's assassination: the scene must be staged as it is later described, and as any educated person knew it to have happened.[39]

Julius Caesar is outstanding for the vivid particularity with which it is visualised, which extends far beyond historical detail. Characters constantly comment on one another – Cicero to Casca: 'Why are you breathlesse, and why stare you *so*?'; Cassius to Cinna: 'where haste you *so*?' Shakespeare, like Shaw, leaves few loopholes to the actor, but his commands are vividly absorbed in the dialogue. Actions are mooted, must be done, and finally are verified. Cassius to Brutus: 'As they passe by, / Plucke Caska by the Sleeue.' Casca to Brutus: 'You pul'd me by the cloake, would you speake with me?'[40] Dialogue at once describes and directs the scene, most sustainedly perhaps in the conspirators' panicky asides as they approach the Capitol. From the text, even the reader can see Popillius (who is not one of the conspirators) coolly dropping a word to Cassius, leaving him in consternation whispering to Brutus, as he passes smoothly on to chat to Caesar, Antony manoeuvred aside by Trebonius . . .

Popillius	I wish your enterprize to day may thriue.
Cassius	What enterprize Popillius?
Popillius	Fare you well.
Brutus	What said Popillius Lena?
Cassius	He wisht to day our enterprize might thriue:
	I feare our purpose is discouered.
Brutus	Looke how he makes to Caesar: marke him.
Cassius	Caska be sodaine, for we feare preuention.
	Brutus what shall be done? If this be knowne,
	Cassius or Caesar neuer shall turne backe,
	For I will slay my selfe.
Brutus	Cassius be constant:
	Popillius Lena speakes not of our purposes,
	For looke he smiles, and Caesar doth not change.
Cassius	Trebonius knowes his time: for look you Brutus
	He drawes Mark Antony out of the way . . .

(Julius Caesar III. 1. 1217ff)

The impression this extract gives is not of a play crushed by a Shavian despotism, but rather of horribly precarious autonomy. Shakespeare, like Stephen Dedalus's artist, seems invisible, remote, paring his finger-nails, while the conspirators struggle to control the drama they have set in motion. In the end their efforts fail, and at Phillippi the 'Courtiers of beautious freedome' die. Such an impression is subtly heightened by Shakespeare's attribution of the panicky, powerless descriptive directions quoted above to the conspirators themselves. They cannot quite harness the events around them; by the same token, their bid for freedom is doomed to fail. This raises the last topic to be discussed in this general introduction to Shakespeare's stage direction – the question of control.

The role of the commentator

Julius Caesar demonstrates Shakespeare's precise control of staging through the dialogue; more than that, it illustrates the implications of his choice of speaker for such directions. For, inevitably, the commentator will dominate our view of the action he describes.

This is simply seen in *Troilus and Cressida*, where we are forced to watch the lovers' first meeting through Pandarus's eyes, and the scene sickens under his salacious commentary. The lovers meet, shyly and in silence. Pandarus busies himself, directing in word and deed, prompting Troilus, rudely unveiling Cressida, and relishing their kisses:

> *Enter pandar and Cressid.*
>
> Pandarus   Come, come, what need you blush? Shames a babie; heere shee is now, sweare the othes now to her that you haue sworne to me: what are you gone againe, you must be watcht ere you be made tame, must you? . . . why doe you not speake to her? Come draw this curtaine, and lets see your picture; alasse the day? how loath you are to offend day light; and twere darke youd close sooner: so so, rub on and kisse the mistresse . . .
>
> (*Troilus and Cressida* III.ii.Q:F2)

The commentator's role is also stressed by his own commentary, which heightens his strength, or his weakness. The difference lies between the commentator who is outside the action, and the one who suffers at what he sees. Troilus and Cressida are Pandarus's puppets here, and he is the *spectator ab extra*, in obtrusive command. Later, when Troilus watches Cressida with Diomed, his impotence is made painfully evident as we hear him observe, 'She stroakes his cheeke'. He is the *spectator ab intra*, who can do nothing but describe the actions that give him pain. Learning from past successes, in *Othello* Shakespeare elaborates and intensifies this scene, when Othello watches Cassio laugh with Iago about what he believes to be Cassio's affair with Desdemona. Here Othello's infuriated asides ('Looke how he laughes already . . . Now he denyes it faintly, and laughes it out . . . Now he tells how she pluckt him to my Chamber') actually control the scene, Shakespeare directing the actors of Cassio and Iago through his words. In effect, though, Othello is the dupe of what he sees, and, ironically, is made to name the very gestures he misinterprets. It is perhaps to be expected that the same technique should be repeated in *The Winter's Tale*, where it takes no elaborately set-up scene to prompt Leontes's jealousy, and we can watch the ironic gulf between Hermione's obedient courtesy, and its distorted image in Leontes's inflamed fancy ('How she holds vp the Neb? the Byll to him? / And armes her with the boldnesse of a Wife / To her allowing Husband'). It is, as we shall see, quite common for a perfected technique to recur.[41]

Elsewhere, the method is reversed, as the spectator dominates the scene, controlling it by his observation. This is typical of those characters who direct the plays in which they find themselves: Richard III, the Duke in *Measure for Measure*, Iachimo (fleetingly), and – ring-master par excellence – Iago.

In the last act of *Measure for Measure*, the Duke has a cruel eye for Angelo's unguarded expressions. When Mariana is sent for, as the witness to disprove Isabella's accusation of Angelo, there is a hard irony in the Duke's affable small talk with his victim. Coolly misinterpreting Angelo's look of relief as a smile at the absurdity of Isabella's accusation, he says, with grim equivocation: 'Doe you not smile at this, Lord Angelo? / Oh heauen, the vanity of wretched fooles!' Poor, vainly optimistic Angelo! He must twist his face into a tight-lipped smile, stiffly maintained till Mariana claims he slept with *her*, as well as Isabella. Then, confidence and anger rising together, he exclaims, 'I did but smile till now, / Now, good my Lord, giue me the scope of Iustice, / My patience here is touch'd.' Yet the Duke's control is unerring. When Claudio is at last brought forward, unmuffled and alive, Angelo's secret relief at his exoneration from manslaughter is once again broadcast to the audience in the Duke's merciless commentary: 'By this Lord Angelo perceiues he's safe, / Methinkes I see a quickning in his eye . . .'[42] Small wonder that Angelo should feel the Duke, like power divine, had looked upon his passes.

Iachimo has an equally sharp eye for Imogen's expressions, when he arrives with letters from Italy. 'Change you, Madam? / The Worthy Leonatus is in safety . . .' His technique is to overact his shocked commiseration for Imogen's insulted beauty, in conspicuous soliloquy, so that Imogen is prompted into the questions ('What makes your admiration? . . . What, deere Sir, / Thus rap's you?') that draw from him his lying tale of Posthumus's infidelity.[43] Yet this moment in *Cymbeline* is a relatively circumscribed reprise of an earlier success. Iago is the unsurpassed *spectator ab extra*, Shakespeare's most wickedly gifted director-cum-author surrogate. Through him, Shakespeare appears to voice his own struggles over the plot ('– – – how, how, – – – let me see . . . tis here, but yet confus'd . . .');[44] through him, also, Shakespeare controls his dramatic details. Much of Iago's power depends on his Shakespearean observation of gesture and expression, out of which he creates his impromptu dramas. When Cassio welcomes Desdemona to Cyprus, Iago watches his affected gestures, and first plans how he can use them:

He takes her by the palme; I well sed, whisper: as little a webbe as this will ensnare as great a Flee as Cassio. I, smile vpon her, doe: I will catch you in your owne courtesies . . .

(Othello II.i.Q:E)

In the event not only Cassio, but Othello himself is caught in this web, in the set-up scene just quoted above. But Iago's real triumph comes, of course, in the great temptation scene of III.iii. Here he manoeuvres Othello into the requisite reactions by pretending, with anxious solicitude, to see them dawning in his victim's face well in advance of their actual appearance. The common critical slurs on the speed of Othello's suspicions take no account of theatre time, which has nothing to do with real time, and furthermore they omit large expanses of text. In reality, Othello's honest, elephantine slowness to take the point is infinitely distressing:

Iago	I see this hath a little dasht your spirits.
Othello	Not a iot, not a iot.
Iago	Ifaith I feare it has.
	I hope you will consider what is spoke
	Comes from my loue.

Still Othello fails to rise.

> – But I doe see you are moou'd,
> I am to pray you, not to straine my speech,
> To groser issues, nor to larger reach,
> Then to suspition.

Othello	I will not.
Iago	Should you doe so my Lord,
	My speech should fall into such vile successe,
	As my thoughts aime not at: Cassio's my trusty friend:
	My Lord, I see you are moou'd.
Othello	No, not much moou'd,
	I doe not thinke but Desdemona's honest.
Iago	Long liue she so, and long liue you to thinke so.
Othello	And yet how nature erring from it selfe.
Iago	I, there's the point . . .

(Othello III.iii.Q:G4ᵛ)

As soon as Othello noses the bait, Iago is swiftly triumphant.

It is gratifying that he should fail in his last attempt at such descriptive manipulation. In the avalanche of the last act, Iago's plots suddenly run out of control. Roderigo bungles Cassio's murder. Iago has to silence Roderigo. In a desperate bid for control, Iago tries to implicate Bianca in the attempt on Cassio, and Cassio in Roderigo's untimely end. In both he affects to detect a guilty pallor, but his obedient puppets revolt at last. Cassio is blank. Bianca, like Emilia later, is healthily bold.

Bianca	O my deare Cassio, O my sweete Cassio, Cassio, Cassio.
Iago	O notable strumpet: Cassio may you suspect
	Who they should be, that thus haue mangled you?
Cassio	No.
	. . .
Iago	Gentlemen all, I doe suspect this trash
	To beare a part in this: patience a while good Cassio:
	. . . he that lies slaine here Cassio
	Was my deare friend, what malice was betwixt you?
Cassio	None in the world, nor doe I know the man.
Iago	What, looke you pale? O beare him out o'th aire.
	Stay you good Gentlewoman, looke you pale mistrisse?
	Doe you perceiue the ieastures of her eye . . .
	Behold her well I pray you, looke vpon her,
	Doe you see Gentlemen? Nay guiltinesse
	Will speake, though tongues were out of vse . . .
	This is the fruit of whoring, pray Emilia,
	Goe know of Cassio, where he supt to night:
	What, doe you shake at that?
Bianca	He supt at my house, but I therefore shake not.
	(*Othello* V.i.Q:L4–L4ᵛ)

It is interesting to note that the entire ruse was first tried out by Richard III.[45]

It must finally be pointed out that the control exerted through Shakespeare's continuous descriptive direction extends to the audience also. Shakespeare conducts us as well as his actors, and we are at the mercy of what he wants us to see.

Take the trial scene of *The Merchant of Venice*, where a descriptive direction is strategically placed. Courtroom and auditorium have just been distracted from the intransigent Shylock by news of the arrival of a messenger from Bellario. Antonio has protested his worthlessness for life in a slow, melancholy speech. The disguised Nerissa enters; the Duke welcomes her; all eyes are on her – when suddenly, cutting across her reply, we hear Bassanio's 'Why doost thou whet thy knife so earnestly?'[46] It is a brilliant juxtaposition of the play's two high points, as the audience's attention is peremptorily torn from Nerissa, herald of the trial's resolution, to a particularly vivid image of its focal point – Shylock, whetting the knife that threatens Antonio's life.

Such juxtaposition is a favourite technique on Shakespeare's part. In *1 Henry IV*, the stage directions (which are almost certainly authorial) demand that the comic and serious climaxes of the battle of Shrewsbury should coincide, in a bewildering profusion of dramatic largesse. Falstaff pretends to die, as Hal kills Hotspur in good earnest: *Enter Douglas, he fighteth with Falstalffe, he fals down as if he were dead, the Prince killeth Percy*. In *Othello*, again, *The Moore runnes at Iago. Iago kils his wife* – simultaneously.[47] (The stage direction is once again most probably authorial.) But in this second example the implications are even more interesting. Shakespeare does not merely run two climaxes together; the second of the two actions (*Iago kils his wife*) is also a prompt and ironic implicit response to Emilia's outburst against Othello, just preceding this stage direction. 'O murderous Coxcombe! what should a foole / Doe with so good a woman?', she cries. And Gratiano's generalised response, following on Iago's attack ('The woman falls, sure he has kild his wife') covers Othello's action just as well as Iago's. Even Emilia's words had a double meaning, for what do Othello and Iago do with so good a woman? Each kills his wife – and the murder of Emilia is an image in little of Desdemona's, as her singing of the willow song reiterates.

In *Hamlet* there is a similar juxtaposition in the last rush of action, as the duel reaches its climax. The audience quickly forgets that Gertrude has drunk the poisoned cup, as the crossed foils of Hamlet and Laertes insist on their attention. The fight suddenly speeds up; rapiers are exchanged, Claudius tries to intervene, the Queen falls, and at the same moment Hamlet and Laertes wound each other.

Laertes	Haue at you now.
King	Part them, they are incenst.
Hamlet	Nay come againe.
Osric	Looke to the Queene there howe.
Horatio	They bleed on both sides . . .

(Hamlet V.ii. Q2:N4ᵛ)

An actress once described to me how the audience reaction appeared from the stage. For a long while her playing of the poisoned Queen went unobserved; at Osric's words the faces of the audience swung round to her (a sudden swamp of pink in her direction), and then, as swiftly, back again, in obedience to Horatio's equally irresistible demand for attention. This account illustrates acutely enough the ultimate function of Shakespeare's internal stage directions. They ensure that he can control the actions and expressions of his players, precisely and permanently, for as long as his words are obeyed. They emphasise the power wielded by some characters, and the weakness of others. Lastly, by these internal directions, Shakespeare grips our own attention, forcing us to see what he wants us to see, and even turning our heads from side to side in obedience to his words.

CHAPTER 2

Position on the stage

For many years the Elizabethan stage had provided its poets with a familiar image of life, as in Raleigh's poem: 'What is our life? The play of passion . . .'[1] Its physical structure was, moreover, a natural frame for the visual image of man's rise and fall from high estate. Most of the stage symbolism of place is related to this theme; most, too, was so commonplace that Shakespeare exploited it only in his earliest plays. In the following account I shall avoid dispute over the details of Elizabethan and Jacobean stage structure by drawing my generalised assumptions from the conclusion of Richard Hosley and T. J. King, both of whom based their research on the stage directions of all the relevant dramatic documents of the time. King concludes that there were four main stage areas, of which any Elizabethan or Jacobean stage would have had the first, and any or all of the rest. These were: 'floor space in front of an unlocalised façade with at least two entrances through which large properties can be *brought on* or *thrust out*'; 'an acting place above the stage'; 'an accessory stage space covered by doors or hangings where actors can hide, or where actors, large properties, or both, can be *discovered*'; 'a trap to a place *below*, which necessitates a platform stage'.[2]

The stage doors

These serve a well-established, common-sense convention clarifying the relationship between groups of characters. They are generally used for the double entry of characters *meeting seuerally*, and, more specifically, for the confrontation of hostile parties – an effect exploited from Shakespeare's earliest plays. Men whose ways part leave, of course, by different doors, and on at least one occasion a significant change of party is clinched by a character's exit through a formerly 'hostile' door. So in *Coriolanus* IV.iii. a Roman and Volsce 'encounter' one another (hence, enter by two doors), the Roman turns out to be a traitor, and they 'go together' – foreshadowing

Coriolanus's shift of allegiance in the next scene. These techniques are too commonplace to be worth further illustration; more interesting is the manner of exit. Hosley noticed the dramatist's provision of an inconspicuous exit-line to get his characters off, but is not concerned with its dramatic implications. In early Shakespeare in particular such exit-lines can be consciously emblematic, somewhat in the manner of the Tudor Interlude. Compare, for instance, the departure of Manhood for a night's roistering, under his new alias of Shame, Folly leading the way with 'Folye before and shame behynde / Lo syrs thus fareth the worlde alwaye', in *The World and the Child*, and the haughty exit of Buckingham, followed by Somerset, in *2 Henry VI*, as Salisbury glosses, 'Pride went before, Ambition followes him'. Later, the emotional impact can be greater, though the implications are less clear-cut, for instance when Lear pointedly leaves his disastrous council scene on Burgundy's arm, in a last, unspoken insult to his daughter.[3]

Dialogue turns the permanent doors into temporary scenery, from the gates of innumerable besieged towns and the Tower, to the doors of tombs and mouths of caves. In *2 Henry IV* and *Macbeth* the norm may well have been effectively varied, since they are specifically left ajar, as the doors leading to two rooms where kings must die.[4]

The discovery-space

The central doors opened, and the aperture covered by a curtain, create the discovery-space in which Portia's caskets are displayed to her suitors, or the arras behind which Hubert's executioners hide, Falstaff snores, and the rat Polonius is caught in his own trap. Similar hangings probably served as the tents of Richard III, Richmond, and Achilles. The play within *The Spanish Tragedy* begins: *Enter Hieronimo, he knocks vp the curtaine*; similarly, the dialogue of *Richard III* makes it clear that the king's tent should be pitched in mid-scene, with all the realism of hammering and whistling that would suggest. Indeed, Richard's speech echoes this: 'we must haue knockes: / Ha, must we not?'[5]

It is generally recognised that no sustained significant action takes place within this confined discovery-space, but flows out onto the stage before it; hence the modern rejection of the unhistoric 'inner stage', whose existence was as much a critical fantasy as the 'upper stage'.[6] The fluidity of place in theatrical practice of the time is neatly illustrated by Shakespeare's last use of the discovery-space in *Henry*

VIII. As on a modern circular stage, locale could change while characters stayed still. So Norfolk and Suffolk decide to visit the King in his private chamber, in spite of warnings not to disturb him. They do not move, but:

> *the King drawes the Curtaine and sits reading pensiuely.*
> Suffolk   How sad he lookes; sure he is much afflicted.
> King   Who's there? Ha?
> Norfolk   Pray God he be not angry.
> King   Who's there I say? How dare you *thrust your selues*
>   Into my priuate Meditations?
>   (*Henry VIII* II.ii.1100ff. SD most probably authorial. My italics)

The versatility of the stage is soon apparent, but it is a versatility which depends, above all, on the well-trained imaginary forces of the audience.

The trap

The author's expectation of a trained audience imagination is most evident in the common allusive use of trap and gallery as familiar stage symbols of heaven and hell – associations which had long been fostered by the conventions of mediaeval pageants.[7] 'All are of the dust, and all turn to dust again.' Earth is naturally associated with death and the grave, and above all with Hell. The stage boards were evidently a perilously thin crust over the infernal regions. Nashe's Backwinter bites, scratches and kicks the ground, crying: 'Earth . . . Ile beate downe the partition with my heeles, / Which, as a mud-vault, seuers hell and thee. / Spirits, come vp; 'tis I that knock for you . . .' In the same franzy Hieronimo *diggeth with his dagger*, swearing, 'ile rip the bowels of the earth, / And Ferrie ouer to th'Elizian plaines'. In a celebrated visual image, Tamburlaine forces Bajazeth to crouch down that he may be *seen* literally to 'treade on Emperours' as he mounts his throne, while the prostrate Bajazeth cries to hell for vengeance: 'Then as I look downe to the damned Feends, / Feends looke on me.' In the actors' memorial version of *2 Henry VI*, the witch Margery Jourdain *lies downe vpon her face* for her incantations, prosaically explaining 'I . . . Do talke and whisper with the diuels be low'. By 1606 Dekker was mocking the cliché: 'Hell being vnder euerie one of their Stages, the Players . . . might with a false Trappe doore haue slipt [the devil] downe, and there kept him, as a laughing stocke to all their yawning Spectators.'[8] Too many stage ghosts and devils rise and sink through the trap, and it is probable that Shakespeare turns this dated spectacle to weird comedy as the old mole grunts in Elsinore's cellerage. Hamlet's hysterical joking may well be explicable in terms of literary satire, as well as apt psychology and good daemonology (and after all, even Lodge was derisive about the original ghost in the Ur-*Hamlet*, so that Shakespeare could hardly have presented him wholly conventionally). The trap's other appearance in *Hamlet* as Ophelia's grave is also turned to literary pastiche, and, apart from the necessary spectacles of *Macbeth*, it reappears in Shakespeare's later work only for a couple of realistic scenes. It must have been too stale for further use.[9]

The gallery

Shakespeare's precocious maturity in the stage symbolism of his colleagues is most obvious in his use of the stage gallery. Its symbolic connotations, with the heavens, the high station of the victor, and the summit of Fortune's wheel, are alternated even in the earliest plays with scenes of ambitious realism.

1 Henry VI is generally recognised to be statistically outstanding in its lavish use of the gallery, but the cocksure orginality and inventiveness of this has been disregarded.[10] The very first gallery-scene is a bold plagiarisation of Marlowe's notorious spectacle of the governor of Babylon, hung out *on the walles* to be shot from the open stage (a spectacle which, in one performance, cost two theatre-goers their lives).[11] In Shakespeare's more dramatic, and historically accurate scene, Salisbury, Talbot, and others appear above, ostensibly *on the Turrets* of the English watch-tower overlooking Orleans, little aware that the French have trained a cannon on them from the stage below, and that this (as the audience already knows) is being watched by the Master-Gunner's boy while his father has lunch. With unconscious irony, Talbot completes his account of his French captivity with 'Ready they were to shoot me to the heart', as Shakespeare directs: *Enter the Boy with a Linstock*. The English men crowd innocently to the watch-tower windows to discuss strategy, the boy discharges the cannon, and Salisbury and Gargrave fall. Yet, unaccountably, the Arden and Cambridge editors concur in placing the firing off-stage, in spite of the precedent of theatrical history in *Tamburlaine*, and the scene's own fidelity to historical detail, of which the boy's triumph was the factual climax. And even Hosley dismisses this as a gallery-scene, in spite of the unequivocal, most

probably authorial stage directions.[12] Moreover, this dénoument had
been clearly promised in the scene's beginning:

	Enter the Master Gunner of Orleance, and his Boy.
Master Gunner	Sirrha, thou know'st how Orleance is besieg'd
	And how the English haue the Suburbs wonne.
Boy	Father I know, and oft haue shot at them,
	How e're vnfortunate, I miss'd my ayme.
Master Gunner	But now thou shalt not . . .
	(*1 Henry VI* I.iv.463ff)

Equally spectacular, and historically literal, is the later surprise attack
on Orleans, in which the probably authorial stage directions instruct
the French to *leape ore the walles in their shirts*, while between these
two fundamentally realistic scenes is the emblematic appearance of
Joan of Arc on Orleans walls, victor of a day's skirmish, to mock the
hangdog English below. Indefatigably, and with real originality,
Shakespeare goes on to stretch his stage to its topmost little hut, in
which De Witt's sketch of the Swan★ shows the trumpeter whose
fanfare announced the beginning of a play. Here Joan emerges after
her successful disguised entry into Rouen, *on the top, thrusting out a
Torch burning* to shout a brief battle-cry, before scampering down to
the gallery for her usual crow over the English, boggling on the
common stage below. Hosley charily takes *the top* to mean the
gallery 'conceived of as the "top" of the tiring-house' (an unprecedented usage), but there is a clear differentiation between Joan's
appearance at the very top, where her three lines are fictionally
inaudible to those on the stage, and her reappearance *on the Walls*
(otherwise why have this direction?), for the usual exchange with
those below. It is characteristic of Shakespeare coolly to repeat this
early felicity in as late a play as *The Tempest*, where Prospero appears
on the top, (fictionally) *inuisible*, and his comments are by the same
convention inaudible to those on the stage below.[13]

1 Henry VI continues with another, standard scene as the General
of Bordeaux prophesies the death of Talbot, uncomfortably standing below. It culminates, however, in a final reversal of the symbolic
cliché, as the defeated Reignier, *on the Walles* of Angiers, must
descend to ransom his daughter, captive to the triumphant Suffolk
on the common stage below.[14] Such ironic reversals of the norm
become subtler in the latter parts of the tetralogy. The end of Cade's
rebellion, for instance, is presented with deceptive straightforward-
ness, King Henry above, *on the Tarras*, Cade's penitent revolution-
aries captive and haltered below, in the approved manner. But the

cardboard traditionalism of this stage picture is promptly undermined by Henry's first words, with their characteristic humility:

> Was euer King that ioy'd an earthly Throne,
> And could command no more content then I? . . .
> Was neuer Subiect long'd to be a King,
> As I do long and wish to be a Subiect?
> (*2 Henry VI* IV.ix.2850ff)

Shakespeare's stilted and excessive use of the gallery in *Titus* (six
shifts of level in the first scene!) is painfully amateurish by comparison. This contrast, and the development just outlined, tend to
confirm the new Arden editors in their several assumptions that the
three parts of *Henry VI* were written in the natural chronological
order, and that *Titus* preceded the lot. Shakespeare's original lack of
skill is further evident in his unquestioning use of the stage symbol,
and his naive eagerness to interpret it. So *Titus*'s first act ends with
Tamora triumphing *aloft*, and the second opens with Aaron labori-
ously explaining. 'Now climeth Tamora Olympus toppe, / Safe out
of fortunes shot, and sits aloft.'[15] In later plays stage symbol and
linguistic metaphor are better integrated, and symbolism itself is
sheltered by realism.

Thus in *Romeo and Juliet* the gallery is primarily the window (or
balcony) of Juliet's bedroom. When Juliet appears there, light probably in hand, the gallery's traditional associations, the lovers' characteristic light imagery, and physical fact all unite as Romeo exclaims,
without undue hyperbole, 'But soft, what light through yonder
window breaks? / It is the East, and Iuliet is the Sun.' Again, at the
turn of their fortunes, Romeo lets himself down from her room,
Juliet unhappily watching. Her frightened vision of him now 'As one
dead at the bottome of a tombe' subtly draws on the stage's
traditional associations with the earth, and so with the grave. At the
same time it is simply realistic, as she sees his white, upturned face –
and, of course, heavily proleptic, for so indeed she next sees him,
dead in the Capulet's monument.[16]

Richard II is as close in technique to *Romeo and Juliet*, as it must have
been in date. Here the sun-image recurs with Richard's appearance,
like 'the blushing discontented Sunne', on Flint Castle walls. Once
again the image has been prepared for by Richard's frequent self-
comparisons to the sun, and it is fully elaborated in Bolingbroke's
long speech on the king's imminent eclipse. Richard himself then
turns the same image to his own ends ('Yet know, my maister God
omnipotent / Is mustering in his cloudes on our behalfe / Armies of

pestilence'). At his descent into the 'base court where Kinges growe base', his classic image continues the theme at the same time as admitting his own regal ineptitude, the weakness that made him no king: 'Downe, downe I come, like glistring Phaeton: / Wanting the manage of vnrulie Iades . . .' In *Titus* the stage symbol was given a lumbering retrospective poetic gloss. In *Romeo and Juliet* and *Richard II*, the familiar stage symbols are the visual culmination of an extended, preceding poetic metaphor.[17]

It is hardly surprising that Shakespeare's later use of the gallery should be briskly functional. Its symbolic, spectacular, and poetic potential had all been fully exploited in the early plays. Now what? A quietly conventional realism. The gallery is pressed into unobtrusive service for the windows of comedy, the pulpit, hill and monument of the Roman plays, the city walls of English and classical history. But even by *Henry V* the technique was evidently so commonplace, that it was enough merely to lean ladders against the gallery to create *Scaling Ladders at Harflew*, and as far as dialogue and directions can tell us, the actual battle-scene proceeded on the flat. The gallery's capacity for subtly original effects, and indeed Shakespeare's apparent interest in them, were soon exhausted.[18]

The throne

It should primarily be remembered that the throne was *raised*, to occupy an elevated and focal position on the stage. Hence directions concerning it use terms like 'ascend', 'go up', 'thus high' and so on. Even more than the stage gallery, the raised throne had an obvious and apparently rigid significance. Consequently dramatic interest lies chiefly in the ironies of who inhabits the throne, and how fit they are for the state it automatically bestows. Its use will thus be similar to that of costume: both are external signs of rank which may belie inherent worth.

The best-known example of this is probably Bolingbroke's premature siezure of the throne in *Richard II*, as soon as he hears of Richard's consent to resign the crown. Hence his line, 'In Gods name, Ile ascend the regall throne.' That he does so is clear from the Bishop of Carlisle's immediate protests at such impiety – protests which are promptly answered by the Bishop's arrest for capital treason to the new 'king'. The sight of Bolingbroke, lofty and enthroned, to hear King Richard's abdication should press home most vividly the fact of his usurpation, and it is, of course,

Shakespeare's invention, having no origin in the historical sources. As usual, stage image and dialogue reinforce each other, and the implications of the tableau are dwelt on by Richard at his entry in full royal regalia:

> Alack, why am I sent for *to a King*,
> Before I haue shooke off the Regall thoughts
> Wherewith I reign'd? I hardly yet haue learn'd
> To insinuate, flatter, bowe, and bend my Knee . . .
>   (*Richard II* IV.i.2084ff. My italics)

Yet this striking staging had already been tried out in one of Shakespeare's earliest plays, when York and his rebels entered the deserted royal palace, and at Warwick's prompting, York 'went up' into the throne. At his later entry, King Henry VI had perforce to stand beneath him, weakly arguing his right to a throne he all too evidently failed to possess (again a partly invented scene). The ironies are subtler in *Richard II*, for here Richard grows in kingly stature as he loses the crown: the actual throne has little to do with his regality.[19] As usual, Shakespeare initially accepts the traditional symbolic associations, and then subverts the pattern. And the better received they are, the more quickly he tends to subvert them.

It is typical, too, that the experimentation of the earliest plays is capitalised in the later. Thus the inventive opening to *3 Henry VI* just described also lies behind a stage image in *Richard III*, as well as *Richard II*. For in *3 Henry VI* York only agrees to take the throne with the words, 'Assist me then, sweet Warwick, and I will'. Warwick the king-maker, and the other rebels, should actually hand York up into the throne with ritualistic clarity ('Wee'le all assist you'). This tableau is repeated with greater emphasis in the later play, when Richard III tells Buckingham to hand him into the throne Buckingham helped him steal. The action is turned into an explicit visual emblem of their relationship in which sound-effects play an emphasising part:

> *Sound a Sennet. Enter Richard in pompe, Buckingham, Catesby, Ratcliffe, Louel.*
> Richard Stand all apart. Cousin of Buckingham.
> Buckingham My gracious Soueraigne.
> Richard Giue me thy hand.
> *Sound.*
> Thus high, by thy aduice, and thy assistance,
> Is King Richard seated.
> (*Richard III* IV.ii.2588ff. SD probably authorial)

'What subiect can giue sentence on his King?' the Bishop of Carlisle had demanded. After God, the King was the supreme judge, and his throne doubled as judgement-seat. In *Henry VIII* the point is clearly made in the staging of Queen Katharine's trial, where, as in Holinshed, *The King takes place vnder the Cloth of State. The two Cardinalls sit vnder him as Iudges*, but the Queen silently walks round the whole court (creating an effective suspended pause) – to kneel at the king her husband's feet, and present her cause to him as her sole judge: 'Sir, I desire *you* do me Right and Iustice.' But the man in the hot seat does not always merit the authority it gives him, and this is the dominant concern of *Measure for Measure*.

This play's theme of 'Judge not, that ye be not judged' is staged in visual terms in the last act, in a series of elaborate changes of place. For here the Duke, returned to Vienna, calls for two judgement seats (and again we should probably think of them as emphatically raised). He installs himself in one, as impartial observer, and Angelo in the other, with the ominous words, 'be you Iudge / Of your owne Cause' – a cause in which Angelo is the only criminal. Later, the Duke makes an excuse to leave, calling on his other deputy, Escalus, to take his place, while he returns in his Friar's disguise to be questioned by the court. As soon as his real identity is revealed, the roles are reversed once again: the Duke reverts from accused to judge, and Angelo from judge to accused. Angelo is pointedly demoted and the Duke takes his place in the judgement seat ('Sir, by your leaue . . .'). Judge not, that ye be not judged . . . What could be a clearer, schematic illustration of the play's theme? Or, indeed, a neater visual summary of its plot? Furthermore, Angelo's unfitness for his position is twice stressed in exactly parallel terms, the angel-devil antithesis boldly underlined. First Isabella's energetic pleas for 'Iustice, Iustice, Iustice, Iustice', which so emphatically proclaim the theme of the last act, as well as of the whole play, are referred by the Duke *to Angelo*. Hence her violent retort: 'Oh worthy Duke, / You bid me seeke redemption of the diuell . . .' The Duke then echoes her protest, in his disguise as Friar (just as Isabella's condemnation had the authority of her novice's habit), when Escalus demands, 'Know you where you are?' 'Respect to your great place', the Duke nods to Escalus, in one judgement-seat; and to Angelo, in the other: 'and let the diuell / Be sometime honour'd, for his burning throne.' Both are deputies who are to be respected for the seats they fill, but in Angelo's case it is the scant honour due to the devil, merely *for* his burning throne. Like Satan, he exalted sits, by illusory merit raised to that bad eminence – a throne whose meaning he has perverted. Thus the scene's sense depends on the visual image, and its staging with two raised judgement seats whose elevation can graphically stress the last act's symbolic changes of place, the enacted epitomisation of the play's theme.[20]

It is typical of *Lear* that the ambiguities of the judgement seat should be dimly evoked in Lear's imaginary court. Here is none of *Measure for Measure*'s schematic symbolism and stern logic, only the pathos of Lear's careful arrangement of Kent, the Fool, and Edgar, as his three judges, seated to hear the cause in which he *stands* – a mere commoner – as plaintiff before them. The effect swings from the phantasmagoric to the clairvoyant, from the confusion as he struggles to get his unruly court in order – 'Come sit thou here most learned Iustice / Thou sapient sir sit here, no you shee Foxes –', to the childish clarity with which he sees his wrongs: 'I here take my oath before this honorable assembly [she] kickt the poore king her father . . .' Conventional employment of the judgement seat, its accepted ironies, even its actual staging, have been left behind in the bewildered fantasy of this scene. And yet its theme is still close to that of *Measure for Measure*. For it is right that Lear should be judged for his unjustified banishment of Cordelia; his other daughters merely repaid him in kind. Even now, Lear has begun to suffer at a dim intimation of his guilt, just as later Kent reports, 'A soueraigne shame so elbows him . . .' Thus his later, conscious humility is prefigured here, as he instinctively associates himself with the suppliant body of common humanity, while lunatic and fool stand judge over him.[21]

Sitting down

Sitting down would appear to differ from the other positions an actor can assume on the stage, in that it is primarily realistic and simple. A quiet domesticity is evoked in several plays as women enter to *set them downe on . . . lowe stooles and sowe*, tell stories, or play with their children. Lovers, too, will cradle their heads in one anothers' laps, Titania stroking Bottom's ass-ears, and even warriors like Mortimer and the fidgety Hotspur nestling their heads in their wives' knees. Hamlet characteristically sours such tenderness in his coarse witticisms ('Lady shall I lie in your lap? . . . Doe you thinke I meant country matters?'),[22] and Webster probably satirises this scene in his Induction to Marston's *Malcontent*, where the actors Sincklo and Sly likewise settle themselves at the side of the stage to mark the play, aping Hamlet and Ophelia's edgy exchange in a feeble, naughty parody:

Sly   O Coosin, come you shall sit betweene my legges heare.
Sincklo   No indeede coosin, the audience then will take me for a viol de gambo, and thinke that you play upon me.
Sly   Nay, rather that I worke upon you, coose.
                        (ll. 18–21)

However, social harmony is also traditionally mirrored in the due order of seated banquet and council. The sedate propriety of the banquet celebrating peace between Spain and Portugal in *The Spanish Tragedy* is later paralleled by the equally old-fashioned banquet-scene in *Pericles*, where the knights placed decorously about Simonides' table remind Pericles of his own father, who 'Had Princes sit like Starres about his Throane, / And hee the Sunne for them to reuerence.' The best-known variant on this traditional stage symbol is its reversal in *Macbeth*, where large-scale disorder is mirrored by the miniature of shattered domestic ceremony, the banquet coinciding with Banquo's murder opening in all harmony ('You know your owne degrees, sit downe'), and ending in chaos ('Stand not vpon the order of your going, / But go at once'). Sitting down may be a primarily naturalistic action, but in drama it is quickly assimilated to more symbolic purposes. Above all, sitting on the boards, and, worse still, lying down, is a familiar image of lost hope and strength, common to the prose as well as the drama. *Qvi iacet in terra non habet vnde cadat.*[23]

The image is a traditional one. In *The Spanish Tragedy* the Portuguese Viceroy mourns his defeat by throwing himself down from his throne, crying, 'But wherefore sit I in a Regall throne . . . Heere let me lye, now am I at the lowest', so giving his audience little opportunity to overlook the clear emblem. Such grovelling is the tragic counterpart to the victorious character triumphing 'aloft', in the gallery, or on his throne. Edward II similarly moralises on the transience of earthly glory, properly suiting his action to his words:

> Stately and proud, in riches and in traine,
> Whilom I was, powerfull and full of pompe,
> But what is he, whome rule and emperie
> Have not in life or death made miserable?
> Come Spencer, come Baldocke, come sit downe by me . . .
>   (*Edward II* IV.vii. 12ff)

When his enemies find him thus, his head in the kindly Abbot's lap, the stage picture is given its appropriate Latin caption: *quem dies vidit veniens superbum, / Hunc dies vidit fugiens jacentem.* About ten years later, Heywood was attributing similar actions and sentiments to Mistress Frankford:[24]

> Bid my coach stay. Why should I ride in state,
> Being hurl'd so low down by the hand of fate?
> A seat like to my fortunes let me have,
> Earth for my chair, and for my bed a grave.
> (*A Woman Killed with Kindness* xvi. 1–4)

Of course the stage symbol has its source in mediaeval drama; compare, for instance, the fall of Skelton's Magnificence:

	Here cometh in Aduersyte.
Magnificence	Alas, who is yonder, that grymly lokys? . . .
	Lorde, so my flesshe trymblyth nowe for drede!
	Here Magnyfycence is beaten downe, and spoylyd from all his goodys and rayment . . .
Adversity	The stroke of God, Aduersyte I hyght;
	I pluke downe kynge, prynce, lorde, and knyght . . .
	Thys losyll was a lorde, and lyuyd at his lust,
	And nowe, lyke a lurden, he lyeth in the dust.
	(*Magnyfycence*, ll. 1898ff)

Shakespeare was wise to it in his earliest work. Titus formally *lieth downe, and the Iudges passe by him*, as he pleads for his sons' lives, and there is a nice implicit contrast between this, and his description of his other sons, who 'died in honours *loftie* bed', on the battle field. His action also has the merit of being one in a long chain of unrequited prayers, thematic to this play.[25] Shakespeare is equally free with this traditional symbol in *Henry VI*. In a scene crammed with significant changes of place, Queen Margaret visits the French King Lewis to ask for aid: the scene opens with the probably authorial direction, *Lewis sits, and riseth vp againe*, to offer Margaret a place beside him. She refuses, ritualistically seating herself on the ground, with the words

> I was (I must confesse)
> Great Albions Queene, in former Golden dayes:
> But now mischance hath trod my Title downe,
> And with dis-honor layd me on the ground,
> Where I must take like Seat vnto my fortune,
> And to my humble Seat conforme my selfe . . .
> (*3 Henry VI* III.iii.1730ff)

Lewis *Seats her by him*; all goes well with her negotiations till a rival English messenger appears, at which Lewis *descends*. *Shee ariseth*, her company are told to *stand aloofe* – and so, for the rest of the scene, its many complicated shifts of party and fortune are clarified by such well-defined, emblematic actions. In the preceding play, Shakespeare had spiced the same symbol with a sharp biblical allusion as Cade, the swashbuckling revolutionary, enters after the failure of his insurrection, and (as the actors verify)

> [Q: *lies downe picking of hearbes and eating them.*]
> Cade Fye on Ambitions: fie on my selfe, that haue a sword, and yet am ready to famish . . . Wherefore on a Bricke wall haue I climb'd into this Garden, to see if I can eate Grasse . . .
>> (*2 Henry VI* IV.x.2906ff; *Contention* Q:G4)

Regular church attendance was enforced by law at the time, and Shakespeare's audience was more likely than ours to recognise this re-enactment of the humbling of Nebuchadnezzar. Characteristically, the stage image is Shakespeare's invention, and owes nothing to his source, which tells us merely that 'one Alexander Iden . . . found hym in a garden, and there in his defence, manfully slewe the caitife Cade'.[26]

As ever, the later plays show Shakespeare's impatient reversal of these norms. In *King John* the traditional humility of such abasement is splendidly overturned by Queen Constance, who, like Margaret before her, sits on the ground to lament her misfortune. But Constance refuses to budge when Salisbury tries to take her to the king. She settles on her chosen throne of suffering, seated with the state of a mater dolorosa:

> To me and to the state of my great greefe
> Let kings assemble, for my greefe's so great
> That no supporter but the huge firme earth
> Can hold it vp: here I and sorrowes sit.
> Heere is my Throne, bid kings come bow to it.
>> (*King John* III.i.992ff)

Richard II, like Edward II, throws himself on the ground to revel in misery ('For Gods sake let vs sit vpon the ground, / And tell sad stories of the death of Kings'), but Shakespeare subtly undercuts what was, in Marlowe, a moving stage image, by debasing the onlookers' comments into the self-indulgence of Richard's own complaints. This is not, as in Marlowe, a tragic climax; it is rather a low point – the beginning of Richard's long climb up to dignity.[27]

So Shakespeare habitually varies and refines the implications of the
traditional stage symbol. Most controlled is its last major appearance
at Antony's disheartened entry after his defeat at the battle of
Actium. Here Shakespeare's skill is apparent in his dovetailing of
some apparently insignificant details from Plutarch's account, making composite sense of them by stage symbolism. Plutarch tells us
that in his flight from Actium in Cleopatra's wake, Antony 'had not
onely lost the corage and hart of an Emperor, but also of a valliant
man, and that *he was not his owne man*'. Later, without making a
connection between the two, Plutarch describes how Antony called
his friends, offering them treasure, 'commaunding them to depart,
and to seeke to save them selves'; at their refusal, he 'very curteously
and lovingly did comfort them, and *prayed them* to depart'.
Shakespeare picks up Antony's loss of self-control ('he was not his
owne man'), extends it to his leadership of his men, whom he can no
longer command, but only entreat, and clinches it by the stage
symbol, as Antony collapses in a state of total self-abandonment:

> Leaue me, I pray, a little: pray you now,
> Nay do so: for indeede I haue lost command,
> Therefore I pray you, Ile see you by and by.
> *Sits downe.*
> (*Antony and Cleopatra* III.xi.2046ff. SD most probably authorial)

The distinction between 'pray' and 'command' came from Plutarch;
Shakespeare simply stresses it by giving it supporting action. Its
rationale, too, came from Plutarch, but is re-stated by Shakespeare's
Antony, who logically if ungrammatically begs his friends to desert
the man who has already deserted his proper self: 'Let them be left /
Which leaues it selfe', he says. Canidius had made the same point at his
flight: 'Had our Generall / Bin what he knew himselfe . . .' But it is
Antony's tragedy that his two rôles of lover and general depend on
each other; one lost, the other perishes. So when Cleopatra enters at
this moment, like Antony to sit down gasping and overcome,
Antony is not aroused. As Iras comments, still harping on the same
theme, 'Hee's vnqualited with very shame'. In his self-abandonment
Antony deserves the Nurse's quibbling reproaches of Romeo, sob-
bing on the floor: 'Stand vp, stand vp, stand and you be a man, / For
Iuliets sake . . . rise and stand.' But Antony does not rise, in any
sense, till Cleopatra has worked on him. His slumped posture
mirrors every aspect of his 'lost command', amatory, military, and
personal, for in him all three are interdependent.[28]

Later use of the symbol is avoided. A recent Stratford production

of *Henry VIII* made Wolsey literally fall at his fall but this was not, in
fact, demanded by the text. It was, perhaps, a little too obvious for
Shakespeare at this stage. His contemporaries continued to use it, a
little dully; in Fletcher's *Bonduca* two Romans, soundly thumped by
the English, *sitt downe*, complaining, 'o. I haue lost myne honor, lost
my name . . .'[29] And Milton continues the same tradition in Sam-
son's first appearance:

Chorus   This, this is hee; softly a while,
           Let us not break in upon him;
           O change beyond report, thought, or belief!
           See how he lies at random, carelessly diffus'd,
           With languisht head unpropt,
           As one past hope, abandond,
           And by himself giv'n over.
                    (*Samson Agonistes*, ll. 115ff)

It is a fine description of everything the action implies.

★ See frontispiece on p. ii.

CHAPTER 3

Taking by the hand

The chief difficulty besetting a study like this one is its inevitable imposition of a false pattern. For instance, Shakespeare's use of the different stage areas, and of an actor's position in them, is obviously not limited to the traditional symbols providing a frame for the preceding chapter. His practice has a multiplicity which defies categorisation, and many significant moments lie well beyond the familiar and somewhat stereotyped associations of Fortune's wheel. When *Falstalffe riseth vp* from the dead beside him, at the battle of Shrewsbury, this resurrection is the last in a series of sacriligeous parodies which have characterised him throughout the play, from his ignoble 'Catechisme' against honour, to a myriad biblical allusions in which he goes so far as to compare himself to the crucified, and now the risen Christ.[1] One longs for the modern producer to take the hint and let himself go, staging this resurrection from the dead on a darkened stage, Falstaff swathed in garish light like Grünewald's risen Christ, for the audience to catch Falstaff's wicked quibbling:

> *Falstalffe riseth vp.*
> Falstaff Inboweld, if thou inbowel me to day, ile giue you leaue to powder me and eate me too to morrowe . . . Counterfet? I lie, I am no counterfet, to die is to bee a counterfet, for he is but the counterfet of a man, who hath not the life of a man: but to counterfet dying when a man therby liueth, is to be no counterfet, but the true and perfect image of life indeed.
> (*1 Henry IV* V.iv.Q:K3–K3ᵛ. SD most probably authorial)

Did Morgann have this stage image at the back of his mind, as the illustrative proof of his words? 'There is in truth no such thing as totally demolishing Falstaff . . . he is safe even in defeat, and seems to rise, like another Antaeus, with recruited vigour from every fall.'[2] Again, when Iago stands over Othello, writhing on the ground in his fit, the stage picture, accompanied as it is by Iago's words, 'Worke on my medicine, worke', irresistibly suggests Iago as an evil spirit possessing Othello – an implication already well established by the

play's persistent use of daemonic images in its language also, and
clinched by a final piece of staging in the last act (discussed in chapter
10).[3] Lying down is not even uniformly symbolic; one of the most
harrowing instances is the moment in *Julius Caesar*, when Brutus and
others approach the dead Cassius, and see another figure prostrate
beside him. They assume it to be Titinius, mourning his master, and
there is uncanny horror as they realise their mistake from the way he
lies:

Brutus	Where, where Messala, doth his body lye?
Messala	Loe yonder, and Titinius mourning it.
Brutus	Titinius face is vpward.
Cato	He is slaine.

(Julius Caesar V.iii.2579ff)

But this pebble of realism throws widening circles. Such mistaken
interpretation of ambiguous phenomena is the leit-motif of the play;
furthermore, Brutus is Shakespeare's mouthpiece as he interprets the
scene to fittingly ominous sound effects. In his awestruck eyes,
Caesar's revenge appears to be accomplished for him, as each of the
conspirators is found dead, by no hand, or his own:

Brutus	O Iulius Caesar, thou art mighty yet,
	Thy Spirit walkes abroad, and turnes our Swords
	In our owne proper Entrailes.
	Low Alarums.

(Julius Caesar V.iii.2583ff)

The interpretation is, of course, Shakespeare's own.[4]

   Thus method brings with it distortion by omission – and, equally,
the distortion of all-inclusiveness. 'There is no great merit in telling
how many plays have ghosts in them, and how this ghost is better
than that,' said Johnson. 'You must shew how terrour is impressed
on the human heart.' Johnson's ideals are noble but impossibly
grandiose. I prefer Eliot's drier recommendation: 'Comparison and
analysis . . . are the chief tools of the critic. It is obvious indeed that
they *are* tools, to be handled with care, and not employed in an
enquiry into the number of times giraffes are mentioned in the
English novel.'[5] Consequently, I shall keep to a few well-hedged
but, I hope, not absurd little fields in the broad plains of Shakespearean symbolism: his use of certain natural, recurrent and meaningful
actions, such as shaking hands, kissing and embracing, and kneeling.
The general implications and development of each will be traced,

before we turn to moments of particular interest, irrespective of their symbolism, realism, or other critical labels.

'Holding eche other by the hande or the arme, whiche betokeneth concorde.'⁶

Taking by the hand is the natural gesture of friendship. One of Timon's servants laments his fall, saying, 'So Noble a Master falne, all gone, and not / One Friend to take his Fortune by the arme, / And go along with him.' Timon repeats the image to Apemantus, the type of the misanthrope he later becomes: 'Thou art a Slaue, whom Fortunes tender arme / With fauour neuer claspt . . .' While Timon affectionately shakes hands with the jeweller and others in the first half of the play, *addressing himselfe curteously to euery Sutor* (authorial stage direction), in the second half, like Apemantus, he too 'With his disease, of all shunn'd pouerty, / Walkes like contempt alone'. The distinction should be made clear in performance. Hamlet, can have similar moments of genuine warmth, or can affect them. He is sincere with Horatio and Marcellus, 'Nay come, lets goe together'; probably not, with Guildenstern and Rosencrantz: 'Harke you Guyldensterne, and you to, at each eare a hearer . . .' (see p. 56 below). It is the gesture of reconciliation; so Puck puns on clapping hands in his valediction, 'Giue me your hands, if we be friends . . .'⁷ It is the symbol of protection: the relatively early *King John* is characteristically explicit:

> *France*   Loe in this right hand, whose protection
> Is most diuinely vow'd vpon the right
> Of him it holds, stands yong Plantagenet.
> (*King John* II.i.542ff)

It is the timeless gesture to clinch a wager, seal a bargain or an oath, to greet and to part; it is the instinctive movement to help the sick, the old, the loved. Shakespeare calls for it naturally and continuously. In *Lear* Edgar leads the blind Gloucester by the hand, Cordelia enters *with her father in her hand*, even Kent comforts the terrified Fool by holding his hand. How easily such warm details can be missed, if our ears aren't attuned to these quiet commands for gesture! Most moving of all, perhaps, is Lady Macbeth's subconscious concern for her husband, in the sleepwalking scene – a tenderness hardly audible in the waking source of her dream: 'Come, come, come, come, giue

me your hand: What's done, cannot be vndone . . .' The hands she
rubbed and scrutinised all through her dream are now held out, as
she leaves, pathetically, for no-one to take.[8]

It is the gesture of relationship. So (an absurd example) the Clown
boasts in *The Winter's Tale*, 'I was a Gentleman borne before my
Father: for the Kings Sonne tooke me by the hand, and call'd mee
Brother: and then the two Kings call'd my Father Brother.' We will
see later how much lies behind Coriolanus's acceptance of his human
ties, as he holds his mother *by the hand silent*, in a supreme acknowledgement of affiliation and concord.[9] In *Lear* the same gesture is
used for painfully opposite effect, as Regan takes her stand by her
sister's side, against her father, and the hostile line-up is marked by
this gesture:

Lear   . . . Beloued Regan,
           Thy Sisters naught: oh Regan, she hath tied
           Sharpe-tooth'd vnkindnesse, like a vulture heere,
           I can scarce speake to thee, thou'lt not beleeue
           With how deprau'd a quality. Oh Regan . . .
           Enter Gonerill . . .
           O Regan, will you take her by the hand?
                       (*King Lear* II.iv.1411ff, 1484)

It is, finally, one of the many formal tokens of marriage. The
Priest in *Twelfth Night* lists them all:

           A Contract of eternall bond of loue,
           Confirm'd by mutuall ioynder of your hands,
           Attested by the holy close of lippes,
           Strengthned by enterchangement of your rings.
                   (*Twelfth Night* V.i.2318ff)

The secret betrothal in the first act of *The Duchess of Malfi* properly
fulfills this list, as the Duchess puts her ring on Antonio's finger,
gives him her hand to raise him (symbolically, to her own rank), and
later embraces him, then disclosing the witness that made all these
acts formal marriage ritual.[10] In Shakespeare the interest lies chiefly in
his developing presentation of this intrinsically dullish staple of
drama: the examples characterise quite accurately his changes in
tone. Thus in the early plays the presentation is often straightforward, *The Taming of the Shrew*, for instance, being plain-spoken,
good-humoured, uninspiring:

Petruchio   Giue me thy hand Kate, I will vnto Venice
           To buy apparell 'gainst the wedding day . . .
                    (*Taming of the Shrew* II.i.1194ff)

By the middle comedies the stock scene is replayed in a series of comic variations. In *As You Like It*, for instance, the hints of *Rosalynde* are acted out in Rosalind's prompting Celia to act as priest for her (note, incidentally, the dialogue's provisions for Celia's embarrassed pause):

Rosalind   Come sister, you shall be the Priest, and marrie vs: giue me
              your hand Orlando: What doe you say sister?
Orlando [———] Pray thee marrie vs.
Celia   I cannot say the words.
Rosalind   You must begin, will you Orlando.
Celia   Goe too: wil you Orlando haue to wife this Rosalind?
Orlando   I will.
                    (*As You Like It* IV.i.2033ff)

In the dark comedies the equivalent scene is correspondingly problematic or unhappy. There is Isabella's notorious failure to rise to the Duke's repeated proposal at the end of *Measure for Measure* ('Giue me your hand, and say you will be mine . . . But fitter time for that'). Her silence is genuinely difficult and can accommodate diverse interpretation.[11] Not so Bertram's stubborn refusal of Helena in *All's Well* – or, worse still, the blunt materialism with which, after some seventy lines, he finally accepts not her, but her dowry. Again, note the pause as he refuses to take her hand:

King   My Honor's at the stake, which to defeate
            I must produce my power. Heere, take her hand,
  [———]   Proud scornfull boy, vnworthie this good gift . . .
            Take her by the hand,
            And tell her she is thine: to whom I promise
            A counterpoize, if not to thy estate,
            A ballance more repleat.
Bertram   I take her hand.
                (*All's Well* II.iii.1052ff)

In the last plays, there is an interesting relationship to the practice of Shakespeare's earlier work; as often, he is re-cycling and modifying. The betrothal of Pericles and Thaisa, falling in the corrupt half of *Pericles*, has the unsubtle, hearty humour sometimes found in Shakespeare's earliest work:

King   Therefore, heare you Mistris, either frame
          Your will to mine: and you sir, heare you;
          Either be rul'd by mee, or Ile make you,
          Man and wife: nay come, your hands,
          And lippes must seale it too.
                              (*Pericles* II.v.Q:D4^v)

In *The Winter's Tale* Florizel shamelessly uses the exotic language of Shakespeare's original young lovers, plagiarising and enriching the imagery of Demetrius and Romeo before him:[12]

Florizel   I take thy hand, this hand,
              As soft as Doues-downe, and as white as it,
              Or Ethyopians tooth, or the fan'd snow, that's bolted
              By th'Northerne blasts, twice ore.
                              (*Winter's Tale* IV.iv.2185ff)

Shakespeare happily elaborates his adolescent style, for the adolescent lover. But for the reunion of the mature lovers he turns the original comedy of situation from *As You Like It* into a moment of grave power. Like Rosalind, Hermione wooes Leontes. But now the gesture is one of forgiveness and reconciliation, all the more compelling for its being made in silence:

Paulina   Ile make the Statue moue indeed; descend,
             And take you by the hand . . .
             Musick; awake her: Strike:
             'Tis time: descend: be Stone no more: approach: . . .
             Start not . . .
             . . . Nay, present your Hand:
             When she was young, you woo'd her: now, in age,
             Is she become the Suitor?
                              (*Winter's Tale* V.iii.3292ff)

And, at last, in *The Tempest*, Miranda and Ferdinand agree on their own betrothal with a direct simplicity that is almost businesslike, and the moment's purity needs no further poetry:

Miranda   My husband then?
Ferdinand   I, with a heart as willing
              As bondage ere of freedome: heere's my hand.
Miranda   And mine, with my heart in't.
                              (*Tempest* III.i.1339ff)

It is the action's essence, heart in hand. Just so were Cassius and Brutus reconciled. 'Giue me your hand.' 'And my heart too.'[13]

When Loue begins to sicken and decay
It vseth an enforced Ceremony'.[14]

But, like all symbols, the gesture can be turned to deception. Quite clear in its significance was the left-handed gesture that Bertram Joseph has suggested to be appropriate in some underhand encounters.[15] Such perversions are, however, hardly deceptive. Dramatically more interesting are the handshakes that have been degraded into the mere exchange of a bribe. Falstaff does it outrageously, as he agrees to cuckold Ford / Brook for him: 'Master Broome, I will first make bold with your money: next, giue mee your hand: and last, as I am a gentleman, you shall, if you will, enioy Fords wife.' In *Cymbeline*, Cloten is characteristically crass, misunderstanding this, like all other symbols, with an absurd literalism:

Cloten	Wilt thou serue mee?
Pisanio	Sir, I will.
Cloten	Giue mee thy hand, heere's my purse.

(Cymbeline III.v.2036ff)

It is a striking contrast with Miranda's proper response of heart in hand.

The ceremony of a handshake can be further perverted, for just as a true handshake creates and acknowledges a bond between two people, so by shaking hands with someone, you can force an unwilling acceptance of such a bond on them. A first attempt at this, in *King John*, is then perfected in *Othello*, where Iago over-rides Roderigo's weak complaints with a bland show of friendship: 'Why now I see there's mettle in thee, and euen from this time doe build on thee a better opinion then euer before, giue me thy hand Roderigo . . .' Before Roderigo knows where he is, he's shaking hands with Iago, and agreeing to murder Cassio.[16]

As might have been expected, the ironies of hollow ceremony are most directly exploited in the earliest plays. In *1 Henry VI* Shakespeare pointedly alters his source to stage a striking scene in which the difference between Gloucester and Winchester's honesty is sharply illustrated. As Gloucester tries to make peace between them, Winchester hangs back, and there is an uncomfortable pause as his handshake is refused:

Gloucester	Here Winchester, I offer thee my Hand.
King [——]	Fie Vnckle Beauford, I haue heard you preach,
	That Mallice was a great and grieuous sinne:
	And will not you maintaine the thing you teach? . . .
Warwick	For shame my Lord of Winchester relent;
	What, shall a Child instruct you what to doe?
Winchester	Well, Duke of Gloster, I will yeeld to thee
	Loue for thy Loue, and Hand for Hand I giue.
[aside] *Gloucester*	I, but I feare me with a hollow Heart.
	See here my Friends and loving Countreymen,
	This token serueth for a Flagge of Truce . . .
	So helpe me God, as I dissemble not.
[aside] *Winchester*	So helpe me God, as I intend it not.

(*1 Henry VI* III.i.1342ff)

On at least five other occasions in the first tetralogy a similar incident is acted out, and in each case the dialogue dwells, as it does here, on the correlation of hands with hearts. (The correlation is a traditional one and can originate in the source, as in Hall's account of the hollow reconciliations at Edward's death-bed: 'And there . . . (as by their woordes appeared) eche forgaue other, and joyned their handes together, when as it after appeared by their dedes their hartes were far a sunder.') In each case the correlation is false, meriting Othello's later, bitter reversal: 'the hearts of old gaue hands, / But our new herraldry is hands, not hearts.'[17]

In these early examples Shakespeare ironically reverses the stage symbol: a handshake visually epitomises enmity and deceit. In *Hamlet* a similar example of what M. C. Bradbrook once called 'moral heraldry' is presented more obliquely, as Hamlet *closes* his disappointing reunion with Guildenstern and Rosencrantz by effusively wringing their hands in *welcome*. Such unnatural reversals have characterised the play from its beginning, and are a theatrical and linguistic leit-motif to stress the central theme. If Guildenstern and Rosencrantz had listened to what Hamlet said, they might have realised that this apparently lunatic 'forcing of his disposition' (as they called it) was a clear warning of insincerity: 'Gentlemen you are welcome to Elsonoure, your hands come then, th'appurtenance of welcome is fashion and ceremonie; let mee comply with you in this garb: [lest my] extent to the players, which I tell you must showe fairely outwards, should more appeare like entertainment then yours.' His genuine pleasure at the players' arrival and his excited, repeated 'welcome maisters, welcome all . . . welcome good friends' contrasts with this admitted enforced ceremony, and corroborates the aphorism of *Timon of Athens*: 'Ceremony was but

deuis'd at first / To set a glosse on faint deeds, hollow welcomes . . .
But where there is true friendship, there needs none.'[18] In both early
instances and here, it is the old theme of appearance and reality once
again.

Typically, too, the increased subtlety of the middle plays is turned
to complex schematic ends in the intellectual *Measure for Measure*.
Here the Duke makes his formal re-entry into Vienna in the last act,
emblematically resting on the arms of his two deputies. Hence his
gloss: 'And good supporters are you', since of course they supported
the state in his absence. But the Duke's praise of Angelo has also a
more critical underlying sense, which undercuts its bland surface
promise that Angelo's merits must be given due public recognition.

> *Duke* . . . Giue [me] your hand
> And let the Subiect see, to make them know
> That outward curtesies would faine proclaime
> Fauours that keepe within.
> (*Measure for Measure* V.i.2361ff)

Like the rest of the Duke's polite overtures at the beginning of this
scene, this is heavily ironic. In his public reception of Angelo
('outward curtesies'), the Duke 'would faine proclaime' what Angelo's actual nature (the 'Fauours that keepe within') really is. The
Duke's words are a secret threat; this very reception will soon make
Angelo's private dishonesty known to the public. Just as Angelo's
accepted reputation wholly belies his nature, so the Duke's reception
of him has an ironic duality. And thus the moment is an image in
little of the play's abiding theme of 'Seeming, seeming'.

Emblematic arrangements

The Duke's entry into Vienna on the arms of his two deputies recalls
the entry of Nashe's Summer, *leaning on Autumnes and Winters
shoulders*, in *Summer's Last Will*, with its equally precise significance,
elegantly explained in a later speech: 'On Autumne now and Winter
must I leane. / Needs must he fall, whom none but foes vphold.'
Such emblematic arrangements have their source in mediaeval
pageantry, and, indeed, Alice Griffin has pointed out that the sight of
the new King Henry V with the Lord Chief Justice would have
evoked a tableau familiar to its original, Elizabethan audience, of 'the
ideal king supported by a sovereigne's chief virtue, Justice'.[19] The
heraldic clarity of this moment is, in fact, untypical of the predomi-

nantly realistic second history trilogy, but it is a bright, auspicious opening to the glorious reign to follow. As such, it is a clear omen. Justice is invested by the Crown, and both stand reconciled, hand in hand. This should be formally, triumphantly acted out:

Prince	Into the hands of Iustice you did commit me:
	For which I do commit into your hand,
	Th'vnstained sword that you haue vsde to beare . . .
	. . . there is my hand,
	You shall be as a father to my youth,
	My voice shall sound as you do prompt mine eare,
	And I wil stoope and humble my intents,
	To your well practizde wise directions.

(2 Henry IV V.ii.Q:K)

It is natural that we should find such traditional tableaux in the first history trilogy, where, for instance, Henry VI joins Warwick and Clarence's hands as joint Protectors of the realm, moralising as he does so, or again that such an antiquated piece of stage symbolism should recur in the first half of *Pericles*, where Helicanus persuades Pericles's impatient lords to wait for his return: 'Then you loue vs, we you, and wee'le claspe hands: / When Peeres thus knit, a Kingdome euer stands.' If not a *Paysage*, then at least *des personnages moralisés!* Similarly in *Merry Wives* there is a comic variant as the Host takes the celestial and terrestrial hands of Evans and Caius, parson and doctor, and reunites them in a humorously balanced speech. Perhaps because the implications of such arrangements were a little more flexible than the symbolism of place described in the last chapter, Shakespeare continues to exploit them throughout the canon. In *Troilus and Cressida* there are two such tableau scenes, which are typical of this play's dramatic method. For this play's premise is its use of a particularly celebrated story whose outcome is foreknown; its miserable effect lies in the characters' ignorance that they are puppets doomed to play out their historical roles. The tableau scenes in particular frankly exploit this inexhaustible source of dramatic irony, as well as the fact that by Shakespeare's time the characters had stiffened into the types of their own attributes. Shakespeare turns them into human beings once again, and then, at the drama's high point, suddenly troubles the illusion by superimposing the type on the individual. In effect, he plays a double-take on the audience similar to that in *Julius Caesar*, where Cassius and Brutus tell the audience that the assassination they have just witnessed is the reality later ages will see dramatised on their stages. By this daring *coup* of evoking the later dramatic fiction Shakespeare at once disturbs and confirms the reality of the present illusion.[20] So Pandarus places Troilus and Cressida in each hand, as all three swear to stand for their own type in times to come:

Pandarus	Go to a bargaine made, seale it, seale it, ile bee the witnes, here I hold your hand, here my Cozens, if euer you proue false one to another since I haue taken such paine to bring you together, let all pittifull goers betweene be cald to the worlds end after my name, call them all Panders, let all constant men be Troylusses, all false woemen Cressids, and all brokers betweene panders; say Amen.
Troilus	Amen.
Cressida	Amen.
Pandarus	Amen.

(Troilus and Cressida III.ii.Q:F4)

This evocation of the type surely makes us all the more aware how much more complex Shakespeare's portraits of the true Troilus and false Cressid are.

Just as this scene is the stark emblem of the Troilus-Cressida-Pandarus story, so another, rather less bold tableau epitomises the Troy story. Both are illustrative stills such as Lucrece might have found in her painting of the siege of Troy. Hector is about to go into battle; he is fully armed. Andromache and Cassandra have both failed to dissuade him; Cassandra shepherds on stage the one man with authority to hold him back. She arranges her human props, and comments on the ominous picture with prophetic authority:

	Enter Priam and Cassandra
Cassandra	Lay hold vpon him Priam hold him fast,
	He is thy crutch: now if thou loose thy stay,
	Thou on him leaning, and all Troy on thee,
	Fall all together.

(Troilus and Cressida V.iii.Q:L^v)

A late, last example of such symbolism occurs in *Henry VIII*, where Gardiner, the King's new secretary, makes his first appearance promptly to have his hand shaken by Wolsey, aside, with the words, 'Giue me your hand, much ioy and fauour to you; / You are the Kings now.' But the undercurrent to this apparently innocuous congratulation is Wolsey's threat of power, as Gardiner's response demonstrates. He changes the handshake into another symbol (and in performance he could quickly bob, to make the point clear): 'But to be commanded / For euer by your Grace, whose hand ha's rais'd me.' As the later dialogue confirms, Wolsey has installed Gardiner in an influential position for his own ends.[21]

There are two plays worth special scrutiny, in which Shakespeare's use of the hand expands from momentary importance, to dominate a scene, or carry a theme.

The relationship between *King John* and what was once commonly assumed to be its source, *The Troublesome Raigne*, is obscure, and no firm conclusion has yet been reached about the two plays' order of precedence.[22] This particular moment does not help the problem. Either Shakespeare picked up a detail mentioned and then forgotten in his source, to turn it into the dramatic focal point of *his* scene, or *The Troublesome Raigne* makes explicit a detail Shakespeare implicitly envisaged, but then fails to make anything of it, in contrast to its Shakespearean source. Thus, in *The Troublesome Raigne*, Philip of France and King John are about to leave the stage to celebrate the marriage-treaty of Blanch of Spain (John's niece) and the French Dauphin, when their way is blocked by the papal legate:

King Philip	Lordings lets in, and spend the wedding day
	In maskes and triumphs, letting quarrells cease.
	Enter a Cardynall from Rome.
Cardinal	Stay King of France, I charge thee joyn not hands
	With him that stands accurst of God and men.
	(*Troublesome Raigne* ll.964ff)

The French King is easily persuaded to drop John, who is excommunicated for disobedience to the Pope. Nothing more is heard of their joined hands; this could have been a mere metaphor. In Shakespeare, conversely, there is a lengthy argument, full of suspense, in which France hangs, undecided, between England on the one hand, and Rome on the other. The handshake, which is never formally introduced, is referred to throughout, providing a visual focus for the entire debate for over some hundred lines, till France's final firm disclaimer, as he lets John's hand drop: 'England, I will fall from thee.' The scene is unfortunately too long for quotation, but later the same effect would appear to be repeated, as Blanch takes her uncle, John, and her French husband in each hand, as the victim to be torn in two by their breach:

> The Sun's orecast with bloud: faire day adieu,
> Which is the side that I must goe withall?
> I am with both, each Army hath a hand,
> And in their rage, I hauing hold of both,
> They whurle a-sunder, and dismember mee.

> Husband, I cannot pray that thou maist winne:
> Vncle, I needs must pray that thou maist lose . . .
> (*King John* III.i.1259ff)

Thus in the same scene the gesture is first used straightforwardly, as a visible symbol of unity ('This royall hand and mine are newly knit,' France protests; 'And shall these hands so lately purg'd of bloud? / So newly ioyn'd in loue? so strong in both, / Vnyoke this seysure, and this kinde regreete? / Play fast and loose with faith?'), then as the graphic image of separation and conflict, in an ironic reversal.[23]

In the second play to be considered in this context, there is no such baldly heraldic use of emblem; rather, a fascinating, impressionistic accumulation of associations. In *Antony and Cleopatra* Shakespeare makes peculiarly loving use of Cleopatra's hand. All references to her past, all the vicissitudes of the present, seem to focus on it. When the luckless Messenger brings her news of Antony's marriage to Octavia, she nervously tries to bribe him to welcome news by proffering her hand as a royal tit-bit:

Cleopatra Anthonyo's dead,
          If thou say so Villaine, thou kil'st thy Mistris:
          But well and free, if thou so yeild him.
          There is Gold, and heere
          My blewest vaines to kisse: a hand that Kings
          Haue lipt, and trembled kissing . . .
                (*Antony and Cleopatra* II.v.1056ff)

Once again, in her ambiguous capitulation to Thidias, she gives him her hand, while keeping her own eyes firmly on its nobler past:

          Your Caesars Father oft,
          (When he hath mus'd of taking kingdomes in)
          Bestow'd his lips on that vnworthy place,
          As it rain'd kisses . . .
               (*Antony and Cleopatra* III.xiii.2251ff)

Her superb, if somewhat ironic, evocation, is interrupted by Antony's entry. By the same token, he then recalls her past in very different terms ('I found you as a Morsell, cold vpon / Dead Caesars Trencher'), exploding in a fit of jealousy over the hand that is *his*:

Antony To let a Fellow that will take rewards,
         And say, God quit you, be familiar with
         My play-fellow, your hand; this Kingly Seale,

And plighter of high hearts . . .
           (*Antony and Cleopatra* III.xiii.2301ff)

Antony may object to Caesar's mercenaries being 'So sawcy with the hand of she heere', but it is another matter when the honour is his to bestow. So, later, in an access of generosity, he gives Cleopatra's hand to Scarus as a unique reward after their one victorious skirmish against Octavius Caesar. We can follow the movements here exactly, for as Cleopatra enters, Antony takes Scarus by the hand, saying: 'Giue me thy hand, / To this great Faiery, Ile commend thy acts, / Make her thankes blesse thee.' But then Antony must drop Scarus's hand as Cleopatra takes him in her arms. Yet Antony does not forget, breaking off his embrace to say:

                 . . . Behold this man,
           Commend vnto his Lippes thy fauouring hand,
           Kisse it my Warriour . . .
                 (*Antony and Cleopatra* IV.viii.2675ff)

Nicely, too, Antony's generosity does not last long, for in the midst of his next speech we hear him jealously reclaiming Cleopatra's hand – 'Giue *me* thy hand'.[24] Thus here, as in many other aspects of the play, its two conflicting themes are forced into unity. Cleopatra's hand carries both the passion of the lover's toy, 'My play-fellow, your hand', and the nobility of its royal function, 'this Kingly Seale, / And plighter of high hearts'. It is flesh, and royal blood. So too, in its glimpsed movements, we see the triumphs and indignities of the present, at the same time as we are reminded of the shameful glories of the past. The technique is reminiscent of a memorable stanza in *The Rape of Lucrece*, analysing Lucrece's picture of Troy:

           For much imaginarie worke was there,
           Conceipt deceitfull, so compact, so kinde,
           That for Achilles image stood his speare
           Grip't in an Armed hand, himselfe behind
           Was left vnseene, saue to the eye of mind,
                 A hand, a foote, a face, a leg, a head,
                 Stood for the whole to be imagined.
                 (*Rape of Lucrece* ll.1422ff)

The necessity of making the part stand for the whole is as fundamental to drama as it is to painting. In the movements of her hand Cleopatra is epitomised.

CHAPTER 4

Kneeling

In one of the many comic interludes in *Thomas of Woodstock*, the virtuous Thomas dubiously eyes a courtier's shoes, their absurdly long toes hitched up to his knees by a chain. Richard II's council sat for three days designing the fashion, the courtier boasts, and hurries on to explain its meaning:

> For these two parts, being in opperatione and quallity different,
> As for example: the tooe a disdayner, or spurner,
> The knee a duetyfull and most humble Orator,
> This chayne, doth as it were, soe tooefy the knee,
> And so kneefye the tooe that between boeth
> It makes a most methodicall coherence or coherent methode.
> (*Thomas of Woodstock*, ll. 1501ff)

'Most excellent, Sir, and full of Art', Thomas politely replies. Artful it may be, but for all its comedy it aptly illustrates even the anonymous Elizabethan author's readiness to read symbolism into dress (the topic of a later chapter), and his easy familiarity with the symbolism of action. The knee is not merely a dutiful and humble orator; kneeling is a visible symbol of order, an illustration of the chain of dependence from Man to God. Its rejection or perversion is an infringement of that order. Its reciprocal action, of raising the suppliant, is a further extension of that order. For true greatness uses its power to support, not humble; perfect justice extends mercy instead of punishment. This, the burden of Portia's famous speech on mercy, re-echoes throughout the canon to die away in Prospero's last words, as he begs his audience to pray for mercy on him, just as they would want to be pardoned for their own crimes:

> As you from crimes would pardon'd be,
> Let your Indulgence set me free.
> (*Tempest*, Epilogue, 2340–1)

Our mercy springs from the knowledge of our own imperfections. Lear's regeneration begins when he realises how others suffer, from his own suffering ('Come on my boy. How dost my boy? Art cold? / I am cold my selfe'), and, thinking of them, forgets to think of himself. So he refuses to enter the hovel, kneeling in the storm to pray for the poor: 'Take Physicke, Pompe, / Expose thy selfe to feele what wretches feele . . .' Kneeling may mirror an earthly order. But it is transcended when the suppliant is raised, and the great man kneels in humbleness. These are the themes to recur in Shakespeare's use of kneeling, and as so often, we will find that in his later work the conventional norms are reversed, to greater poignancy and strength.[1]

Order

The traditional chain of dependence is continually affirmed by ritual kneelings, too simple and numerous for illustration. Spirits kneel to their gods; men kneel in prayer and on oath. King kneels to his country; men to their king. Suppliants kneel for forgiveness or a boon, in humbleness or gratitude, and are raised to favour. Wife kneels to her husband, and, if she is the reformed Kate, even *laies her hand vnder her husbands feete*. The child kneels to its parents, and is blessed by them.[2]

Such implicit order is often further elaborated in speech. Thus in *All's Well* Helena prefigures Cordelia in her admission of natural order, in which a woman's duty is first to her husband, and then to her parents, when she kneels to the Countess of Rousillon to admit her love for Bertram: 'Then I confesse / Here on my knee, before high heauen and you, / That before you, and next vnto high heauen, / I loue your Sonne.' In *1 Henry VI*, Talbot kneels equally formally before his king, declining the sword that had won back so many of Henry's French territories, 'And with submissiue loyaltie of heart / Ascribes the Glory of his Conquest got, / First to my God, and next vnto your Grace.' And in a more highly charged scene in the second history trilogy, Hal kneels to his dying father in contrition, saying: 'there is your crowne: / And he that weares the crowne immortally, / Long gard it yours . . .'

But it is typical that this later scene should have more than its most obvious symbolic sense. When Hal, like two other cut-purse usurpers soon to follow him, steals the crown – not from its shelf, but from the King's sleeping side (much like the later Player King in Hamlet's *Mousetrap*), he simply, metaphorically re-enacts his father's usurpation of the crown. For both father and son, in the dying king's words, 'it seemd . . . But as an honor snatcht with boistrous hand'. But Hal goes on to absolve himself from his inherited crime by kneeling to render the crown back to its original possessor. Thus the contracted stain is symbolically lifted: his father forgives him, seats him by him, confesses his own crime of usurpation to him, and finally, formally, bestows the crown on his son:

King	How I came by the crowne, O God forgiue,
	And grant it may with thee in true peace liue.
Prince	You won it, wore it, kept it, gaue it me,
	Then plaine and right must my possession be.

(2 Henry IV IV.v.Q:12^v)

Balance and rhyme stress the harmony. Interestingly, both Hal's theft of the crown and his restitution of it, the kneeling and formal inheritance come from *The Famous Victories*. It is one of the rare occasions in which a crucial stage symbol has come intact from the source. Shakespeare has simply expanded and clarified the implications of the scene.[3]

Disorder

Refusal to kneel is a clear rejection of order, and as such it is hardly surprising that we find it most frequently exploited in the straight-forward symbolism of Shakespeare's earliest plays. The mannish Joan of Arc's habitual flouting of natural order is ultimately, incontrovertibly demonstrated in her denial of her father, as she is led off, impenitent, to the stake. The English lords helpfully comment aside: 'Gracelesse, wilt thou deny thy Parentage?' 'This argues what her kinde of life hath beene, / Wicked and vile . . .' Yet even in this self-confessedly emblematic encounter, invented by Shakespeare for this purpose, her shepherd father's pleas momentarily hit off a comically clumsy pathos:

> Fye Ione, that thou wilt be so obstacle:
> God knowes, thou art a collop of my flesh . . .
> Kneele downe and take my blessing, good my Gyrle.
> Wilt thou not stoope?
> (1 Henry VI V.iv. 2657ff)

It is a characteristically blunt early stage image of that Shakespearean commonplace, the impious isolationism of his villains, later ably expounded by the future Richard III:

> I haue no Brother, I am like no Brother:
> And this word (Loue) which Gray-beards call Diuine,
> Be resident in men like one another,
> And not in me: I am my selfe alone.
>   (*3 Henry VI* V.vi.3156ff)

In his quieter turn, Richard parallels Joan. He kneels to his mother, but cynically mocks his pretence of piety aside. It is hardly a preferable substitute.[4]

Disorder in the state is similarly mirrored by the misplaced kneelings of its citizens – a dramatic image somewhat overused in the troubled society of these early plays. So York's campaign for the crown is initiated in a slightly comic scene in which he expounds his regal claims in an undigestibly lengthy speech. His two feeds, Warwick and Salisbury, delightedly exclaim 'What plaine proceedings is more plain then this?', kneel to their new sovereign, are grandly acknowledged ('*We* thanke you Lords'), till poor York has to add, a little uncomfortably, 'But *I* am not your King, till I be Crown'd'. Once again an invented scene, its submerged comedy surfaces unmistakeably in its also invented counterpart at the other end of the play, when York openly disputes his right before Henry VI for the first time. York refuses to kneel to the King, absurdly but effectively demonstrating his better fitness for the crown by insisting on taking the obeisance of the newly entered Clifford as his own:

> Clifford   Health, and all happinesse to my Lord the King.
> York   I thanke thee Clifford: Say, what newes with thee?
>   Nay, do not fright vs with an angry looke:
>   We are thy Soueraigne Clifford, kneele againe:
>   For thy mistaking so, We pardon thee . . .
> Clifford   To Bedlem with him, is the man growne mad?
>   (*2 Henry VI* V.i.3121ff)

The sequence culminates, of course, in York's self-investiture in the throne at the beginning of the next play – a scene already discussed in chapter 2. In each case Shakespeare is inventing theatrical ways of presenting un-visual material from his historical sources.[5]

Knighting was evidently a popular civic and stage ritual, and as such recurs frequently in these early histories, but here again disorder is imminent as Henry VI twice contrives to honour two future traitors in a tragically misguided ceremony.[6] Again, the due order so perfectly mirrored in the knighting of Talbot (quoted above) is pointedly reversed in one of Shakespeare's most succinct and successful early symbolic scenes, the *self*-knighting of the revolutionary leader, Jack Cade. As he tells his rabble, 'then are we in order, when we are most out of order'. By all the rules of decorum, the agents of disorder must themselves be disordered (an idea staged with some subtlety later in the canon).[7] Then what apter image of revolution – the seized illegitimate power of a subservient class – could there be, than the sight of a man kneeling to himself, in order to receive the honour he lacks, from himself? The theatrical vignette is, once again, Shakespeare's addition to his historical sources:

Michael	Fly, fly, fly, Sir Humfrey Stafford and his brother are hard by, with the Kings Forces.
Cade	Stand villaine, stand . . . He is but a Knight, is a? . . . To equall him I will make my selfe a knight presently; Rise vp Sir Iohn Mortimer. Now haue at him.

(2 Henry VI IV.ii.2432ff)

The actor-reporters appear to have missed the point completely in their attempt to repeat what was evidently a popular joke, because in their version Cade goes on to knight Dick Butcher as well. This characteristic vulgarisation is a necessary warning against too ready an assumption that the actors, let alone the contemporary audience, fully understood Shakespeare's theatrical symbolism. As Jonson said of his elaborate devices on the Fenchurch arch, designed for James I's triumphal entry into London, such symbols 'might, without cloud, or obscuritie, declare themselues to the sharpe and learned: And for the multitude, no doubt but their grounded iudgements did gaze, said it was fine, and were satisfied.'[8]

'Arise Dissembler'

Order and disorder as imaged by various kneelings was evidently sufficiently standard dramatic practice for Shakespeare to loose interest in its subtle variation after his earliest history plays. His development here follows the pattern already noted in his use of the symbolism of place on the stage. But where kneeling subserves the dominant Shakespearean theme of seeming, we find it scattered throughout the canon. Here the significant development is not in the manner of staging (after all, little more can be done with kneeling than to kneel), but in the linguistic commentary accompanying the action.

Naturally kneeling, like all other 'outward' symbols, is turned to deceit by the dissemblers, and often we find that such moments of significant stage action are introduced by Shakespeare, rather than coming from his sources. This is best seen in some of the history plays. So Bolingbroke's easy 'tribute of his supple knee' is sneered at in the beginning of *Richard II* (compare Froissart: 'he was a pleasaunt knight . . . curtesse and swete, and meke to every man'). Such hints are twice put into practice, first in the invented moment as Boling-broke kneels to the testy York on his return from banishment:

Bolingbroke	. . . my noble Vnckle.
Yorke	Shew me thy humble heart, and not thy knee,
	Whose duety is deceiuable and false . . .
	(*Richard II* II.iii.Q:E2ᵛ)

and then again, when Richard II descends into Bolingbroke's power, in the base court of Flint Castle:

Bolingbroke	Stand all apart,
	And shew faire dutie to his Maiestie:
	he kneeles downe.
	My gratious Lord.
King	Faire coosen, you debase your princely knee,
	To make the base earth proud with kissing it:
	Me rather had my hart might feele your loue,
	Then my vnpleased eie see your curtesie:
	Vp coosen vp, your hart is vp I knowe . . .
	(*Richard II* III.iii.Q.G2. SD most probably authorial)

At this point, in Holinshed Bolingbroke kneels three times to Richard, and is accepted without irony. But on the stage dramatic irony needs a warning commentary to make it clear to the audience. Thus, in Shakespeare's hands, the comments of York and Richard clearly warn the audience of Bolingbroke's insincerity. A similar moment recurs in *Julius Caesar*, when Antony's servant kneels, and even falls prostrate in order to deliver his master's conciliatory message. Audience reaction is firmly guided by Cassius's voiced suspicions; in his own words, his 'misgiuing still / Falles shrewdly to the purpose'. The incident is not in Plutarch, and paves the way for Antony's betrayal of the conspirators' trust in his funeral oration.[9] A final example, although from an earlier play, is dramatically more interesting. There is no account in the chronicles of Richard III's wooing of Lady Anne. By a particularly bold theatrical stroke, Shakespeare stages this invented encounter over the corpse of Henry VI, murdered by Richard and furthermore Anne's former father-in-law (her husband also being dead by Richard's hand). Thus Richard's choice past has its prone, concrete embodiment on the stage at this ticklish moment. Richard then kneels at Anne's feet, bares his breast to the sword he has put in her hands, and urges her to kill him, who murdered her husband and her husband's father for love of her alone. As she nervously *fals the Sword* (SD most probably authorial), his victory is won:

> Richard   Take vp the Sword againe, or take vp me.
> Anne   Arise Dissembler . . .
> (*Richard III* I.ii.377ff)

Thus, with characteristic wicked perversity, Richard turns the traditional act of helplessness and humility into one of disguised power. Anne is trapped by it, but not duped. This highly theatrical moment has no origin in the play's recognised historical sources, although it may have been suggested by some merely metaphorical hyperboles in Thomas Legge's *Richardus Tertius*, a Latin play on the same theme (the Latin would seem to be sufficiently simple for Shakespeare's reputedly small powers).[10] Such perversion of the act into its opposite is later paralleled by Middleton and Rowley's *The Changeling*. When Beatrice kneels to De Flores, begging him not to make her sleep with him in payment for his murder of Alonso, he raises her, saying, ironically, 'Thy peace is wrought for ever in this yeilding' – so perverting his act from its proper meaning, the granting of a request, to its refusal. And instead of the suppliant being raised to a happier state, De Flores' action here marks the inescapable fact that she is now 'the deed's creature' and his corrupt mate.[11]

'Seeming, seeming' is dwelt on with greater poetic and philosophical complexity later in the canon. Hal, kneeling to his father, carefully distinguishes between the impulse, and the act by which it is expressed: 'my most inward true and duteous spirit, / Teacheth this prostrate and exterior bending.'[12] The theme proposed in his balanced antithesis is elaborated soon after, as Angelo and Claudius in turn corroborate Hal's observation of the discrepancies between outward act and inward intention. As so often, in this sequence we see Shakespeare replaying the same scene till he gets it pat, as well as moving from the verbal to the staged. Angelo first expounds the theme in his soliloquy:

> When I would pray, and think, I thinke, and pray
> To seuerall subiects: heauen hath my empty words,
> Whilst my Inuention, hearing not my Tongue,

> Anchors on Isabell: heauen in my mouth,
> As if I did but onely chew his name,
> And in my heart the strong and swelling euill
> Of my conception . . .
>> (*Measure for Measure* II.iv. 1003ff)

The soliloquy is crucial to the play, promptly turning to a general statement of its theme:

> . . . oh place, oh forme,
> How often dost thou with thy case, thy habit
> Wrench awe from fooles, and tye the wiser soules
> To thy false seeming?
>> (*Measure for Measure* II.iv. 1014ff)

Angelo concludes with a paradox of such blinding simplicity, that the play's commentators still stand bedazzled and uncomprehending:

> Let's write good Angell on the Deuills horne
> 'Tis not the Deuills Crest.
>> (*Measure for Measure* II.iv. 1018–9)

But he means exactly what he says: we should write a sign on the traditional devil's horn, saying 'Good Angel', for it is not by horns that a *devil* can be recognised. The devil, indeed, is most likely to look angelic (as of course Angelo does); by the same token an angel may appear devilish (an aphorism we could extend to the much maligned Duke). Angelo has simply restated a common aphorism particularly crisply. In Nashe's words, 'It is not to be gain-said, but the diuell can transforme himselfe into an angell of light.' So Hamlet: 'the deale hath power / T'assume a pleasing shape'. Iago, too, knows this 'diuinity of hell': 'When diuells will their blackest sins put on, / They doe suggest at first with heauenly shewes.' 'Diuels soonest tempt resembling spirites of light', Berowne concurs, and indeed this is corroborated in the play's action, as Angelo knows to his cost, since he is tempted by the virtue of Isabella, rather than by vice. Hence his complaint: 'Oh cunning enemy, that to catch a Saint, / With Saints dost bait thy hooke . . .' Angelo, as ironically named as the Angel of *Tess of the d'Urbervilles*, has reason to know the shams of outward show. How, then, can the devil be recognised? Not by his horns, his obvious crest; those might as soon show him to be an angel.[13]

There is no clear sign, however, that Angelo kneels for his futile prayers. It is Claudius who stages the discrepancies posed by Hal and verbally elaborated by Angelo, and here we see Shakespeare finally get his sums right. In this disturbing scene that so distressed Johnson's moral sense,[14] there is at once a pathetic irony in Claudius's weak optimism as he tries to pray, and a harder irony in the baffling of Hamlet's calculated obduracy, as he determines not to kill his praying victim in case he might save his soul.

King	. . . helpe Angels make assay,
	Bowe stubborne knees, and hart with strings of steale
	Be soft as sinnewes of the new borne babe,
	All may be well.
	Enter Hamlet.
Hamlet	Now might I doe it, but now a is a praying,
	And now Ile doo't, and so a goes to heauen . . .
	No . . .
	Vp sword, and knowe thou a more horrid hent,
	When he is drunke, a sleepe, or in his rage . . .
	Then trip him that his heels may kick at heauen . . .
	Exit.
King	My words fly vp, my thoughts remaine belowe.
	Words without thoughts neuer to heauen goe.
	(*Hamlet* III.iii.Q2:I^v–I2)

Hamlet (who knows not seems) has fallen for the false seeming of Claudius's 'exterior bending', when, ironically, it is an act 'That has no relish of saluation in't'. He has naively taken the angel's crest to designate an angel. It is a final, brilliant staged version of the recurrent theme.

Mercie then will breathe within your lips / Like man new made

It is sad that Johnson's overdeveloped moral sense should lead him to condemn the end of *Measure for Measure* for its failure of justice, Angelo, in his opinion, not getting the punishment he deserved. So Johnson demonstrates his incomprehension of a central Shakespearean theme, that of mercy mitigating justice. Shakespeare's attitude to this, like his attitude to seeming, does not change from his earliest plays; the tenets that are there aphoristically, categorically expounded, are simply explored more fully and subtly in the dramatised ethical problems of the later plays. The moral assumptions do not alter; their presentation progresses to become philosophically more complex and technically more theatrical. This can best be seen if we begin by outlining the moral argument, before turning to its presentation.

The rival claims of justice versus mercy are often argued out, and on several occasions a character is made to present the fair argument that 'Nothing imboldens sinne so much, as Mercy.'[15] Shakespeare frankly allows the truth of this. It is the starting-point of *Measure for Measure*: corruption has, demonstrably, been encouraged by the Duke's lenience. But, for all the validity of this concessive point, Shakespeare invariably comes to rest on the greater claims of mercy, primarily basing his argument on divine precedent, as it is argued by Isabella:

> Why all the soules that were, were forfeit once,
> And he that might the vantage best haue tooke,
> Found out the remedie.
> (*Measure for Measure* II. ii. 825ff)

Divine justice was turned to mercy in Christ's redemption of mankind; so Shakespeare repeatedly ranks mercy with divinity, above the tyranny of earthly justice. The monarch's sceptre, says Portia, 'showes the force of temporall power . . . But mercie is aboue this sceptred sway . . . It is an attribut to God himselfe; / And earthly power doth then show likest [God's] / When mercie seasons iustice.' Repentance is, of course, the due prerequisite; hence at the end of *The Tempest* Prospero is merciful: 'the rarer Action is / In vertue, then in vengeance: they, being penitent, / The sole drift of my purpose doth extend / Not a frowne further.'[16]

Shakespeare's second, humanly persuasive argument is the simple one of Mrs Doasyouwouldbedoneby; sinners all, 'we doe pray for mercy, / And that same prayer doth teach vs all to render / The deedes of mercie.' This argument is not only thus convincingly expounded by Portia in the dry atmosphere of the Venetian court. It is vividly evoked in *King John*, when Arthur, pleading with Hubert not to blind him, wishes Hubert had 'a gnat, a wandering haire' in his own eye, that, 'feeling what small things are boysterous there', he could not bring himself to put out Arthur's eyes. The theme *poetically* so well presented here is then sharply *staged* in *Henry V*, in a scene Shakespeare significantly adapts from his historical source, on his own initiative making Henry invent a test-case for the historic traitors, Scroop, Cambridge and Grey. Henry proposes mercy for a

man who supposedly swore at him in drunkenness; the traitors argue
for severity; their chosen harshness is then meted out to them when
their treachery is made known. Forgive us our trespasses, in the same
way as we forgive them that trespass against us . . . The whole
scene, not only its stress on Scroop's fall from apparent integrity, is a
clear precursor in miniature of *Measure for Measure*.[17]

Kneeling is naturally associated with this theme, simply because
the suppliant kneels for mercy. Characteristically, Shakespeare develops from his early, straightforward use of the action, where the
point is made by repetition rather than finesse, to economy and
complexity. *Titus* suffers from a pointed and theatrically significant
embarras de richesse in this respect. The tragedy is initiated by Titus's
rejection of Tamora's pleas for mercy for her son, his captive by war.
(Titus's intransigence here significantly prefigures Lear's *hamartia*.)
In Tamora's words, Shakespeare voices his two great arguments for
mercy, for the first time. Human sympathy demands it:

> Victorious Titus, rue the teares I shed,
> A mothers teares in passion for her sonne:
> And if thy sonnes were euer deare to thee,
> Oh thinke my sonne to be as deare to mee . . .

Divine example prompts it:

> Wilt thou draw neere the nature of the Gods?
> Draw neere them then in being mercifull . . .
> (*Titus* I.i.Q:B)

But Tamora prays in vain, her sons are sacrificed to Titus's family
honour, and the chain of futile kneelings, prayers and tears begins. It
is hardly surprising that *Titus* is statistically outstanding in its
quantity of kneelings; they continually evoke the good order in
which prayer is answered by indulgence and justice gives way to
mercy – the order Titus destroyed, to his own irreparable loss. Only
in the last act is harmony restored, as 'The poore remainder of
Andronicie' kneel to Rome, and are gently raised again.[18]

Shakespeare learnt economy from *Titus*, and in *Richard III* the
same point is made by a single tableau, an invented incident particu-
larising a general observation from the historian Hall. *Hall* describes
Edward IV's guilt at Clarence's untimely execution, all subsequent
pleas for mercy for common malefactors prompting his grief for
Clarence, whom nobody defended. *Shakespeare* sends in Derby, hot
on the news of Clarence's execution, to throw himself at Edward's

feet begging a reprieve for his servant, condemned to death for murder. Once again Shakespeare portrays a world bereft of pity; once again the point is stressed by a kneeling figure. Derby, prostrate for pardon, is an image of the ideal; its contrast to Edward's pitiless court is eloquently elaborated before Edward allows Derby to rise, his pardon granted. The speech is a wonderful early triumph of persuasive rhetoric, unfortunately too long for quotation here (and selection would break its impassioned flow). Quite different in dramatic style is a moment in *Lear*, where Shakespeare draws on the ambiguity of gesture in order to stage a significant point in the regeneration of both Gloucester and Lear. When the blind Gloucester hears the voice of the newly entered king, he recognises it, saying, 'Is't not the King?' As Nevill Coghill points out, he should kneel in homage at these words. But Lear, in his madness, does not recognise Gloucester, and takes the abject figure before him to be kneeling for mercy. With magnificent insight, he forgives the unknown penitent for the crime that first caused all his subsequent suffering:

Lear   I, euery inch a King.
When I do stare, see how the Subiect quakes.
I pardon that mans life. What was thy cause?
Adultery? thou shalt not dye: dye for Adultery?
No . . .

(*Lear* IV.vi.2554ff)

The action makes superb dramatic sense out of an otherwise undirected, merely 'mad' speech. So Gloucester is forgiven for his illegitimate son. And so Lear, in his turn, learns the mercy that outgoes justice.[19]

The theme is, of course, most fully argued in *Measure for Measure*, with extraordinary logical and dramatic cogency. Kneeling helps punctuate and emphasise the argument. Thus the last act opens with Isabella throwing herself at the Duke's feet, calling for the four-times repeated ideal, Justice. Her plea, and her action, are then repeated by Mariana later in the scene, as she too begs for justice in the adjudication of her claims on Angelo. But as soon as Angelo's guilt is clear, and the Duke has pronounced rigid *justice*: 'An Angelo for Claudio, death for death', the pattern is repeated in reverse. Mariana now throws herself down before the Duke, pleading for *mercy* with all the anguish of love: 'Oh my most gracious Lord, / I hope you will not mocke me with a husband? . . . Oh my deere Lord, / I craue no other, nor no better man.' Mercy is prompted, above all, by love. But it must also be supported by moral logic: Mariana's pleas must be seconded by Isabella, Angelo's victim. Mariana knows that the sight alone would be enough: 'Sweet Isabel, doe yet but kneele by me, / Hold vp your hands, say nothing: I'll speake all.' Yet, for all his love of the silent figure, Shakespeare cannot afford it here; Isabella kneels, but she must also give her reasons for pleading for Angelo.

It is an indication of *Measure for Measure*'s dialectical neatness that Isabella and Angelo must both abide by the same painful consistency during its course. Forgive us our trespasses as we forgive them . . . The standards each had chosen at the beginning of the play must now be applied where they would least desire. Angelo must condemn himself to the death he first meted out to Claudio, since their crimes are the same, and it is to his credit that he does so sincerely ('such sorrow I procure, / And so deepe sticks it in my penitent heart, / That I craue death more willingly then mercy'). And the mercy Isabella required for Claudio, she must now beg for Angelo. Again, it is to her credit that she corrects her original sophistries, when she tried to plead for Claudio's life, in her present argument in Angelo's favour: 'Let him not die: my Brother had but Iustice, / In that he did the thing for which he dide. / For Angelo, His Act did not ore-take / His bad intent . . .' But her argument is more generous than truthful. Angelo may not have slept with her, but he did spend the night with Mariana, with whom he had a pre-contract (just as Claudio had with Juliet). And, as far as Isabella knows, he did moreover break his word and kill Claudio – a fact she magnanimously glosses over in her plea that the Duke should look on Angelo 'As if my Brother liu'd'.

Isabella's generous compassion effects the miracle; a muffled figure is brought on stage, and disclosed to her as her living brother. So, in all justice, she is repaid by the standards she had set up at the play's beginning. There she had reminded Angelo of Christ's sacrifice:

> Why all the soules that were, were forfeit once,
> And he that might the vantage best haue tooke,
> Found out the remedie . . .
>   Oh, thinke on that,
> And mercie then will breathe within your lips
> Like man new made . . .
> (*Measure for Measure* II.ii.825ff)

Now she has brought about the embodiment of her own image. At her mercy to Angelo, Claudio rises from the dead, and Angelo, effectively guiltless by his resurrection, can live also. Mercy breaths within her lips, and Claudio rises, like man new made, from the dead. It is a subtle and beautiful instance of a Shakespearean verbal image being brought to life in the visible action of the play; linguistic metaphor unfolds into stage symbol.[20]

Order, broken order, order transcended

This chapter's *leit-motif* of order, disorder, and transcended order is perhaps most poignantly seen in its last broad topic, the kneeling of parent and child.

It is in the due order of things that the child should kneel to its parents. Even in its earliest, comic appearances, this moment has a subterranean gravity linking it with the later plays. Launcelot Gobbo's teasing of his blind father by pretending that he is not himself, and that Launcelot is dead, is an uncanny early premonition of the deceptions Edgar practices on his blind father. And when Launcelot tires of his 'confusions' and tries to disabuse old Gobbo, the scene distantly prefigures the reunions of the last romances. Their recognitions are heard in Launcelot's anxious, repeated demands, 'doe you know me Father . . . Doe you not know me Father?' The blessings likewise marking all the later reunions of parent and child are first seen here, as Launcelot kneels, saying, 'giue mee your blessing . . . I am Launcelot your boy that was, your sonne that is, your child that shall be.'

The moment constitutes what might be called an early theatrical image-cluster. Tears and benediction constantly recur in the reunions of the last plays, as the child kneels, to be blessed and acknowledged. Marina, like Launcelot, finally convinces Pericles of the truth when she names her mother, his wife: 'Thaisa was my mother, who did end the minute I began'; 'Now blessing on thee, rise th'art my child'. Thaisa too raises her up as her own – a pair of words to re-echo through all these scenes: 'Looke who kneeles here, flesh of thy flesh Thaisa'; 'Blest, and *mine own*'. The same chimes are rung again and again. Cymbeline unwittingly grants a pardon to Imogen, disguised as Fidele, page to the Roman general Lucius, saying to her: 'Thou hast look'd thy selfe into my grace, / And art *mine owne*'. When Imogen's identity has been disclosed, she too kneels for her father's blessing: 'Your blessing, Sir'; 'My teares that fall / Proue holy-water on thee'. Tears turn into a heavenly blessing in *The Winter's Tale*, when Hermione raises Perdita: 'You Gods looke downe, / And from your sacred Viols poure your graces / Vpon my daughters head: Tell me (*mine owne*) / Where hast thou bin preseru'd?' By *The Tempest* Shakespeare's interests have expanded beyond the narrow family circle, and although Ferdinand kneels to Alonso and rises with his blessing, as usual, all an older generation's tears are epitomised in Gonzalo, who pronounces the divine blessing: 'I haue inly wept, / Or should haue spoke ere this: looke downe you gods / And on this couple drop a blessed crowne.' 'Mine owne', finally, is entrusted to Prospero, as he reminds Alonso and himself of patrician rather than paternal obligations, pointing to Stephano, Trinculo and Caliban: 'Two of these Fellowes, you / Must know, and *owne*, this Thing of darkenesse, I / Acknowledge *mine*.' The family is universal.[21]

Hence the visible proof of thwart disnature, when the child denies its place in this natural order, like Joan of Arc, refusing to kneel. Equally unnatural is the sight of parent kneeling to child – a sight which finally prompts Coriolanus's doomed *volte face* outside the walls of Rome. Here, as so often, we find that Shakespeare has introduced the visible acts that highlight his historical narrative. Earlier in the play Shakespeare had made Coriolanus kneel to his mother, at his triumphal entry into Rome after the victory over Corioli (he did not do so in Plutarch). Such is the proper order of things. Now it is significantly reversed. Coriolanus, reluctantly going to meet his family outside the walls of Rome, is made by Shakespeare to kneel to his mother once again. But she raises him, to kneel herself (again without historical precedent), so compelling him to recognise what unnatural acts his own treachery forces on his family:

Volumnia	Oh stand vp blest!
	Whil'st with no softer Cushion then the Flint
	I kneele before thee, and *vnproperly*
	Shew duty as mistaken, all this while,
	Betweene the Childe, and Parent . . .
	(*Coriolanus* V.iii.3402ff. My italics)

Coriolanus's speech of outraged hyperbole at this is all that she could wish, as her confident response implies ('Thou art my Warriour, I hope to frame thee'). Nor is her confidence misplaced. After her great speech of persuasion, which ends with the entire family kneeling once again (this time only as in Plutarch), Coriolanus gives in. If he cannot allow such disruption of natural order, then he must take his due filial place, and by the same token cannot war against his own people. The family is universal.[22]

Should the conventional chronology be correct, Volumnia's exploitation of the abhorrent abnormality of such a scene might have its origin in *Lear*. In a far more intensely unpleasant moment, Lear kneels to Regan, sarcastically asking:

> Do you but marke how this becomes the house?
> Deere daughter, I confesse that I am old;
> Age is vnnecessary: on my knees I begge,
> That you'l vouchsafe me Rayment, Bed, and Food . . .
>
> (*Lear* II.iv.1434ff)

Lear, like Volumnia, is justified; his daughters' inhumanity forces
him into equally grotesque humiliation. Disorder, if you like, in
family and state is epitomised by this distasteful scene. But when
Lear kneels to Cordelia, on waking from his healing sleep, there can
be no such simple interpretation, as comparison with the sources
shows.

The original reunion between Leir and Cordella was dominated
by an absurd alternation of kneelings, daughter to father, father to
daughter, father to daughter again, daughter to father, father to
daughter. The gist of this tedious 'loving controversy' was that Leir
wanted forgiveness for his unjust cruelty to his daughter; she wanted
to be blest by him. It was, in fact, a crucial admission of fault in Leir.
There is no question that Shakespeare also intends this implication,
for this is how Lear later remembers the scene, as one of perfect
harmony: 'When thou dost aske me blessing, Ile kneele downe / *And
aske of thee forgiuenesse*: So wee'l liue, / And pray, and sing . . .'[23]

As Lear kneels to Cordelia, he implicitly admits his fault, for
actions speak as loud as words. Yet, at the actual moment,
Shakespeare deliberately avoids the straightforward moral declara-
tions of his source. As he presents it, Lear's first feeling is simply one
of confusion. He is not sure of his own existence, or the truth of his
sensations; he does not know where he is. He is surrounded by
unknown faces; he is in unfamiliar dress. He does not even know
where he last slept. He is conscious only of being an old man – no
King, since the storm disabused him of such delusions. There is no
question now of what 'becomes the house'. When he sees this
woman kneel, aware that the dignity cannot be for him, he simply
kneels as well, in humbleness and a kind of bewildered mimicry.
Only many lines later does he dimly realise that she is Cordelia and
has cause to hate him.

Lear's very absence of intention gives his kneeling its absolute
force. Some falls are means the happier to arise. So Gloucester knelt
on Dover cliff, to fall to a failed death that brought him resignation,
and reunion with his son. So Lear kneels beside Cordelia, and in
humility finds peace. The normal order of the natural world is
irrelevant here; the tragedy is that this is not the end of the play.

CHAPTER 5

Kissing and embracing

Unlike most of the stage action discussed so far, kisses need little historic or symbolic gloss. 'Poore hope's first wealth, ostage of promist weale, / Breakefast of Love' – their essential meaning does not change. The approach of this chapter will consequently differ slightly from those preceding it. After an initial discussion of certain identifiable types of kiss, I will be more concerned to describe the different *effects* of kisses in different plays. The chapter will end with an account of a remarkable dramatised image-cluster, that recurs in various verbal and enacted forms, in the embraces of dying lovers from the earliest plays to the last, and with a special account of the lovers' three kisses in *Othello*.

   Conventional kisses need no illustration. People kiss in welcome and in parting; warriors hug the men they have tried to kill, and, indeed, just as in the lovers' stories 'kiss' and 'kill' are tragically allied, so in the military plays 'embrace' is often a euphemism for 'fight'. The kiss is the seal of amity and patronage as well as of love, and one of several formal seals of marriage. As usual, the early plays are explicit: 'Vpon thy cheeke lay I this zelous kisse, / As seale to this indenture of my loue.' Later instances are more suggestive. So Goneril hangs a lover's favour about the kneeling Edmund's neck, kisses him, and raises him up, encouraging his political and sexual ambitions simultaneously, both by her act and by her insistent metaphor:

> . . . Weare this; spare speech,
> Decline your head. This kisse, if it durst speake
> Would stretch thy Spirits vp into the ayre:
> Conceiue, and fare thee well.
> (*King Lear* IV.ii.2289ff)

In this illicit, amatory variant on the knighting ceremony Goneril is offering, in her own quibbling words, 'A Mistresses command'.[1]

'To see him kisse his hand'!

A kiss's essential meaning may not change, but the fashion and occasion for certain kinds of embrace do vary, both from Shakespeare's time to our own, and also within the Shakespearean canon. It is worth considering such kisses within the context of their own type.

For instance, to kiss one's hand first appears, a little ignobly, as a groom's gesture. So Grumio prepares his servants for the arrival of the newly wed Petruchio and Kate: 'let their heads bee slickely comb'd, their blew coats brush'd . . . let them curtsie with their left legges, and not presume to touch a haire of my Masters horse-taile, till they kisse their hands.' Suffolk, in *2 Henry VI*, is appalled by the prospect of his undignified end, killed by a plebeian, protesting: 'The honourable blood of Lancaster / Must not be shed by such a iaded Groome: / Hast thou not kist thy hand, and held my stirrop?' From such low origins it becomes a fop's gesture – an affectation shared by Armado and Boyet in *Love's Labour's Lost*, and later satirised by Touchstone and Lavache, who defines a courtier by the negatives, 'hee that cannot make a legge, put off's cap, kisse his hand, and say nothing . . . were not for the Court'. Osrick, Hamlet's water-fly, is just such a courtier, whose hat is always off his head, and hand is ever at his lips, bidding fair words.[2]

Given the gesture's clear social colouring, Malvolio and Cassio's use of it becomes an evident stigma. Malvolio, sober Puritan though he may once have been, affects the gesture of the silliest of courtiers in a well-visualised scene, in which he grossly misinterprets Olivia's concern for his health as an invitation to intimacy:

Olivia	Wilt thou go to bed Maluolio?
Malvolio	To bed? I sweet heart, and Ile come to thee.
Olivia	God comfort thee: Why dost thou smile so, and kisse thy hand so oft?

(Twelfth Night III.iv.1552ff)

Even Cassio's pleasant charm, that 'daily beauty in his life' so galling to Iago, appears in a different light when we realise that he is presented like a more fully characterised Boyet, that 'Ape of Forme, Mounsier the nice . . . That kist his hand away in courtisie'. For, when he welcomes Desdemona ashore at Cyprus, Iago's malignant commentary allows us to see him use the gesture again and again: 'it had beene better you had not [kiss'd] your three fingers so oft, which now againe you are most apt to play the sir in . . . yet againe, your

fingers at your lips? Would they were Clisterpipes for your sake . . .'
And thus both Cassio and Othello are entangled in the web of his
affections, for, to jealous eyes, Cassio's social graces are as suspect
as the earlier Boyet's. As Berowne once said, so would Iago have
Othello believe: 'Had he bin Adam he had tempted Eue.' Moreover,
at Cassio's first important appearance, the disembarkation at Cyprus, his very first act is to kiss Emilia on the lips – under her
husband's eyes – with an insulting parade of superior manners:

> *Cassio* Let it not gall your patience, good Iago,
> That I extend my manners, tis my breeding,
> That giues me this bold shew of courtesie . . .
> (*Othello* II.i.Q:D4)

There is little true breeding in such insolence. Nor is the impression
allowed to fade. When Cassio's casual maintenance of Bianca is
added to his soiled behaviour in this early scene, he does seem
well-qualified, in manners at least, for the role Iago creates for him.
And thus a single gesture, to whose social overtones we are no longer
sensitive, can shed an important light on intended character. Cassio's
libertine foppery, properly presented, should fit him for the nasty
part Iago prepares, and at least partially mitigate Othello's gullibility
in believing Iago's lies.[3]

The Judas kiss

Shakespeare's use of the Judas kiss of treachery neatly illustrates the
observed pattern of his straightforward acceptance of traditional
stage symbols in the early plays, and their later elaboration, modification, and even reversal. The pattern can be illustrated in miniature by the kiss of loyalty – a kiss presented baldly in the early plays,
then turned to simple comedy, for instance when Armado ridicu-
lously over-refines fealty with 'I will kisse thy royall *finger*, and take
leaue'. Finally, characteristically, Lear repudiates even this, the
simplest form of homage, with all the other trappings of kingship,
'The Sword, the Mase, the Crowne Imperiall, / The enter-tissued
Robe of Gold and Pearle . . .'

> *Gloucester* O let me kisse that hand.
> *Lear*   Let me wipe it first,
> It smelles of Mortality.
> (*King Lear* IV.vi.2574ff)[4]

The same pattern obtains elsewhere.

So the first history tetralogy replaces the subject's kiss with the Judas kiss of treachery, with predictable frequency and frankness. The Judas kiss is, however, a literary platitude; later, it is presented more subtly, or not at all. In *Richard II* Shakespeare goes out of his way to make the point by an ironic parallel, whose careful engineering is shown up by a comparison with the sources. In his staging of the lists between Mowbray and Bolingbroke, Shakespeare makes Bolingbroke ask to kiss Richard's hand in parting homage. His demand is ceremoniously repeated three times, first by himself, then by the Martial, and finally by Richard himself, as he descends to take him in his arms. This incident does not appear in Holinshed or Hall. However, the sincerity of this formal embrace is later significantly undercut when Bolingbroke, a patently disloyal exile, new-entered into England in defiance of royal decree, a rebel army marching at his side, sends Northumberland to Flint Castle to convey his humble embrace and obeisance to the King. Once again the message is thrice repeated, first by Bolingbroke, then by Northumberland – but now repudiated at its actual occurrence, as Bolingbroke kneels to Richard and is grimly raised by him: 'Me rather had my *hart* might feele your loue.' The second incident is historic; the commentary undermining it is not. Shakespeare has clearly planned ahead for it by its earlier ironic foreshadowing.[5]

Elaboration is followed by modification, and in *Julius Caesar* Shakespeare presents a theatrical *volte face* of considerable thematic importance. What appears to be a Judas kiss of treachery is in fact its opposite, a warning against *self*-betrayal.

Plutarch vividly describes the scene at the Capitol, just prior to the assassination: the conspirators' importunate pleas for Publius Cimber as they jostled round Caesar and 'tooke him by the handes, and *kissed his head and brest*', till he literally had to shake himself free.[6] The ruse was evidently a practical one: so the victim was surrounded. Yet, according to Antony's later account, Shakespeare envisaged the scene with an important difference:

Antony   You shew'd your teethes like Apes,
          And fawn'd like Hounds,
          And bow'd like Bondmen, *kissing Caesars feete* . . .
                    (*Julius Caesar* V.i.2374ff. My italics)

It has already been argued in an earlier chapter that, to have an effect, such retrospective descriptions should have been given their due dramatic embodiment in the original scene. And indeed, the dialogue at the assassination bears this out. Evidently Shakespeare intended his fictional moment of blatant idolatry *to be staged*, as Metellus Cimber and Cassius's lines both make clear:

Metellus	Most high, most mighty, and most puisant Caesar
	Metellus Cymber *throwes before thy Seate*
	An humble heart . . .
Cassius	Pardon Caesar: Caesar pardon:
	As lowe as to thy foote doth Cassius fall,
	To begge infranchisement for Publius Cymber . . .
	(*Julius Caesar* III.i.1239ff. My italics)

By their acts and by their words the conspirators go out of their way to make a god of Caesar, a deification he smugly approves in his self-comparison to the Northern Star. So he is caught in his own trap: it is fitting that for such hubris the mortal man should die.

But when Brutus joins his pleas to the rest, he distinguishes himself from his grovelling accomplices, and we would be wrong to take his plea as the arch hypocrisy, kissing where he means to kill:

Brutus	*I kisse thy hand*, but not in flattery Caesar:
	Desiring thee, that Publius Cymber may
	Haue an immediate freedome of repeale.
	(*Julius Caesar* III.i.1259ff. My italics)

This is no Judas kiss of treachery, but a warning. Shakespeare makes Brutus forestall misinterpretation by word and deed, triply differentiating him from his fellow conspirators. His tone is one of insistent sincerity ('but not in flattery'), rather than hyperbolic entreaty. His admonition is grave, as he 'desires', rather than abjectly 'begs' pardon for Publius Cimber. And he kneels to kiss Caesar's hand, an act of intimate urgency and legitimate respect, while they throw themselves at his feet in palpable idolatry. So Caesar is given his last chance to admit human fallibility and retract. It is a moment of profound tension, the assassination's rationale hanging in the balance. It could, and perhaps should be played with Caesar momentarily uncertain, wavering ('What, Brutus?') rather than lofty, as he is conventionally presented, before Cassius hastily breaks in with his fawning 'Pardon Caesar . . .' The moment passes, and Caesar's arrogance returns. 'This eare is deafe', and he does not hear.

Lovers' kisses

Shakespeare's developing technique is less crisply illustrated by the main topic of this chapter, his many lovers' kisses. Here the interest is rather in the light such embraces throw on each play's mode and themes. The progress from theatrical clarity to complexity remains true to pattern. Of the early plays, *The Taming of the Shrew* is numerically outstanding for its embraces, which are presented with as robust an exuberance and realism as the play's tears, discussed in the next chapter. But they are explicitly demanded with such damnable iteration that a modern musical version of the play justifiably took for its title the refrain, 'Kiss Me Kate'. In the later plays, fewer kisses are demanded and are reserved for more powerful impact. *Othello* only calls for three specific embraces between its lovers, each significant, and even *Romeo and Juliet* is hardly more restrained.

Here the lovers are made to kiss on surprisingly rare, loaded occasions, while their first embrace is a perfect example of this play's dramatic technique, in which basically simple stage action has its meaning heightened and deployed by literary elaboration (an approach already illustrated in the play's use of the balcony). 'These lovers parled by the touch of hands', like others before them; the chaste lovers' 'kiss' of palm joined to palm had been staged in earlier plays.[7] But here Shakespeare's unprecedented pun of 'Palmers kis' is supported by a sustained metaphor of religious idolatry, in the sonnet shared by the lovers. So the lovers' future union is prefigured in their spontaneous collaboration over a complex poetic form. Their isolation from the other maskers is intensified by their absorption in the sonnet's interlocking rhymes (the rest of the scene is conducted in blank verse or rhyming couplets). And their growing interdependence in the composition of the sonnet is matched by a series of increasingly intimate embraces, physical closeness thus mirroring their poetic merging. It is a perfect example of literary and theatrical techniques tranquilly united.

Thus Romeo takes the lead and the first quatrain, as he formally kisses his hand to Juliet, and then lays it on her waist – a recognised respectful embrace that occurs elsewhere in the canon:[8]

> Romeo   If I prophane with my vnworthiest hand
> This holy shrine, the gentle sin is this,
> My lips two blushing Pylgrims did readie stand,
> To smoothe that rough touch with a tender kis.
>   (*Romeo and Juliet* I.v.Q2:C4)

Juliet takes the second quatrain to encourage his advances, as she offers her hand in the 'Palmers kis'. But this innocuous gesture carries the profounder connotations of marriage, as Chapter 3 has shown. In her turn, her quatrain ends with 'kis', and her own inviting gesture as she takes his hand:

Juliet Good Pilgrim you do wrong your hand too much
    Which mannerly deuocion showes in this,
    For saints haue hands, that Pilgrims hands do tuch,
    And palme to palme is holy Palmers kis.
       (*Romeo and Juliet* I.v.Q2:C4)

The tempo rises in the semi-stychomythic third quatrain, as Romeo begs to kiss Juliet:

Romeo Haue not Saints lips and holy Palmers too?
Juliet I Pilgrim, lips that they must vse in praire.
Romeo O then deare Saint, let lips do what hands do.
    They pray (grant thou) least faith turne to dispaire.
       (*Romeo and Juliet* I.v.Q2:C4)

Consummation comes with the climax of the sonnet's couplet, equably shared, one line each as their lips touch:

Juliet Saints do not moue, thogh grant for praiers sake.
Romeo Then moue not while my praiers effect I take.
       (*Romeo and Juliet* I.v.Q2:C4)

It is a laughably exact embodiment of Keats's lines, 'his erewhile timid lips grew bold, / And poesied with hers in dewy rhyme.'

Yet, since Rowe, the editorial stage direction for the kiss has been postponed till after Romeo's next line.[9] This not only breaks up the literary and physical structure of the present sonnet, but disregards the fact that, as soon as one sonnet and one embrace is completed, with true lovers' insatiability, Romeo and Juliet spill over into *another* sonnet. The abab rhyme-scheme (found nowhere else in the scene) starts them off again; now Juliet begs a kiss of Romeo, and total involvement is reached as they split a single line between them, its caesura marked by their second kiss:

(Romeo) Thus from my lips, by thine my sin is purgd.
Juliet Then haue my lips the sin that they haue tooke.
Romeo Sin from my lips, ô trespas sweetly vrgd:
    Giue me my sin againe.
Juliet   You kisse bi'th'booke.

Nurse   Madam your mother craues a word with you.
                    (*Romeo and Juliet* I.v.Q2:C4–C4ᵛ)

At last prose, in the person of the Nurse, interrupts them. There is, I
think, no comparable instance in Shakespeare's work of such an
exquisite matching of physical action with literary form, one
echoing the other. It is, of course, Shakespeare's invention, replacing
an absurd, if homely encounter in Brooke's *Romeus and Juliet*.[10]

The kisses of the middle comedies and histories are inevitably pale
by comparison. In general, the comedies are characterised by brilliance of dialogue, rather than theatrical éclat, and they rarely
provide material of interest to a study of Shakespeare's stage direction. The prime concern of the histories also lies elsewhere. Much as
one may distrust the bald category of 'problem plays', these are also
true to form in their embraces. None, significantly, are demanded in
Measure for Measure; in this respect the play's bleak key-note is set by
Mariana's song:

> Take, oh take those lips away,
>   that so sweetly were forsworne . . .
> But my kisses bring againe, bring againe,
> Seales of loue, but seal'd in vaine, seal'd in vaine.
>   (*Measure for Measure* IV.i.1770ff)

In *All's Well* those lips are taken away even more painfully and
emphatically, as Bertram callously ignores Helena's tentative plea
that he should kiss her, now she is his wife. His refusal clearly warns
the audience that this is but the first of so many marriage rites to be
rejected by him:

Helena   Pray sir your pardon.
Bertram   Well, what would you say?
Helena   I am not worthie of the wealth I owe,
                  Nor dare I say 'tis mine: and yet it is,
                  But like a timorous theefe, most faine would steale
                  What law does vouch mine owne.
Bertram   What would you haue?
Helena   Something, and scarse so much: nothing indeed,
                  I would not tell you what I would my Lord: Faith yes,
                  Strangers and foes do sunder, and not kisse.
Bertram   I pray you stay not, but in hast to horse.
                    (*All's Well* II.v.1354ff)

Johnson, impaled once again on the barbs of his own rigid moral
system, is surely mistaken in his belief that Bertram is 'dismissed to

happiness', for the play's ending is pointedly ambivalent, as a comparison with the source shows. Life with Helena scarcely seems to promise happiness to Bertram, and his continuing disinclination is suggested not only by his jingling acceptance of the bride, but by the fact that at the end, as at the original marriage, his words are addressed to the king whose authority forced the match: '*If* she my Liege can make me know this clearly, / Ile loue her dearely euer, euer dearly.' The King's dubious closing couplet is as queasily conditional as Bertram's: 'All yet *seemes* well, and *if* it end so meete . . .' – surely a heavily ironic qualification of the play's title! And finally, even if both these pointers are dismissed as accidentally equivocal (which is hardly flattering to the author), the calculated pessimism of the play's ending is strongly suggested by its divergence from Painter, whose hero raised up his wife, 'imbraced and kissed her', publicly acknowledged her, and caused her dress to be changed from pilgrim's weeds to the robes befitting her rank. Shakespeare knew well enough the weight of such symbolic acts, and had exploited them often enough before. Had he intended the play to end on the traditional happy note, there would have been no difficulty in following Painter's lead. That he elected not to do so has its own force; action *dropped* from the source can be as significant as action *introduced* in the dramatised version. Bertram never knowingly makes any physical approach to his unhappy wife; the fact that he does not kiss her even now fosters the play's ending on a note of lurking disappointment. The note is characteristic of this thoroughly unhappy play.[11]

The kisses in *Troilus and Cressida* betray its tenor equally precisely, as love is perpetually corrupted from without and within. The lovers' first embraces are sullied as they occur, first by Pandarus's grotesque running commentary ('so so, rub on and kisse the mistresse'), then by his nasty parody of the betrothal kiss in terms of a business deal ('what billing again: heeres in witnesse whereof the parties interchangeably'), last and worst of all by his physical, rather than verbal intrusion at their final parting. Here he thrusts himself forward to make a threesome in their desperate last embrace – a sight extremely repulsive in performance:

Pandarus	Here, here, here he comes, a sweete ducks.
Cressida	Oh Troylus, Troylus.
Pandarus	What a paire of spectacles is here, let me embrace too.

                  (*Troilus and Cressida* IV.iv.Q:H3)

Nor is such intrusion limited to Pandarus. All Troy forces the lovers apart. Troilus has reason to complain,

Iniurious time now with a robbers hast
Cram's his ritch theeu'ry vp hee knowes not how;
As many farewells as be starres in heauen
With distinct breath, and consignde kisses to them,
He fumbles vp into a loose adewe . . .
    (*Troilus and Cressida* IV.iv.Q:H3ᵛ)

This 'single famisht kisse' is almost emblematically staged shortly after, as their last embrace is crushed between two imperious off-stage summons:

Aeneas within	Nay good my Lord?
Troilus	Come kisse, and let vs part.
Paris within	Brother Troylus?

(Troilus and Cressida IV.iv.Q:H4)

The poverty of this, their last kiss, contrasts unhappily with the largesse with which Cressida is welcomed by the Greeks, as Agamemnon, Nestor, Achilles, and Patroclus embrace her in turn. The obvious parallel between Cressida's eager coquetry here, and the play's central emblem of Helen's infidelity, is evoked by the usual baiting of the cuckolded Menelaus, in which Cressida takes such a pert and confident part. As kiss follows kiss it seems indeed as if (to quote Othello's grievance) 'the generall Campe, / Pyoners, and all, had tasted her sweete body', and Ulysses' disdainful dismissal of her, after her exit, needs no further justification. Her future infidelity with Diomed has been well prepared for.[12]

Yet in this scene of many kisses, as in Cressida's night meeting with Diomed later, one senses a pitiful vulnerability in her eagerness to please, her anxious need to be courted and loved. Her discomfort in the scene with Diomed is acutely perceptible to the audience, the unhappy flux of her feelings being accurately mirrored by the to-and-fro of Troilus's favour, from her hands to Diomed's, and back, and back again . . . Cressida is more than her stereotype, 'the very crowne of falsehood'; behind these two Greek scenes lies her involuntary confession to Troilus: 'I haue a kind of selfe recids with you: / But an vnkinde selfe, that it selfe will leaue, / To be anothers foole.' Troilus repeats the essence of her confession when they are separated, warning her: 'something may be done *that we will not*, / And sometimes we are diuells to our selues . . .' Cressida is at the mercy of her worser nature, a nature she recognises but cannot control. In her own way, she is as pitiable as the upright Troilus she betrays.[13]

The meaning of Cressida's kisses of the Greek generals is clear
enough; well presented, however, their effect could be more complex. *Antony and Cleopatra*, on the other hand, has two kisses in
particular whose meaning is paramount. They are the audience's
signpost, an emphatically marked stage emblem of the lovers' choice
between the play's two pivots, the opposed goals of worldly,
military prowess, and private harmony in love. So the play opens
with Antony's flamboyant, enacted creed, as he kisses Cleopatra:

> Kingdomes are clay: Our dungie earth alike
> Feeds Beast as Man; the Noblenesse of life
> Is to do *thus* . . .
> (*Antony and Cleopatra* I.i.46ff. My italics)

And *thus*, as he kisses her, the general turns lover. After the crucial
defeat at Actium, he repeats his creed again, as he takes the remorseful Cleopatra in his arms:

> Fall not a teare I say, one of them rates
> All that is wonne and lost: Giue me a kisse,
> Euen this repayes me . . .
> (*Antony and Cleopatra* III.xi.2100ff)

Scarus can justifiably exclaim, 'we haue kist away / Kingdomes, and
Prouinces'; it is Antony's explicit gloss on both occasions. Predict-
ably, too, each embrace and its accompanying commentary is
Shakespeare's invention, having no source in Plutarch. He has
provided the audience with two clear stage images to guide it
through the conflicting cross-currents of the play.[14]
   Curiously, this balancing of military and amatory is echoed in
reverse in *Coriolanus*. Antony rates a lover's embrace above all that
war can win; in *Coriolanus* the opposition is resolved and two
warriors' embraces are suffused with the intensity of married love.
First Coriolanus hugs Cominius on his triumphant return from
Corioli:

> Oh! let me clip ye
> In Armes as sound, as when I woo'd in heart;
> As merry, as when our Nuptiall day was done,
> And Tapers burnt to Bedward.
> (*Coriolanus* I.vi.640ff)

The embrace is historic, the imagery Shakespeare's. But Shakespeare
invents in its entirety the later parallel, when Aufidius welcomes

Coriolanus, his enemy turned ally, with the same excited comparison to the wedding night: 'Let me twine / Mine armes about that
body . . . that I see thee heere . . . more dances my rapt heart, / Then
when I first my wedded Mistris saw / Bestride my Threshold.' The
tone is more descriptive and less epigrammatic than in *Antony and
Cleopatra*; as a result the effect seems to me to differ. There is not the
same emblematic precision; rather, the flushed, almost erotic comparison heightens this play's pervading sense (and one that is not
limited to Coriolanus alone) of total immersion in war and the affairs
of a man's world. Family feeling, whether filial, marital, or paternal,
is not opposed to public concerns in *Coriolanus*, as love and war
collide in *Antony and Cleopatra*; on the contrary it is subordinate, and
yet closely linked to military zeal. A single energy impels both; just
as Volumnia, 'poore Hen', clucked Coriolanus to the wars and home
again, so a private intensity governs his acts. Enmity with Aufidius
or alliance with him are equal passions; wounded personal pride
drives him to war against Rome, and love of his family causes him to
abandon the assault. All his military doings have a private fierce
commitment, whose quality is partly created by the imagery of these
parallel embraces.[15]

The dying kisses of Antony and Cleopatra bring this chapter to its
penultimate theme.

Dying kisses

The Shakespearean image-cluster has become a cliché of modern
criticism. Like the Cheshire Cat's disembodied smile, elusive and
often enigmatic fragments of an idiosyncratic image-cluster bob up
from play to play, only to be fleshed out by our knowledge of the
invisible Cat – the full nexus of associations as cumulatively suggested by other fragments of the same cluster elsewhere in the
canon.[16] However, it has not yet been sufficiently recognised that this
tendency is not limited merely to Shakespeare's linguistic imagery. It
is a frequent phenomenon in his work that the *staged* image of one
play turns into the *spoken* image of another, and vice versa.
Shakespeare's tendency to metaphoric thought remains a constant,
although its expression will oscillate continually between the linguistic and theatrical modes, or a combination of the two. A particularly curious example of this is the collocation of ideas surrounding
lovers' dying kisses.

Three dominant ideas can be seen to recur in conventional lovers' kisses: their restorative power to bestow life; their equal and opposite potential to suck the soul away, both in life and death; and, finally, the Elysian bliss of such a 'death'. Marlowe merely turns the sentimental commonplace of the first idea to Byronic irony in *Hero and Leander*:

> By this, sad Hero, with love unacquainted
> Viewing Leanders face, fell downe and fainted.
> He kist her, and breath'd life into her lips,
> Wherewith as one displeas'd, away she trips.
> (*Hero and Leander* II. 1–4)

Obviously, such a kiss of life has its origin in fact as well as literary tradition, and it recurs from age to age.[17]

It is equally natural that the lover should be imagined as rendering up his soul in his dying kiss. In *Hydriotaphia* Sir Thomas Browne notes this among the pre-Christian rites of the ancients:

That they sucked in the last breath of their expiring friends, was surely a practice of no medical institution, but a loose opinion that the soul passed out that way, and a fondnesse of affection from some Pythagorical foundation, that the spirit of one body passed into another; which they wished might be their own.

In Castiglione's *Courtier* Pietro Bembo reiterates the idea in neo-Platonic terms, now referring it to the kiss of the living, rather than dying:

a kisse . . . is the opening of an entrie to the soules, which drawne with a coveting the one of the other, poure them selves by turne the one into the others bodie, and bee so mingled together, that each of them hath two soules.

And one alone so framed of them both ruleth (in a manner) two bodies. Whereupon, a kisse may be saide to be rather a coupling together of the soule, than of the body . . .

This whole passage provides an apt commentary for Donne's poem, 'The Extasie', and the doctrine is broadly echoed by innumerable other writers of the time. So Sidney writes, 'O kisse, which soules, even soules together ties / By linkes of Love, and only Nature's art.' It is ironically evoked by Marlowe, whose Faustus literally loses his soul by kissing the succuba of Helen of Troy. 'Her lips sucke forth my soule, see where it flies' is no erotic hyperbole but doctrinal fact. It is turned to the deathly pain of a parting kiss by Donne: 'So, so,

breake off this last lamenting kisse, / Which sucks two soules, and
vapors Both away.' Plato recedes as the idea of death becomes
increasingly prominent, for instance in Pope's plagiarising improvement on Oldham:

> Thou, Abelard! the last sad office pay,
> And smooth my passage to the realms of day;
> See my lips tremble, and my eye-balls roll,
> Suck my last breath, and catch my flying soul!
> (*Eloisa to Abelard*, ll. 321ff)

So (to return to my third element) the dying lover is transported into
Elysium.[18]

Curiously, Pope's lines are closest to Shakespeare's first projection
of the lovers' dying embrace, Suffolk's parting speech from Margaret:

> If I depart from thee, I cannot liue,
> And in thy sight to dye, what were it else,
> But like a pleasant slumber in thy lap?
> Heere could I breath my soule into the ayre,
> As milde and gentle as the Cradle-babe,
> Dying with mothers dugge betweene it's lips.
> Where from thy sight, I should be raging mad,
> And cry out for thee to close vp mine eyes:
> To haue thee with thy lippes to stop my mouth:
> So should'st thou eyther turne my flying soule,
> Or I should breathe it so into thy body,
> And then it liu'd in sweete Elizium.
> (*2 Henry VI* III.ii.2105ff)

In this remarkable speech all the recurrent elements of Shakespeare's
later dying lovers' embraces are intimated. The last three lines
encapsulate the three recurrent potentialities of the dying kiss, either
to restore life ('So should'st thou eyther turne my flying soule'), or to
end it in a mutual mingling ('Or I should breathe it so into thy body')
which transports the beloved to a better world ('And then it liu'd in
sweete Elizium'). However, true to the form of the image-cluster, in
this speech such conventional and rational elements lie tangled with
the idiosyncratic and bizarre. The restorative quality of death is to
remain a Shakespearean constant, and Suffolk's suckling image is
partly an incoherent intimation of this life-giving power. But why
should the baby die at the breast? There is no logical reason, and yet

the image is an extraordinary premonition of its staged rationalisation in *Antony and Cleopatra*, many years later.

Suffolk's speech is merely the descriptive projection of his desires; in fact, he is nowhere near dying. Later, such a projection gradually finds its stage embodiment. So Juliet, waking by Romeo's corpse, actually tries to join him in death by kissing him and taking the poison from his lips:

> Juliet   O churle, drunke all, and left no friendly drop
> To help me after; I will kisse thy lips,
> Happlie some poyson yet doth hang on them,
> To make me dye with a restoratiue.
> Thy lips are warme.
> (*Romeo and Juliet* V.iii. Q2:L4)

Like Suffolk, she thinks of death as a 'restoratiue'; like Suffolk, she longs for the death–dealing kiss; unlike him, she tries to take it. But the inherent realism of the play cannot allow her success; to die, she has to stab herself with Romeo's dagger. Yet the same realism, which makes her wish (but not the kiss accompanying it) as illusory as Suffolk's, prompts the unnerving immediacy of 'Thy lips are warme'.[19]

Romeo's suicide is less immediately connected with the central collocation of ideas that are my chief concern, except that his last words echo the paradoxical implications of Juliet's 'restoratiue' in their pun on 'quicke' as "alive" and "promptly efficacious": 'O true Apothecary! / Thy drugs are quicke. Thus with a kisse I die.' However, his dream at Mantua, before he has even heard of Juliet's death, does join the dominant collocation of ideas. For here, in a suspicious echo of Marlowe's lines quoted earlier (p. 91),[20] Romeo describes his version of the sweet Elysium Suffolk imagined after death:

> I dreamt my Lady came and found me dead,
> Strange dreame that giues a deadman leaue to thinke,
> And Breathd such life with kisses in my lips,
> That I reuiude and was an Emperor.
> (*Romeo and Juliet* V.i. Q2:K4)

The deprecatory parenthesis ('Strange dream . . .') is typical of this play's basis of careful realism. Juliet *will* find the dead Romeo, but she cannot revive him. Later, though, Shakespeare is to have no difficulty in staging the dream.

Thus, in *Lear*, Cordelia echoes Juliet as she kisses her father in his healing sleep: 'O my deere Father, *restauratian* hang / Thy medicine on my lippes . . .'[21] But her kiss revives Lear to a state far different from the grandeur of Romeo's dream: 'You do me wrong to take me out o' th'graue, / Thou art a Soule in blisse, but I am bound / Vpon a wheele of fire . . .' The poetic narrative of Romeo's dream is translated into the modest stage reality of Lear's painful delusion.

Lear stages what is factually plausible. In reality there is nothing impossible in Lear's awakening, or Gloucester's leap. But both Gloucester and Lear project a metaphysical reality which encloses and transforms the unremarkable fact of their falling over, or waking up. So Shakespeare simultaneously presents plausible stage action, and the vast spiritual nebula it casts in the mind of the sufferer – Gloucester floating like unharmed goassamer down Dover Cliff, to survive to a life of humble patience; Lear waking to scalding remorse, Cordelia a spirit before him. In *Lear* the metaphysical only has its origins in a physical form, and is not directly staged.

But in *Antony and Cleopatra*, it is. Here the correlation between the two is absolute, and, in the culmination of all the strands of this cluster, literary images are given an apt physical origin, while at the same time the demands of realism are left behind in the staging of what may be spiritually true, but is factually impossible.

So, Suffolk's powerful *image* of himself as a child, 'Dying with mothers dugge betweene it's lips' is translated into the more powerful stage *fact* of Cleopatra placing the asp at her breast (this last detail in itself a departure from Plutarch). The original oddity is lost in Cleopatra's modified reversal, in which nurse, not child, falls asleep instead of dying, and thus the uneasy extravagance of Suffolk's fantasy turns into the placid naturalism of Cleopatra's last appearance. 'No more but [e'en] a Woman', she suckles death as a tired mother her child: 'Peace, peace: / Dost thou not see my Baby at my breast, / That suckes the Nurse asleepe . . .'[22]

Again, the death-dealing kiss, that realism forbade in *Romeo and Juliet*, is now given theatrical life. There, Juliet found no trace of poison on Romeo's lips, although he had just drunk poison; here, Iras dies at Cleopatra's embrace, although Cleopatra has not yet been bitten by the asps. Past commentators have, I believe, worried unnecessarily about the improbability of this moment (did Iras die of grief? or apply an asp herself?). The precise manner of her death is clearly unimportant, by the simple token that Shakespeare provides no further explanation than Cleopatra's words: 'Haue I the Aspicke in my lippes? Dost fall?' At her approaching death, Cleopatra (the

'Serpent of old Nyle') carries death within her, and at her kiss Iras dies.[23]

The dying kiss has dual potential, to restore life or to end it, and Cleopatra carries life as well as death in her embrace. When Antony, brought dying to the monument, proudly importunes death until they have shared their last embrace, Cleopatra hoists him up, welcoming him, kissing him: 'Dye *when* thou has liu'd, / Quicken with kissing' (Pope's emendation to 'where' obscured this essential point). Lear merely awoke; Antony actually revives. But Cleopatra, like Antony, admits their ineluctable mortality; they can only 'importune death a-while', not dismiss it. Hence her lines, 'Had my lippes that power, / Thus would I weare them out.' Yet Cleopatra achieves the miracle Romeo had only dreamt of, as Antony, invigorated by their embrace, redeems the indignity of his bungled suicide in his last words: 'please your thoughts / In feeding them with those my former Fortunes / Wherein I liu'd. The greatest Prince o'th'world, / The Noblest . . .'[24] What else is this but the fleeting dramatic enactment of Romeo's dream?

> I dreamt my Lady came and found me dead . . .
> And Breathd such life with kisses in my lips,
> That I reuiude and was an Emperor.
> (*Romeo and Juliet* V.i. Q2:K4)

So Antony momentarily lives, to die with imperial dignity.

Thus all the recurrent themes come to rest in their dramatic embodiment. Whether consciously or not, Shakespeare has staged here the image of death like a child at the breast, the kiss that is now restorative, now mortal, the resurrection that had hitherto remained a fantasy. But, lest it be imagined that this account assumes the pre-eminence of staged over linguistic imagery, let it be added that within the present context, Shakespeare also makes poetry stand alone, with no stage backing. For Cleopatra not only effectively brings about Romeo's dream, she also echoes it later:

> I dreampt there was an Emperor Anthony.
> Oh such another sleepe, that I might see
> But such another man.
> (*Antony and Cleopatra* V.ii. 3292ff)

Her subsequent description of the emperor of her dreams neither needs, nor could have found, a physical reality to support it.

Othello

The extraordinary dramatised emergence of an image-cluster in *Antony and Cleopatra* illustrates a Shakespearean tendency noted often enough before – his practice of absorbing clichés of thought and staging, or proverbial ideas, and gradually translating them into highly original staged versions. The modern reader or watcher is often unaware of the traditional nature underlying such stage imagery. However, the lovers' embraces in *Othello* have no part in this pattern. And yet they are well worth analysis, if only for their very scarcity. Shakespeare envisages only three specific embraces – the lovers first kiss at their reunion at Cyprus; thereafter, their lips never meet in mutual consciousness. Othello kisses Desdemona as she sleeps, before killing her, and he then allows himself the same luxury, kissing her corpse as he dies. Such controlled paucity warrants attention and epitomises their tragically truncated love.

Othello has obvious affinities with *Romeo and Juliet* and *Antony and Cleopatra* – and even with the early tragicomedy of Pyramus and Thisbe. But the other lovers find a peace in death that was denied to them in life, whereas in *Othello*, this high point of harmony within the enclosing storm comes at the very heart of the play, rather than its end. For, at the reunion in Cyprus, Othello longs for the perfect *liebestod* – a death which is not, in fact, achieved by any of the other lovers, since a true *liebestod* is a death mutually chosen at a moment of absolute content, for no outward cause (as in *Tristan und Isolde*, II.ii).

Othello   . . . If it were now to dye
　　　　　T'were now to be most happy, for I feare
　　　　　My soule hath her content so absolute,
　　　　　That not another comfort like to this
　　　　　Succeeds in vnknowne Fate. .
　　　　　　　　(*Othello* II.i.Q:E^v)

None of the other lovers' deaths are freely chosen in this way; in each case the hero, be it Pyramus, Romeo or Antony, mistakenly believes his love to be dead, killing himself to join her, she then dying to join him. The deaths are triggered off by fate working against human plans. Not so with Othello; at this supreme moment, his love potentially outgoes even that of Antony and Cleopatra in its life-rejecting positivism. But, tragically, the lovers do not die, and the play can only decline from this ominously prophetic peak.

So Desdemona sensibly rejects Othello's flamboyant *liebestod* for the natural increase of their life and love, and Othello replies:

> Amen to that sweete power,
> I cannot speake enough of this content,
> It stops me heere, it is too much of ioy:
> And this, and this, the greatest discord be,
> *they kisse.*
> That ere our hearts shall make.
> (*Othello* II.i.Q:E^v. SD probably authorial)

This ominously worded kiss lies like a kernel at the heart of the play. Jealousy can only grow out of love: it is that most powerful expression of love in which all love's instincts are perverted to their opposite. The other lovers' dying kisses united paradoxes in harmony: even the death-dealing kiss was longed for as a restorative, and in death the lovers aspired to union ('come lye thou in my arme'; 'Husband, I come').[25] In *Othello* there is no such harmony, only the dissonant reversal of *concordia discors*. The key-note so quietly struck in Othello's imagery here is acted out in musical terms, later in the play, in the cacophony of the Clown's first scene; its implications reverberate through the other two embraces. Symbols, traditionally, of unity, these kisses are shattered by images of disjunction – love grotesquely fuelling loathing, pity whipping on vengeance, the life-giving and death-dealing in jarring consort.

In the mock brothel-scene, Othello's lines suggest that the actor playing him should take Desdemona's face in his hands, drawing it close as though about to kiss her, before forcing himself away:

> O thou blacke weede, why art so louely faire?
> Thou smell'st so sweete, that the sence akes at thee,
> [——] Would thou hadst ne're bin borne.
> (*Othello* IV.ii.Q:K4)

Certainly the same terrible internal conflict, image, act, and awareness of Desdemona's sweet breath, recur as Othello kisses her on her death-bed:

> . . . when I haue pluckt the rose,
> I cannot giue it vitall growth againe,
> It must needes wither; I'le smell it on the tree,
> A balmy breath, that doth almost perswade
> Iustice her selfe to breake her sword. Once more . . .
> . . . once more, and this the last.
> *He kisses her.*
> (*Othello* V.ii.Q:M. SD probably authorial)

So Othello vainly strives to make contradictory feelings one. Her sweetness, instead of softening him, is a spur ('So sweete was ne're so fatall'); his pity confirms his resolve ('I must weepe, / But they are cruell teares'); even his perplexity is dignified into a divine perversity ('this sorrowes heauenly, / It strikes when it does loue').[26] His tears, which drop on his wife and wake her, are equated with his pitying vengeance about to fall on her. The paradoxical image is exact, epitomising the double pull suffered from the start, of loving jealousy and grieving, implacable justice.

The idea of justice is, indeed, essential to our understanding not only of Othello, but of his bewilderingly glib last couplet, which at first seems chillingly epigrammatic and hollow. Othello needs must sublimate his irrational jealousy, which all the play's objective observers – Iago, Emilia, Rymer, the audience – know to be causeless, self-fuelling. Jealousy, Iago mockingly informs Othello, is 'the greene eyd monster, which doth mocke / That meate it feedes on'; ''tis a monster, / Begot vpon it selfe, borne on it selfe',[27] Emilia later concurs, in a rare moment of conjugal agreement. Desdemona's naïve commonsense is inadequate here:

Desdemona	Alas the day, I neuer gaue him cause.
Emilia	But iealous soules will not be answered so,
	They are not euer iealous for the cause,
	But iealous for they are iealous.

(Othello III.iv.Q:12)

But Othello's actions must be anchored on the belief that his jealousy has a cause. His words lie in direct contrast with Emilia's:

> It is the cause, it is the cause, my soule,
> Let me not name it to you, you chaste starres:
> It is the cause.
> (*Othello* V.ii.Q:M)

Without cause he could never decide to kill Desdemona. For his own self-credence his actions must be founded on a stern sense of cause and right retribution, a delusion quickly fostered by Iago. 'Strangle her in her bed, euen the bed she hath contaminated', Iago prompts; 'Good, good, the iustice of it pleases; very good', Othello replies. And when, after the murder has been done, the vehemence of Emilia's protestations at last begins to make some impression on him, he cries (in his first words echoing Iago's vocabulary): 'Cassio did top her, aske thy husband else, / O I were damn'd beneath all depth in hell, / But that I did proceed vpon iust grounds / To this extremity'.[28] So, as he kisses Desdemona sleeping, it is his sense of justice which he wields over his reluctance and his love:

> A balmy breath, that doth almost perswade
> Iustice her selfe to breake her sword . . .
>
> (*Othello* V.ii.Q:M)

But Desdemona, in the panic of this last scene, twice associates him, not with divine justice, but mercy.[29]

And so the eternal Shakespearean debate between justice and mercy is played out once again. For in the appalling downward rush of this last scene, in which Othello's intended ritual sacrifice degenerates into rank murder, the limitations of his mistaken ideal are bitterly contrasted with the supreme generosity of Desdemona's dying lie. It is she, not he, who embodies mercy, the greatest of all divine attributes. Just as Othello surpassed all Shakespeare's other lovers at his moment of greatest joy, so she outgoes them all in her death. For, in Othello's eyes, she squanders her soul in her last breath, consigning it to no lovers' Elysium but to Hell, as she damns herself by false witness, accusing herself of Othello's crime and absolving him of guilt. Like them but greater than them, she makes death the ultimate expression of her love, and of her mercy.

Not so Othello. The polite justice tendered by Lodovico is equally coolly brushed aside by him, to be replaced by his own simplistic concept of what is right. He matches the ritual sacrifice he had intended for Desdemona, with all its naïve fiction of appositeness ('Strangle her in . . . the bed she hath contaminated'), by his own ritual execution as infidel and traitor. It is extraordinary that a critic of Eliot's intelligence should miss the categoric self-condemnation here. Othello simply executes himself as a 'circumcised dog', the molester of a Venetian and traitor to the state.

But Othello matches this public justice by the private justice of his last words. Their banality betrays the terrible simplicity of his moral code. For, in a pathetic last display of equity, he allows himself exactly the respite he had granted Desdemona:

> I kist thee ere I kild thee, no way but this,
> Killing my selfe, to die vpon a kisse.
> *He dies.*
>
> (*Othello* V.ii.Q:N2)

The discord so lightly evoked in the play's central embrace finds its final embodiment in the neat chiasmus of this couplet and its accompanying action, as love and death unite at last, and 'kiss' and 'kill' are visibly made one.

Othello's last words echo Romeo's. 'Thus with a kisse I die.' But the effect is very different. As Desdemona protested earlier, 'That death's vnnaturall, that kills for louing'.[30] It is the inverse of the equally unnatural death that dies for loving, that took Romeo, Juliet, Antony and Cleopatra. But it is the more tragic, for in it there is no joy, and no hope of union.

CHAPTER 6

Weeping

'Excess of sorrow laughs. Excess of joy weeps.'
(Blake: *The Marriage of Heaven and Hell*)

Presentation

In practice, crying appears to have raised as few problems for the
Elizabethan actor as for his modern counterpart. Hamlet's envy of
the Player suggests that even a ranting minor among the King's men
was capable of raising real tears in a dream of passion. For the less
accomplished, an onion did the trick, as the Lord's advice to his boy
player admits:

> And if the boy haue not a womans guift
> To raine a shower of commanded teares,
> An Onion wil do well for such a shift,
> Which in a Napkin (being close conuei'd)
> Shall in despight enforce a waterie eie.
> (*Taming of the Shrew* Ind. i. 135ff)

In the last resort, however, blushes, sweat, tears, and all the other
faint watermarks of expression that may lie beyond a poor actor's
range, or the sight of his audience, are created and proclaimed
primarily by the dialogue, and it is on this that our attention will
concentrate.

Shakespeare's first problem was the control and placing of a
rhetoric which both created a character's anguish, and elicited its
echo in the audience. The obvious solution is for the weeper to point
to his own tears. Thus, in one stylistically ambitious scene, Titus
pleads for his sons' lives, imagining his tears laying the summer dust
and melting the winter snows. Scorned by the Senators, he contrasts
their flinty hearts with the impressionable pavings, worn away by
his tears. Lamenting with Lavinia, he likens her sighs to the gusty
sky that raises his sea-storm of tears; consoling her, he pictures them
weeping into a fountain till its waters turn to brine. Such rhetorical

elaboration may well be defended on the grounds of the preponder-
ant formalism of drama at this date, and yet in other highly written
moments, both in this play and *Henry VI*, Shakespeare appears to
succeed better (for instance in Margaret's baiting of York). At this
point, I believe, Titus's laments fail by their very excess: we cannot
credit such inventive misery. Shakespeare's later development takes
two concurrent and divergent paths. On the one hand, the direct
rhetoric of misery is intensified and refined, to reach its heights in
Cleopatra's passionate laments, or Lear's irresistible commands –
'Howle, howle, howle: O [you] are men of stones . . .' On the other
hand is the equal and opposite tendency to obliqueness and understatement. This second tendency is clearly illustrated by a chronological sequence of examples related to the original passage from *Titus*.
The original gap between rhetorical vehemence and dramatic effect
narrows to equilibrium, and finally inverts to awesome imbalance,
so that understatement can whelm, whelm, and overwhelm us.[1]

Thus in *Romeo and Juliet* a similar moment is improved stylistically, and given the necessary dramatic twist. Here Shakespeare transfers a trimmer version of the skies–sighs, seas–tears platitude from
mourner to mourner's observer. With comfortable callousness,
Capulet points out Juliet's desperate tears at her threatened marriage
to Paris:

> How now a Conduit girle, what still in tears,
> Euermore showring in one litle body?
> Thou counte[r]faits [a] Barke, a Sea, a Wind:
> For still thy eyes, which I may call the sea,
> Do ebbe and flowe with teares, the Barke thy body is,
> Sayling in this salt floud; the windes thy sighes . . .
>   (*Romeo and Juliet* III.v.Q2:H4ᵛ, F:2170)

But now the rhetoric is undercut both by allocation and style.
Capulet's catalogue of comparisons is comically dated: it is an old
man's summary of a poem that had been all the rage in his youth –
Wyatt's sonnet, 'My galy charged with forgetfulnes' (c.1535). And
this detail is part of a larger scheme: the play's revaluation of
traditional love-poetry. Shakespeare takes the clichés of the Petrarchan sonneteers and transfers them to a setting where the meaningless paradoxes are factually true. Romeo's speech on discovering the
fray of the first act is the crucial example. 'Heres much to do with
hate, but more with loue: / Why then ô brawling loue, ô louing hate'
proclaims the worn Petrarchan formula which will be for real in this
play, where public hatred and private love are thrown in violent

conflict, while on the comic plane brawling servants threaten in sexual innuendo ('My naked weapon is out . . .'). In the rest of Romeo's speech, Shakespeare condemns the Petrarchan convention when it lacks a living source (just as Romeo merely imagines he is in love with Rosalind): 'O any thing of nothing first create[]: / O heauie lightnesse, serious vanitie, / Mishapen Chaos of welsee[m]ing formes.'[2] At the same time, these clichés provide an intensifying contrast with the spontaneous originality of the lovers' poetry when they meet. In this highly literary play, dead metaphors are continually played off against reality. And in little, Capulet's derivative similes emphasise, by contrast, the simple authenticity of Juliet's unspoken grief.

Richard II is subtler still. Here Richard is the sufferer (like Titus) and failed poet (like Titus and Capulet), but both are consciously played against him. Furthermore, the adverse audience reaction, inadvertently aroused in *Titus*, is now deliberately prompted and forestalled by an implicit stage direction:

> King   Aumerle thou weepest (my tender-hearted coosin)
>   . . . shall we play the wantons with our woes,
>   And make some prety match with sheading teares,
>   As thus to drop them still vpon one place,
>   Till they haue fretted vs a paire of graues
>   Within the earth, and therein laid there lies
>   Two kinsmen digd their graues with weeping eies:
>   Would not this ill do well? well well I see
>   I talke but idlely, *and you laugh at me* . . .
>   (*Richard II* III.iii. Q:G^v–G2. My italics)

The flaws of *Titus* are preserved, but in their new arrangement they are dramatically flawless. Stage observers and theatre audience alike laugh uncomfortably at Richard's maudlin fantasy, and the self-indulgent image-spinning which was Shakespeare's error in *Titus* is turned into an effective piece of characterisation.

As Shakespeare's control of tone becomes assured, Titus's hyperbolic analogies are not jettisoned, but changed, changed utterly. The surreal artifice of 'O earth, I will befriend thee more with raine / That shall distill from these two auntient [vrnes] / Than youthfull Aprill shall with all his showres'[3] is simply ill-judged. But what was pathetically laughable in *Titus* is turned to controlled comic pathos in *Two Gentlemen*. Launce cries over his account of parting from his family, watched by Crab, impassive as the Senators that drove Titus to his anguish: 'now the dogge all this while sheds not a teare:

nor speakes a word: but see how I lay the dust with my teares . . .'[4]
We know from the entering Panthino that Launce should indeed be
in tears. His last line has a pathos that is comically misplaced, but in
Lear the same image is raised to the awesome imbalance from which I
began. Lear, caught by Cordelia's attendants, breaks down to think
himself alone and in enemy hands:

> No Seconds? All my selfe?
> Why, this would make a man, a man of Salt
> To vse his eyes for Garden water-pots,
> [I and laying Autums dust] . . .
>   (*King Lear* IV.vi.2638ff, Q:14ᵛ)

Titus's cold pastoral, his absurd pseudo-classical urns are trans-
formed into prosaic watering-cans. And yet the familiar is not
laughable: a heart-rending beauty is born.

There is a sympathetic magic uniting stage observers and theatre
audience, as Richard's reproach of his snickering courtiers suggests,
and Shakespeare habitually splashes tears among his extras to
prompt our own. In the earlier work such tactics are often ill-judged.
Portia somewhat unexpectedly compares the ordinary Bassanio,
puzzling over her caskets, to Hercules, herself to Hesione, while
'The rest aloofe are the Dardanian wiues / With bleared visages come
forth to view / The issue of th'exploit.' Shakespeare out-writes his
source, Golding's Ovid,[5] and the showy classical analogy evidently
has a structural function. The casket-scene, previously a light interlude with Arragon and the Moor, is now laden with heroic ballast to
equal its Venetian counterpart, Shylock's trial scene. That, however,
is naturally dramatic, the play's true climax; the casket-scene, third
time round, risks tedium and its outcome is secure. Few productions
would attempt the grave suspense Portia's lines demand. An audience of obedient extras is there to be prompted; the auditorium has
the prerogative of caprice. Casual remarks are more likely to touch
us unaware. Richard, newly submitted to Bolingbroke and about to
return in ignomy to London, turns suddenly to York, now of the
usurper's party: 'Vncle giue me your handes, nay drie your eies . . .'[6]
Such pluck in the central character often contrasts powerfully with
the breakdown of his followers. Hermione in *The Winter's Tale* is
unjustly hurried off to prison, consoling her women, 'Doe not
weepe (good Fooles)', just as Cleopatra had tried to rouse her maids
at Antony's death: 'How do you Women? / What, what good

cheere? Why how now Charmian? / My Noble Gyrles?' How subtly
Shakespeare changes her tone from rallying courage to the return of
grief! 'Ah Women, women! Looke / Our Lampe is spent, it's
out . . .'[7]

Nor was he ignorant of such effects in his earliest plays, although
the presentation there can be more awkward. Margaret, crowing
over York in the superb baiting-scene that ends in his death, turns
suddenly to her companions – 'What, weeping ripe, my Lord
Northumberland?' But Northumberland had already twice nudged
the audience about his tender feelings, which are offered in smart
fulfilment of York's prophecy: 'And if thou tell'st the heauie storie
right . . . euen my Foes will shed fast-falling Teares.'[8] Instead of the
natural, suggestive empathy between stage witnesses and auditorium expertly tapped later, Shakespeare conducts a self-defeating
frontal attack on the sensibilities of his audience.

Rhetoric and dramatic manipulation are the besetting problems of
the early plays. From the start Shakespeare has a natural gift for
psychology and simple pathos; he stumbled scaling tragic heights. In
the converging pincer movement of his development, as rhetoric is
tamed and placing mastered, simplicity turns complex – not in
expression, but in implication and tone. The early plays triumph
most often in moments of lucid authenticity. Take Kate's angry
misery when Petruchio fails to turn up to his wedding on time. It is
more credible than Titus's lachrymose eloquence, simply because its
cause is the unheroic and familiar one of wounded pride:

> *Kate* Now must the world point at poore Katherine,
> And say, loe, there is mad Petruchio's wife
> If it would please him come and marry her . . .
> Would Katherine had neuer seen him . . .
> *Exit weeping.*
> (*Taming of the Shrew* III.ii. 1406ff. SD probably authorial).

Similarly, in *King John*, Arthur's unsuspecting gentleness to Hubert,
his red-eyed would-be murderer, is a transparent tear-jerker ('Are
you sicke Hubert? you looke pale to day').[9] This is too contrived to
be moving, while his entirely credible mortification at the bickering
of his mother and grandmother works at once:

> *Queen*   Come to thy grandame child.
> *Constance* Doe childe, goe to yt grandame childe,
> Giue grandame kingdome, and it grandame will
> Giue yt a plum, a cherry, and a figge,
> There's a good grandame . . .

Queen Mother   His mother shames him so, poore boy he weepes.
                          (*King John* II.i.46off. SH probably authorial)

But in the great tragedies, moments of apparently translucent pathos
can have a fine ambivalence escaping the casual observer. When Lear
first wakes from madness, his dawning recognition of Cordelia is
immediately followed by 'Be your teares wet? / Yes faith: I pray
weepe not . . .' The gentle commiseration for Cordelia we sen-
timentally expect is a bare afterthought to this analytic anxiety.
Lear's first concern is the fumbling verification of his senses. 'Let's
see, / I feele this pin pricke . . . Be your teares wet?' He must touch
Cordelia's cheek, experimental, absorbed. 'Yes faith . . .'[10]

Grace

Lear's dry-eyed absorption raises the dominant question of tears'
moral significance. Here Shakespeare's practice can be defined by a
neat square-dance in which two proposals set to their mirror oppo-
sites. Thus tears are associated with grace, while the graceless are
impassive to emotion. And on the other hand the graceless can affect
an unfelt grief, while pain's ultimate expression may be an apparent
indifference. Although Shakespeare learns to flesh such skeletal
schema, behind Hamlet's Keatsian awareness of the feel of not to feel
it this simple set of equations still obtains, viz:

> Tears equals grace; no tears equals no grace;
> Tears equals no grace; no tears equals grace.

The correlation of tears and grace is explicitly made by the
gardener's sentimental scene-stopper in *Richard II*:

> Here did she fall a teare, here in this place
> Ile set a banke of Rew, sowre hearb of grace.
> Rew euen for ruth heere shortly shall be seene
> In the remembrance of a weeping Queene.
>   (*Richard II* III.iv.Q:G4)

In *Romeus and Juliet* Brooke provides the token aphorism: 'teares are
as true messengers of mans ungyltie mynde.'[11] The standard moral is
often all too glaring. Arthur has nothing more to fear when Hubert
breaks down to weep instead of skewering his eyeballs on a red-hot
poker. Flavius's honesty is attested by his frank tears for Timon, in

contrast with the smooth commiseration of his creditors. Of all Alonso's fickle courtiers honest Gonzalo alone weeps at his distraction. As ever, it is the palpable linguistic or dramatic texture that makes an impression, not its high moral gloss. For instance, we may hear report of Parolles' incipient repentance with some scepticism, but are disturbed by the Wordsworthian warmth of a maternal image, as, stocked and apprehensive, 'he weepes like a wench that had shed her milke' and cannot feed her child.[12]

So much depends on what is made of the moment. Tourneur is explicit and stylised in his post-Shakespearean staging of the regenerative tears of patience:

> *Vindice* I'faith, 'tis a sweet shower, it does much good.
> The fruitful grounds and meadows of her soul
> Has been long dry: pour down thou blessed dew,
> Rise Mother; troth, this shower has made you higher.
> (*The Revenger's Tragedy* IV.iv.47ff)

But as he raises his mother from her knees, his image acts out in formal terms the association of moral refreshment and growth invigorating many memorable tears / rain images in religious poetry from Herbert to Hopkins. It is dominant in two related moments in *Lear* and *Othello*. Lear's scalding tears at his awakening are, psychologically, a simple sign of longed-for physical release – the relaxation of his original intransigence in 'No, Ile not weepe, I haue full cause of weeping'. At the same time, they are at once penitential and spiritually healing, as his image of purgatorial torment implies.[13] Othello's tears in his last speech have the same double force. Like Emilia's violent outburst against him just before, they relax tension for him and the audience. Further, for all Eliot's thin-lipped scepticism, they restore Othello to some kind of heroic stature, *because* the last speech is his first, crucial acknowledgement of fault. His rich, biblical imagery combines the confession

> . . . of one whose hand,
> Like the base Indian, threw a pearle away,
> Richer then all his Tribe,

with the penitence

> . . . of one whose subdued eyes,
> Albeit vnused to the melting moode,
> Drops teares –

and the balm of absolution:

> — as fast as the Arabian trees
> Their medicinall gum.
> (*Othello* V.ii.Q:N2)

In a curious parallel, Crashaw accurately recapitulates these emotional implications:

> There is no need at all
> That the Balsame-sweating bough
> So coyly should let fall
> His med'cinable Teares . . .
> Yet let the poore drops weepe . . .
> They, though to others no reliefe,
> May Balsame bee for their own grief.
> ('The Weeper', sts.12–13)

In rigid moral terms, tears may be a sign of spiritual mollification. In
blunt reality, they are at once painful and shaming, an intense and
mixed relief to the weeper.

The converse is correspondingly modified also. In absolute terms,
the unregenerate are as incapable of instinctive, self-castigating tears
as they are of blushing at their crimes. The close cross-weave of the
first history tetralogy is incidentally illustrated by Richard's inability
to weep at his father's atrocious death in *3 Henry VI*, and his uneasy
reminiscence of the occasion in his courtship of Lady Anne in *Richard
III*.[14] He chooses Clarence's murderers for a comparable callousness,
gallantly flattering them: 'Your eyes drop Mill-stones, when Fooles
eyes fall Teares: / I like you Lads' – a compliment they later return to
him, in a moment uncannily prophetic of *King Lear*.[15] Launce rages at
his dog Crab that he 'has no more pitty in him then a dogge: a Iew
would haue wept to haue seene our parting' from his family.[16] But at
every stage this canine behaviour is a carefully manipulated parallel
to the literally beastly Proteus (whose classic prototype's animal
metamorphoses are clearly suggested). Here, for instance, Crab's
impassivity is a sharp reminder of Julia's tearful parting from Proteus
just previously, and Proteus's own impassive calm. Again,
Shakespeare ill-advisedly follows Marlowe's crude example in attributing a supposed Semitic indifference to Shylock, who weeps, like
Barabbas, for his ducats and his daughters indiscriminately. There is
small grace in mercenary tears like these.[17] Significantly, however,
such examples come from the early plays: ostentatious cruelty soon

becomes too coarse a means of caricaturisation. By *Othello*, Shakespeare elicits a subtler frisson of fear and loathing, as the shaken Desdemona and Emilia turn to Iago for support. Their pathetic, feminine weakness is implicit in the generic, most probably authorial stage direction as Iago jollies them off-stage:

Iago   Goe in, and weepe not, all things shall be well.
         Exit women.
                    (*Othello* IV.ii.Q:L)

Gleefully dry-eyed himself, he begs them not to cry . . .

As Iago demonstrates, the unregenerate are not only impervious to grief themselves, but indifferent to the grief of others. Gertrude is more than crassly insensitive in her reasoning with Hamlet: 'Thou know'st tis common all that liues must die . . . Why seemes it so perticuler with thee?' Her moral sloppiness must be taken seriously, because it is intimately allied with Claudius's vice. He merely translates her plaintive prevarication to high-sounding admonition when he continues: 'to perseuer / In obstinate condolement is a course / Of impious stubbornes . . . It showes a will most incorrect to heauen.' Like Satan, Richard III, Shylock and Iago,[18] both Claudius and Gertrude pervert pious argument to evil ends, in order to defend the hollowness of their mourning for a brother and husband eliminated and forgotten in flagrant defiance of heaven's will. Claudius's guilt, and Gertrude's feebler fault, are further emphasised by parallel elsewhere. Shakespeare presents a rare moral absolute in the fairytale wickedness of Cymbeline's Queen, who muses grimly on Imogen's tears at the banishment of Posthumus: 'Weepes she still (saist thou?) / Dost thou thinke in time / She will not quench, and let instructions enter / Where Folly now possesses?'[19] Such advice, however sound to the unattuned, pragmatic modern reader, is unacceptable. Leaving aside the cruel dismissiveness of 'Folly', the scorn of 'quench', the attitude itself is redolent of evil, a mockery of sorrow most incorrect to heaven. Such advice is never offered by trustworthy characters in Shakespeare, who are far more likely to encourage the expression of grief, and their negative witness underlines the positive moral taint implicit here.

Othello's heartless stage-management of Desdemona's tears is similar in kind. Desdemona turns to go from the Venetian ambassador, smarting and in tears at Othello's public slap (a detail that was often cut from performances of the play).[20] Othello calls her back in mocking compliance with Lodovico's shocked request, parading his wife as a whore for hire:

What would you with her sir?
. . . you did wish that I would make her turne:
Sir, she can turne, and turne, and yet go on,
And turne againe, and she can weepe sir, weepe;
And shee's obedient, as you say, obedient;
Very obedient, proceed you in your teares.
                              (*Othello* IV.i.Q:K2ᵛ)

There is perhaps nothing more horrible than the sight of a character playing in such cold mockery with his victim's bewildered compliance. The baiting of York in *Henry VI* and Gloucester in *Lear*, the cruel games of *The Birthday Party*, the debasement of the Captain in *The Dance of Death* – all have the same, nauseating force. And yet Othello's callous manipulation here cannot be neatly docketed as archetypal malignant indifference to grief. He baffles absolute moral condemnation because the reasons for his undeniable cruelty, like Heathcliff's, have been made too intimately clear for easy judgement. Once more Shakespeare has complicated the issues deployed straightforwardly in his earlier work.

By contrast, in *Titus* indifference to tears is the unquestionable original sin – a denial of common humanity that cuts Titus off from mercy and makes him vulnerable to the evil first exercised by himself. Titus begins by denying Tamora's anguished pleas for the life of her captive son, whom he sacrifices to his family honour. This 'cruell irreligious pietie'[21] is then logically and inexorably repaid by its obverse, Tamora's impious religion of revenge. Titus's original intransigence is mirrored in a series of ironic parallels, as, blind with tears, he prostrates himself in vain to the Senators, who execute his sons; fruitlessly, Lavinia weeps before Tamora and her sons, who rape and mutilate her in return. The play is set in a world devoid of pity, as Helen Gardner has pointed out,[22] and its long series of futile tears and prayers derided culminates in a strikingly ridiculous stage image, as all the surviving Andronici shoot arrows tagged with prayers up to the gods. In the source a mere ruse to feign madness, in Shakespeare it epitomises the theme already explored at length in speech and stage action. It is superficially reminiscent of a silly anecdote from Copley's jest-book: 'One seeing a Meteor fal down when an Astronomer was taking the height of a Starre with his Jacobs staffe, cryed out unto him, O well shot ifaith!'[23] But in *Titus* the patent absurdity has point: not even divine pity will be found in a world which Titus himself has made pitiless.

Lying tears

The reverse of the original paradigm is illustrated as comprehensively as its straightforward positive. Flip the coin, and tears, like all other external signs of grace, are ably simulated by the corrupt. They may not weep naturally, but craftily they can. The idea is stated most clearly in *Cymbeline*, a curious and difficult play comprehensively devoted to all the intestinal convolutions of 'seeming', Shakespeare's perennial theme. Imogen reflects bitterly on her apparently loyal husband's suspicions of her fidelity. Speech and tears, she observes, are both undermined by their corrupt use:

> . . . Oh!
> Mens Vowes are womens Traitors. All good seeming
> By thy reuolt (oh Husband) shall be thought
> Put on for Villainy . . .
> True honest men being heard like false Aeneas
> Were in his time thought false: and Synons weeping
> Did scandall many a holy teare: tooke pitty
> From most true wretchednesse.
> (*Cymbeline* III.iv.1724ff)

And indeed the Sinon of *The Rape of Lucrece*, 'eyes wayling still', heads a long, lachrymose procession. Perhaps Shakespeare's first epitome of deception in every aspect, his ever-more sophisticated progeny throng the plays to follow. In *Henry VI* the guilty Queen Margaret squeezes out heroic tears in a diversionary interlude worthy of Lady Macbeth, when she sees Henry's suspicions at Duke Humphrey's empurpled and strangulated corpse. Richard III is the arch archetype. He preens himself for his own histrionic versatility ('Why I can smile, and murther whiles I smile, / And cry, Content, to that which grieues my Heart, / And wet my Cheekes with artificiall Teares'), and accepts Buckingham as an accomplice only when he has promised a similar competence. Richard pretends to cry in his courtship of Lady Anne,[24] but the most brazen demonstration of his boast is his public grief at Hastings' execution. With wicked irony he receives the head he ordered, lapsing into a tearful denunciation of the very sin he is practising, while attributing it to his innocent victim:

> So deare I lou'd the man, that I must weepe:
> I tooke him for the plainest harmelesse Creature
> That breath'd vpon the Earth, a Christian . . .
> So smooth he dawb'd his Vice with shew of Vertue.
> (*Richard III* III.v.2110ff)

Oliver draws Charles's attention to his distress at the iniquities of a brother he is reluctantly constrained to have killed. But Hubert is the neatest illustration of Imogen's words. A curious variant on Shakespeare's obsessive theme, Hubert *seems* worse than he is. King John picks him out for villainy, and calls him 'A fellow by the hand of Nature mark'd, / Quoted, and sign'd to do a deede of shame.' Hubert, however, does not murder Arthur, and retorts to John, 'you haue slander'd Nature in my forme, / Which howsoeuer rude exteriorly, / Is yet the couer of a fayrer minde / Then to be butcher of an innocent childe.' His villainous looks work against him, so that he is commonly maligned. Confronted with Arthur's corpse, he breaks into bitter tears, at which Salisbury remarks, 'Trust not those cunning waters of his eyes, / For villainie is not without such rheume.'[25] This unjustified slur on Hubert's genuine distress shows exactly how Sinon's weeping can scandal many a holy tear.

Shakespeare's Sinons have their Aeneases: many lovers slip into moist vows, often innocent of the fact that they will break them. *A Midsummer Night's Dream* persuasively stages love's fanatical faith in its own illusion, and we laugh at, but do not loathe, Lysander's sudden desertion of Hermia to run after Helena with tearful protestations. Yet his vows contrast with her real distress, as she attacks his perjury, and cries at a courtship she interprets as mockery. Less pardonable is the early deceiver Proteus, who coaches Thurio in the *ars amandi* of winning his lady with 'walefull Sonnets'. 'Write', he says, 'till your inke be dry; and with your teares / Moist it againe.' Lucetta rightly mistrusts the 'Ocean of his teares' that Julia foolishly built her hopes on. 'All these are seruants to deceitful men' – and women too. Enobarbus warns Antony from the start about Cleopatra's divine dissembling (incidentally capitalising on the clichés used by Titus and Capulet): 'We cannot cal her winds and waters sighes and teares: They are greater stormes and Tempests then Almanackes can report . . . she makes a showre of Raine as well as Ioue.' Her gifts are well demonstrated after Antony's defeat at Actium (Antony: 'Fall not a teare I say, one of them rates / All that is wonne and lost . . .'). Cressida, too, promises to tear her bright hair and crack her voice with sobs at her enforced departure from Troy. But lingering behind this sudden passion of grief is the ominous banter of the first scene:

Pandarus	Ile be sworne tis true, he will weepe you an'twere a man borne in Aprill . . .
Cressida	And Ile spring vp in his teares an' twere a nettle against May.

(Troilus and Cressida I. ii. Q:B^v)

For all her distraught protestations, Cressida neither tears her hair nor cracks her voice, just as she cannot keep her last words closing the scene, 'I will not go from Troy.' She goes, and thrives. Cressida, like Lysander, cannot help her duplicity, but now the drama is history, not a dream.[26]

As verisimilitude increases the distinctions become blurred. Who cared more for Ophelia, Hamlet or Laertes? Hamlet rightly ridicules Laertes' grave-side hyperboles, but perhaps Hamlet is jealous of an extrovert grief he has already envied in the Player. His oath of love at this late stage sounds as much like a defiance of Laertes as a disinterested avowal, and its interpretation would depend on the actor. Again, as Bradley points out, we would sooner trust Octavius Caesar's public grief over Antony's death if he had wept in private, as he does in Plutarch.[27] The change is significant, its implications being underlined by Caesar's brisk interruption of his elegy for the 'businesse' brought by a messenger. Antony's public tears in *Julius Caesar* are similarly suspect; it is telling that he does not cry over Caesar's corpse till a messenger's grief prompts his own. In retrospect, his sincerity is emphatically questioned by Enobarbus and Agrippa in *Antony and Cleopatra*: 'When Anthony found Iulius Caesar dead, / He cried almost to roaring: And he wept / When at Phillippi he found Brutus slaine.' 'That year indeed, he was trobled with a rheume . . .'[28] Yet in the play itself, can one doubt his horror at the assassination? Antony is a sentimentalist, *and* a born orator in his manipulation of others' grief. His tears can be at once maudlin and sincere (as in his premature farewell to his servants, before his only victory), and politic (as in the funeral oration). 'What willingly he did confound, he wail'd', but he wept willingly too. His simultaneously sentimental and controlled exploitation of others' tears is historic. Plutarch's account of the Parthian campaigns includes a tear-jerking ploy, parallel to Antony's manipulative valediction to his household, so sharply undercut by Enobarbus's aside ('What does he meane?' 'To make his Followers weepe').[29] Shakespeare had to cut the campaigns completely, but the trait is evident enough elsewhere.

Hal is open to similar reservations. At his father's apparent death, we may *hear* him promise his due of 'teares and heauy sorowes of the blood', but we only *see* him seize his own due, the crown. We have been warned sufficiently often against the relative credibility of words and deeds to take the point. Matters are quickly rectified, however, as Warwick enters to describe Hal duly crying in an antechamber. Later Hal himself replies to his father's long rebuke by protesting that he would have defended himself sooner, 'but for my

teares, / The moist impediments vnto my speech'.[30] Moreover,
Shakespeare has clearly introduced a carefully planted exchange with
Poins, two acts previously, in order to forestall any criticism:

Prince	. . . I tel thee, my heart bleeds inwardly that my father is so sick, and keeping such vile company as thou arte hath in reason taken from me all ostentation of sorrowe.
Poins	The reason.
Prince	What wouldst thou thinke of me if I should weep?
Poins	I woulde thincke thee a most princely hypocrite.
Prince	It would bee euery mans thought, and thou arte a blessed felow, to thinke as euery man thinkes.

(*2 Henry IV* II.ii.Q:C4–C4ᵛ)

In spite of the warning, critics rashly lay themselves open to Hal's
charge. Shakespeare has parried condemnation of his future hero by
a ruse whose efficacy is undermined by the greater complexity of his
characterisation.

'To weepe is to make lesse the depth of greefe'

Hal's slow response might well be an instance of our fourth proposition: that in Shakespeare's practice dry-eyed grief is the trustworthy
counterpart to lying tears. Yet such grief needs preparation, and,
though startling, is relatively rare. Most often Shakespeare presents
silent tears as his truthful positive. As often, he capitalises on
accepted psychology, later well summarised by Herbert:

> Joys oft are there, and griefs as oft as joyes;
> But griefs without a noise:
> Yet speake they louder, then distemper'd fears.
> What is so shrill as silent tears?
> ('The Familie')

So Beatrice, shocked for the first time into silence by Hero's
nightmare wedding, cannot speak for crying ('Lady Beatrice, haue
you wept al this while?'). So Duke Humphrey at the beginning of the
canon, and his counterpart Cranmer at the end, each 'strangled his
language in his teares' – sure proof of honesty. Most flamboyant is
the early *tour de force* in *Titus* to which we will return in the next
chapter. Here Titus fails to ransom his two sons' heads by chopping
off his own hand. When a messenger returns with all three bloody
orts, Marcus and Lucius break into heady laments. Only many lines

later does Titus rouse himself from a dazed and slumberous silence, to laugh. 'Why, I haue not another teare to shed.'[31] The moment roughly blocked out here is perfected later, when Othello leaves Desdemona after the harrowing brothel-scene:

Emilia	How doe you Madam, how doe you my good Lady?
Desdemona	Faith, halfe asleepe.
Emilia	Good Madam, what's the matter with my Lord?
Desdemona	With who?
Emilia	With my Lord Madam.
[*Desdemona*	Who is thy Lord?
Emilia	He that is yours, sweet Lady.]
Desdemona	I ha none. Doe not talke to me Emillia,
	I cannot weepe, nor answer haue I none,
	But what should goe by water . . .

(*Othello* IV.ii.Q:K4ᵛ, F:2802–3)

For all the clumsy contrivance of the exchange ('Who is thy Lord? . . . I ha none'), Desdemona's sheer exhaustion, her numbed indifference, are unsurpassed. 'Faith, halfe asleepe . . .'

Othello, typically, excels at such purely realistic pathos. Elsewhere the startling substitution of indifference for grief is less effective and more meaningful. Brutus does not weep at Cassius's death, unlike the more accomplished Antony bewailing Caesar's corpse. Nor is he seen to mourn Portia. 'No man beares sorrow better.' Malcolm and Donalbain's seeming indifference to Duncan's death contrasts with the ostentatious grief of the murderers and is yet another instance of 'faire is foule, and foule is faire.' Even the apparent stupidity of 'Your Royall Father's murther'd' – 'Oh, by whom?' is pointed. Its flatness contrasts directly with Macduff's parallel exchange with the histrionic Lady Macbeth just before: 'Our Royall Master's murther'd' – '*Woe, alas:* / What, in our House?' Its significance is stressed later. While Macbeth embroiders elegantly on silver skin with golden blood, and Lady Macbeth swoons, the brothers comment aside: 'Why doe we hold our tongues, / That most may clayme this argument for ours?' 'What should be spoken here? . . . Let's away, / Our Teares are not yet brew'd.' When they are left alone, Malcolm concludes, 'To shew an vnfelt Sorrow is an Office / Which the false man do's easie.' Such dramatisation of the perennial theme of seeming is, however, more interesting than moving.[32]

'Strange times that weepe with laughing, not with weeping'

Titus's laughter at his sons' execution raises the broadest and most fascinating aspect of Shakespeare's dramatisation of crying: his exploitation of the contradictory union of laughter and tears. A mixture of modes abhorrent to classical purity is experimented with from the earliest plays, and passes through a clear evolution from the stated to the enacted, and from the local episode to the extended effect. In its finest forms, this complicated fusion of feelings is not only staged but elicited from the audience also, and can come to be seen as characterising an entire play's mood. It is rare for Shakespeare's development to be seen so clearly, and with such a consistent movement towards perfection.

In the earliest plays, Shakespeare twice presents the sickening glee the debased find in others' misery. Queen Margaret taunts the captive York, crowned as in the mocking of Christ: 'I prythee grieue, to make me merry, Yorke.' This abhorrent clash of mutually exclusive emotions is intensified by stressing their unnatural unity. Just so Aaron confesses that he pried on Titus when his hand and his sons' heads were returned to him, and 'laught so hartelie / That both mine eyes were rayinie like to his', while Tamora, peeping beside him, nearly swooned, but for pleasure rather than pain.[33] This grotesque inversion of what should be, and indeed looks like sympathy to its monstrous and indistinguishable opposite is never to recur with such strength again. It is a violent felicity characteristic of the early plays.

In the comedies, Shakespeare turns to a lighter variant on the theme, still tentatively approaching it in the described, rather than staged scene. Boyet recalls the nervously happy Lords, rehearsing their Muscovite masque for the French ladies, falling over themselves at one of Moth's feebler jokes:

> With that they all did tumble on the ground,
> With such a zelous laughter so prof[o]und,
> That in this spleene rediculous appeares,
> To check their follie, pashions solembe teares.
> (*Love's Labour's Lost* V.ii.Q:G3)

This improbable vignette is then expanded and (for the first time) embodied, in the comic tragedy ('very tragicall mirth') of *Pyramus and Thisbe*. The telescoping of opposite emotions becomes a dramatic reality, as stage audience, and surely theatre auditorium also, share Philostrate's reaction, that Pyramus's tragedy 'made mine eyes water; / But more merry teares the passion of loud laughter / Neuer shed.'[34] This comic sequence culminates in its least strained and most effective manifestation during Hal and Falstaff's amateur theatricals, when Falstaff grandiosely exploits his giggling stage audience for a moment of high tragedy:

Falstaff   . . . stand aside Nobilitie.
Hostess   O Iesu, this is excellent sport ifaith.
Falstaff   Weepe not sweet Queene, for trickling teares are vain.
Hostess   O the father, how he holds his countenance?
Falstaff   For Gods sake Lords, conuay my tr[i]stfull Queene,
        For teares do stop the floudgates of her eyes.
              (*1 Henry IV* II.iv.Q:E2ᵛ)

It is the perfect, happy reversal of the theme's origin. Aaron and Tamora turned tears to laughter: now laughter is turned into tears.

Yet in its most rounded form, Shakespeare presents neither the grotesque clash of glee with grief, nor the comic mistaking of laughter for sorrow, but their simultaneous union in one man's feelings. This conflicting emotion can find a variety of disturbing forms. It is twice suggested as early as *Richard II*, where York describes Richard's ignominious return to London, dust thrown on him by the jeering crowd, 'Which with such gentle sorrow he shooke off, / His face still combating with teares and smiles, / The badges of his griefe and patience.' The moment clearly anticipates Cordelia's also reported smiles and tears, 'Sun shine and raine at once' when Lear is found. But in an earlier scene Richard's mixed feelings are staged in his greeting of England after the Irish expedition. He kneels. 'As a long parted mother with her childe / Playes fondly with her teares and smiles in meeting; / So weeping, smiling, greete I thee my earth.'[35] Not the image alone points forward to the mother-child reunions of the last romances, for both share the fine balance of pathos and joy.

Gradually the complex union of feeling becomes absorbed in the texture of the plays, rather than surfacing in the isolated incident. 'How much better is it to weepe at ioy, then to ioy at weeping?' Leonato recapitulates, and continues the theme, in *Much Ado*.[36] Here, however, comedy and tragedy still alternate in the bold interplay of the double plot, in a partial advance on *The Comedy of Errors*, the farce with the near-tragic frame, and *The Merchant of Venice*, with the contrasting tone of its parallel narratives. Shakespeare first succeeds outright in this difficult combination of moods with the melancholy undercurrents of *Twelfth Night*, while the grim humour of Malvolio's discomfiture is a clear premonition of the sterner version of this theme to emerge in the problem plays.

Here the callousness of the earliest plays recurs in a more credible form in the distorted natures of the central figures. Cressida mockingly prophesies how she will flourish in Troilus's tears, while Bertram sulks at what should be his gain, marriage to Helena, and rejoices at her supposed death. 'I am heartily sorrie that hee'l bee gladde of this', one Lord says at this point, to which the second Lord replies: 'How mightily sometimes, we make vs comforts of our losses'. 'And how mightily some other times, wee drowne our gaine in teares' is the response.[37] Comments like these suggest Shakespeare's abiding interest in the theme; the play itself illustrates them *in extenso*. As in *Measure for Measure*, the comedy is too near the bone to be honestly laughable; it is too unsettling a portrayal of human weakness. And yet Shakespeare deliberately turns the despicable and detestable to comedy, in a further attack on the inadequacies of human response – an attack which is clearly voiced in Isabella's famous denunciation:

> . . . But man, proud man . . .
> Plaies such phantastique tricks before high heauen,
> As makes the Angels weepe: who with our spleenes
> Would all themselues laugh mortall.
> (*Measure for Measure* II.ii.874ff)

Instead of merely describing, or even staging a transitory mixture of laughter and tears, Shakespeare elicits this response from his audience. We laugh uncomfortably at an anatomisation watched to our general shame, a comedy at which the angels weep.

But in *Coriolanus* Isabella's lines find a further permutation, when Volumnia kneels to her son, and he gives in to her:

> . . . O Mother, Mother!
> What haue you done? Behold, the Heauens do ope,
> The Gods looke downe, and this vnnaturall Scene
> They laugh at . . .
> (*Coriolanus* V.iii.3540ff)

Shakespeare once again intensifies audience reaction by drawing on the unexpected response: just as the comic follies of *Measure for Measure* are pitiable, so the unnatural perversities of Coriolanus's story, like his mother's kneeling to him here, are laughable to divine eyes. Indeed, in terms of audience response, *Coriolanus* is as much of a problem play as the rest.

Such uncomfortable comedy reaches a further mutation in *Lear*, where the Fool sings:

> . . . then they
> For sodaine ioy did weepe,
> And I for sorrow sung,
> That such a King should play bo-peepe,
> And goe the Foole[s] among.
> (*King Lear* I.iv.687ff, Q:D)

Feste's submerged melancholy in *Twelfth Night* finally surfaces in the songs, puns and riddles that are 'for sorrow sung' in *Lear*, and in his greatest tragedy Shakespeare presents his King as the fool. His audience, weeping angels at last, mourn the comedy.

The profound confusion of comedy and tragedy in *Lear* not only completes and transforms the development begun in the comedies, but looks forward to the last plays. Regardless of whether Bradley's optimistic reading of Lear's death is correct, Kent, Gloucester and Cordelia's experiences all foreshadow the intolerable joy of the last plays. So Gloucester's 'flaw'd heart . . . twixt two extremes of passion, ioy and greefe, / Burst smilingly'. Joy is often indistinguishable from pain, in the true Keatsian manner: 'Ay, in the very temple of delight / Veil'd Melancholy has her sovran shrine . . .' Kent provides the ruling aphorism: 'Nothing almost sees miracles / But miserie': it is only in the extremity of grief that joy's ultimate can be felt. This principle, applied by the Duke to Isabella as by Prospero to Ferdinand, governs the action of the last plays.[38] Indeed, it is almost overstressed. It is brusquely defined by Jupiter in *Cymbeline*: 'Whom best I loue, I crose; to make my guift / The more delay'd, delighted.' It recurs in a verbal form again and again. Miranda exclaims at Ferdinand's love, 'I am a foole / To weepe at what I am glad of.' It is a kind of running continuo to the last act of *The Winter's Tale*. Camillo and the King 'look'd as they had heard of a World ransom'd, or one destroyed.' 'Our King being ready to leape out of himselfe, for ioy of his found Daughter, as if that Ioy were now become a Losse, cryes, Oh, thy Mother, thy Mother . . .' 'But oh the Noble Combat that 'twixt Ioy and Sorrow was fought in Paulina. Shee had one Eye declin'd for the losse of her Husband, another eleuated, that the Oracle was fulfill'd.'[39] Such a chord, not key-note, is indeed only proper to these plays, which are the perfection of tragi-comedy, where tragedy is not skirted, but passed through, to attain to a more strenuous joy. It finds its gentlest, most playful form in the discovery of Ferdinand and Miranda, all political rivalries shrunk to a game of chess, all family hatred dwindled to tender teasing:

Miranda   Sweet Lord, you play me false.
Ferdinand   No my dearest loue,
               I would not for the world.
                    (*Tempest* V.i.2143–5)

It finds its most passionate expression in Pericles' cry as Marina is discovered:

> Oh Hellicanus, strike me honored sir,
> Giue mee a gash, put me to present paine,
> Least this great sea of ioyes rushing vpon me
> Ore-beare the shores of my mortalitie,
> And drowne me with their sweetnesse.
>   (*Pericles* V.i.Q:I)

CHAPTER 7

Silence and pause

Loue, therefore, and tongue-tide simplicity,
In least, speake most to my capacity.
(*A Midsummer Night's Dream* V.i.Q:G4)

'Nothing short of a procession or a fight should make anything so extraordinary as a silence during a Shakespearean performance,' Shaw once rashly dogmatised to Ellen Terry. Yet Shakespeare continually orchestrates his own silences. The *reader* must be on the look-out for minute signs pointing to them, from bystanders' remarks, metrical lacunae, and the speaker's own repetitions and stressed hesitations. Examples have incidentally occurred already, and many more can be found.[1]

For instance, Clarence's murderer, doubled up by a sudden cramp of conscience, begs his accomplice: 'I prythee stay a little: / I hope this passionate humor of mine will change, / It was wont to hold me but while one tels twenty.' There should, then, be a twenty-second pause, before the other's impatient demand, 'How do'st thou feele thy selfe now?' Arragon, unlocking the silver casket, must stand aghast at the 'pourtrait of a blinking idiot' long enough to justify Portia's line: 'Too long a pause for that which you finde there.'[2] What did Shakespeare care for Shaw's timorous orthodoxies? Or for those of Stoppard's crass drama critic, staring at an empty stage?

> (*They look at it. The room. The BODY. Silence.*)
> Birdboot Has it started yet?
> Moon Yes.
> (*Pause. They look at it.*)
> Birdboot Are you sure?
> Moon It's a pause.
> Birdboot You can't start with a *pause*!
> (*The Real Inspector Hound*)

The Temple Garden scene, Shakespeare's invented source for the Wars of the Roses, is emphatically marked by its opening with a pause, finally broken by York's 'Great Lords and Gentlemen, / What meanes this silence? / Dare no man answer in a Case of Truth?'[3]

Such experimentation is characteristic of the beginner Shakespeare; for all the obvious flaws of his earliest plays, they constantly excite admiration for their technical iconoclasm and daring. Take his gleeful dramatisation of the death of Salisbury, in *1 Henry VI*. It is another experiment in silence, and more. The episode is skilfully turned to solve the recurrent structural problem in this trilogy, of creating an orderly sequence out of a confused variety of historical events. In these early histories Shakespeare is particularly concerned with the continual transference of power from victor to victim, from French to English, from one dying generation to the next. This pattern is partly stressed by Shakespeare's juxtaposition of a dying hero with his spiritual heir, as in the invented scene where a moribund Mortimer expounds to York his claims to the throne.[4] The same trick is worked to better theatrical effect in the death of Salisbury, who hands on to Talbot his own role as terror of the French. Every detail of Salisbury's demise is historical, down to his facial mutilation, but in the play the episode is turned into a stage symbol. Talbot literally takes over Salisbury's part, speaking the lines that he can no longer pronounce, and interpreting his gestures for him, just as he will inherit his military role in the battles to come.

	Here they sho[o]t, and Salisbury falls downe . . .
Talbot	Speake Salisbury; at least, if thou canst, speake . . .
	One of thy Eyes, and thy Cheekes side struck off? . . .
	Salisbury cheare thy Spirit with this comfort,
	Thou shalt not die whiles ———
	He beckens with his hand, and smiles on me:
	As who should say, When I am dead and gone,
	Remember to auenge me on the French.
	Plantaginet I will . . .
	Here an Alarum, and it Thunders and Lightens.
	What stirre is this? what tumult's in the Heauens? . . .
	Enter a Messenger.
Messenger	My Lord, my Lord, the French haue gather'd head . . .
	Here Salisbury lifteth himselfe vp, and groanes.
Talbot	Heare, heare how dying Salisbury doth groane,
	It irkes his heart he cannot be reueng'd.
	Frenchmen, Ile be a Salisbury to you . . .

(*1 Henry VI* I.iv.539ff. SDs probably authorial)

Shakespeare has tricked out Salisbury's necessary, historical muteness with a barrage of effects – thunder, lightning, gestures, groans.
But at the centre of the scene is the wordless figure that was to haunt
him in so many plays to come.

Most striking of all these figures is the early heroine Lavinia, raped
and lopped, handless and tongueless. Her grotesque disabilities do
not seem to me to make the good theatre some critics claim, and yet
this was clearly Shakespeare's hope. Yet the horrors of her mutilation (taken direct from the source) become the pretext for conscious
theatrical experimentation in which Shakespeare discovers what can
be done with the actor who is deprived of his two most obvious
means of expression, speech, and gesture.

The potentialities of silence are first exploited in the scene referred
to in the last chapter, when Titus is brought his executed sons' heads,
in spite of the ransom he paid to save them by severing his hand.
Here the inadequacies of language are played off against silence, as
Marcus and Lucius break into extravagant laments. Titus says not a
word, till Lavinia tries to comfort him the only way she can, by
kissing him. *Then* his silence is broken by the weary understatement
that, even at this early stage, Shakespeare knew to be more moving
than any rhetoric.

Marcus	Now let hote Aetna coole in Cycilie,
	And be my hart an euerburning hell . . .
Lucius	Ah that this sight should make so deepe a wound
	And yet detested life not shrinke thereat:
	That euer death should let life beare his name,
	Where life hath no more interest but to breath.
Marcus	Alas poore hart, that kisse is comfortlesse,
	As frozen water to a starued snake.
Titus	When will this fearefull slumber haue an end?

(Titus III.i.Q:F2ᵛ–3)

Evidently Shakespeare only later realised the implications for
drama raised by Lavinia, and, to a lesser extent, by Titus himself.
Consequently it seems probable that he wrote in an entire scene in
order to explore them. This is the fly-scene (III.ii), which appears
only in the later, Folio text of the play, and not in the original Quarto
text. It follows directly on the scene just described, and elaborately
verbalises all the peculiarities of Lavinia's dumb role to the audience,
in poor drama but interesting theory.

Thus Titus begins by expatiating on the handless man's inability
to gesture: 'Marcus vnknit that sorrow-wreathen knot: / Thy Neece

and I (poore Creatures) want our hands / And cannot passionate our ten-fold griefe / With foulded Armes.' He puns on their handicap: 'What violent hands can she lay on her life . . . O handle not the theame, to talke of hands!'[5] He draws particular attention to her maimed sign language:

> . . . Harke Marcus what she saies:
> I can interpret all her martir'd signes . . .
> Thou shalt not sighe nor hold thy stumps to heauen,
> Nor winke, nor nod, nor kneele, nor make a signe,
> But I (of these) will wrest an Alphabet.
> (*Titus* III.ii.1494ff)

Such is the theory that lies behind all Shakespeare's use of gesture. But here, probably for the first time in his dramatic career, he draws attention to the emotive power of the silent figure – a power staged and perhaps discovered without comment in the preceding scene. And thus *The Rape of Lucrece* aptly summarises the impact of Lavinia's silent kiss, and all her later 'martir'd signes':

> To see sad sights moues more then heare them told:
> For then the eye interpretes to the eare
> The heauie motion that it doth behold,
> When euerie part a part of woe doth beare.
> Tis but a part of sorrow that we heare.
> (*Lucrece* ll.1324ff)

As Herbert said, 'What is so shrill as silent tears?' As early as *Titus* and *Lucrece*, Shakespeare had discovered the positive force of silence, which he was to exploit in all his plays.

'Why should calamity be full of words?'

Behind the emphatic and consistent positivism of Shakespeare's use of silence lies the familiar Senecan tag, *Curae leves loquuntur, ingentes stupent*. It was not only commonly quoted, often untranslated, in Elizabethan and Jacobean drama; it has remained a literary platitude from Jane Austen to Marianne Moore (see the Appendix at the end of this chapter). It was also staged, though often hesitantly and with little skill, by Shakespeare's contemporaries. In *The Spanish Tragedy* Hieronimo is faced by his mirror image when Don Bazulto stands before him, silent in a rabble of petitioners, proffering a paper demanding justice for the murder of his son. He cannot speak for grief. And in Gascoigne's *Supposes*, the humourless source for *The Taming of the Shrew*, when Erostrato is reunited with his father, he too is speechless while Pasiphilo nudgingly comments aside, 'Beholde the naturall loue of the childe to the father: for inwarde ioye he cannot pronounce one worde.' Great grief and joy may both be dumb.[6]

At first Shakespeare seems to have been undecided whether or not true emotion should be articulate, and both views are argued in the same imagery, in *Venus and Adonis*, *Titus*, and *Two Gentlemen*. But here Proteus finally decides the issue as Julia leaves him, overwrought and in silence: 'Iulia, farewell: what, gon without a word? / I, so true loue should doe: it cannot speake, / For truth hath better deeds, then words to grace it.'[7] The theoretic debate is ended. Thereafter the virtues of silence are so often canvassed, that by *Troilus and Cressida* it is a cliché to be relegated to the garrulous Pandarus, wheezing over the parted lovers:

Oh heart, as the goodly saying is, Oh heart, heauy heart, why sighst thou without breaking: where hee answers againe, because thou canst not ease thy smart by friendshippe nor by speaking: there was neuer a truer rime . . . We see it, we see it . . .

(*Troilus and Cressida* IV.iv.Q:H3)

We do indeed: it is dramatised in all Shakespeare's work.

As early as *Henry VI* Duke Humphrey and the King are outstanding for their vituous sincerity, and their silence. On one occasion Humphrey suffers five speeches of attack, leaves unostentatiously, without a word, and only returns when he can say, 'Now Lords, my Choller being ouer-blowne / With walking once about the Quadrangle . . .' He practises a restraint unknown to Coriolanus; at his wife's banishment, as Hall says, he 'toke all these thynges paciently, and saied litle', parting from her in silent tears. When his murder is discovered, the insincere outcry from the guilty Cardinal, Suffolk and Margaret contrasts with Henry's silent swoon.[8] The technical interest this scene held for Shakespeare is evident from his recasting of it in *Macbeth*, where Lady Macbeth's swoon (inherited from the blameless Henry) is as ambivalent as Macbeth's rhetoric at the crime. The producer must decide whether she faints from genuine feeling (of whatever kind), or as a tactic to divert attention from her husband's ill-judged elegy. Such complication and blurring of the cliché is typical of the great central plays, but at the end of his career Shakespeare sometimes seems worryingly content to crawl back to his archetypes. One of the many similarities between the first history plays and the last is the polar contrast between Duke Humphrey and Cardinal Beaufort in *Henry VI*, and Cranmer and Cardinal Wolsey in *Henry VIII*. Here Cranmer, interrogated by the King, refuses to speak in his own defence, in marked contrast to the loquacious Cardinal. Neither King nor audience have any difficulty in interpreting his silent tears: 'I sweare he is true-hearted . . . He ha's strangled his Language in his teares.' Minor instances could be indefinitely multiplied: Bolingbroke going to banishment in *Richard II*, chaffed for his miserable, silent parting from his friends; Pisanio, unable to say a word as he hands Imogen the letter that requires her death, and, like Don Bazulto, proffering the paper that can best speak for him; Posthumus ending his remorseful prayers in prison with the unsayable: 'Oh Imogen, / Ile speake to thee in silence.' Or Shakespeare, in his own poetry: 'O learne to read what silent loue hath writ.'[9] It is in love, and women, that Shakespeare's staged, rather than merely spoken estimation of silence comes into its own.

Women and silence

Unsteady voiced boy actors are the obvious potential practical cause for Shakespeare's frequent association of women and silence. *Twelfth Night* and *Othello* both show signs of playhouse alteration to lighten the female lead of a song: all Viola's unspoken love-longing was probably first expressed by her, rather than Feste, singing 'Come away, come away death' to Orsino. It has been suggested that Cordelia's part was so small for a similar reason. Hence Lear's affectionate memory, which turns playhouse apology into *idée reçue*: 'Her voice was euer soft, / Gentle, and low, an excellent thing in woman.' As the proverb had it, 'Silence is the best ornament of a woman'; women, like little children, should be seen and not heard.[10]

The theme is, naturally, most fully explored in Shakespeare's early work: *The Taming of the Shrew* is devoted to it. It is interesting to compare this play with Jonson's *Epicoene*, which came out in 1609, the approximate date of *Cymbeline*. Jonson's hero(ine) is the reverse of Shakespeare's: a mute metamorphosed by marriage into a shrew, rather than a shrew trained by marriage into dumb submission. Yet *Epicoene* is a most disappointing play in its extensive use of silence, especially after all the subtlety of Shakespeare's practice could have shown Jonson the way. Silence is dutifully passed, like port, around the cast, from Epicoene to Morose's mute to Morose himself, and action, so deftly used by Shakespeare, frequently takes the place of

words. But it is never more imaginative than a nod, or *Makes a leg*.
Theatrically at least, Jonson contrives to make almost nothing of its
potential. Now Shakespeare, like Morose, subscribes to the orthodoxy Gratiano mocks: 'silence is onely commendable / In a neates
to[n]gue dried, and a mayde not vendable.'[11] But he works out his
theme in terms of speech and silence, in a play sufficiently full of
humour and psychological vitality to obscure this arid thesis. Kate
passes through a series of changes, from rant to silence to controlled
speech, and her training in womanhood is charted in articulate
terms.

At her first appearance, as at the end of the play, she is pointedly
contrasted with her sister. One is the apparent ideal; the other, any
man's nightmare of a wife. The key quality is proclaimed by the
onlookers, Tranio saying of Kate: 'That wench is starke mad, or
wonderfull froward', Lucentio of Bianca: 'But in the others *silence* do
I see / Maids milde behauiour and sobrietie.' The same point is
reiterated in the next scene, when Kate's father reproaches her for
attacking Bianca: 'When did she crosse thee with a bitter word?', and
Kate retorts, 'Her *silence* flouts me, and Ile be reueng'd'.[12] Kate has, of
course, every reason for her miserable, attention-seeking resentment
at her father's favouritism, and at her sister's shrewd pretence of
mildness. As soon as Petruchio begins his bizarre courtship, she no
longer needs to yell for attention, and her training in womanly
muteness begins. It is camouflaged by the robustness and speed of
the dialogue, and yet its course can be accurately plotted. Her
protests at the betrothal and wedding are drowned by Petruchio,
leaving her nothing but a silent exit at his side (but 'silence is
consent', as Shakespeare would have known).[13] As Petruchio takes
her railing role on himself, she becomes progressively quieter and
more reasonable, to moderate his wildness. The climax comes,
however, when Petruchio can dominate her in speech as well as
silence. At his peremptory insistence she swallows absurdity to call
the sun the moon, the ancient Vincentio 'Yong budding Virgin,
faire, and fresh, and sweet'.[14] Yet the absurdity is not only comic but
symbolic: a wife has no words but her husband's, however silly they
may be. Now at last the victory is hailed:

Hortensio   Petruchio, goe thy waies, the field is won.
                        (*Taming of the Shrew* IV.v.2320)

After this somewhat ironic climax, the last scene merely demonstrates Kate's obedience to the rest of the cast. Of three wives (one

hastily invented merely for this scene), she alone obeys her husband's summons. To their vociferous indignation, she wordlessly treads on her cap at Petruchio's command: silent action symbolises her submission. It is fitting however that the play should end with Kate finding her tongue in a persuasive speech of loving obedience to mankind. Language has found its proper place, and the irony of Shakespeare's earlier climax is tempered by Kate's sober account of mutual married dependence and respect.

The theme is played out in *The Taming of the Shrew*. Later, Shakespeare's lesser women show such a traditional silent submissiveness. Hermione says nothing to encourage Polixenes to stay in Sicilia until Leontes prompts her ('Tongue-ty'd our Queene? speake you'); significantly, the tragedy is entirely of his own making. Faced by her indignant parents, Anne Page cannot defend her elopement in *Merry Wives*; her husband has to speak for her. But in *Troilus and Cressida* the roles are reversed. Here Troilus is tongue-tied, his first words to Cressida being 'You haue bereft me of all wordes Lady', while Cressida launches into a long confession of her love, whose coquettish volubility and continual self-contradiction warn us that her heart, like Richard III's, is figured in her tongue. Yet her fault does not lie in her taking what she calls 'mens priuiledge / Of speaking first'. Many of Shakespeare's virtuous heroines have such an attractive directness – Miranda, for instance, who corners the delighted Ferdinand with 'Hence bashfull cunning, / And prompt me plaine and holy innocence. / I am your wife, if you will marrie me . . .' Cressida's rottenness is on the contrary clear from her bashful cunning, playing on Troilus's enraptured silence to draw her 'confession' from her.[15]

Opposing Cressida is Virgilia, the type of silent womanhood, Coriolanus's 'gracious silence'. She first appears in silence and in tears; weeping and speechless she stands unnoticed, as Volumnia welcomes Coriolanus home to his triumph; at his banishment she is rebuked by husband and mother-in-law for her 'faint-puling', all speech choked in tears. And yet her part is not one of monotonous lachrymose inarticulacy. At her first appearance, she refuses to go out of the house while Coriolanus is campaigning, for all Volumnia and Valeria's frivolous insistence, and the quality of her refusal is emphasised by a humorous comparison with Penelope. At her last appearance before Coriolanus, encamped outside Rome, Shakespeare pointedly alters Plutarch to make her the first to speak to him, just as Miranda confronted Ferdinand.[16] For the first time, Coriolanus rather than his wife is at a loss for words, an actor who unaccountably has dried. The dialogue requires this pause before he speaks:

Virgilia	My Lord and Husband.
Coriolanus	These eyes are not the same I wore in Rome.
Virgilia	The sorrow that deliuers vs thus chang'd
	Makes you thinke so.
Coriolanus [—]	Like a dull Actor now, I haue forgot my part,
	And I am out, euen to a full Disgrace. Best of my Flesh,
	Forgiue my Tyranny . . . O a kisse
	Long as my Exile, sweet as my Reuenge!
	(*Coriolanus* V.iii.3386ff)

Throughout the rest of the play, Virgilia's gracious silence contrasts with Coriolanus's violent hyperboles, and the energetic boldness of his mother. It has a potential force only paralleled by Shakespeare's other great, silent woman – Cordelia.

'Loue, and be silent'

Cordelia's laconic words – the first she ever speaks – epitomise one of the most important commonplaces lying behind Shakespeare's use of silence. Not only great cares are silent, as Seneca affirms, but any strong feelings, and above all love. 'True love is mute, and oft amazed stands', wrote Marlowe in *Hero and Leander*. Shakespeare accepts the aphorism, but dramatises it with increasing skill. As early as *1 Henry VI*, the accomplished Suffolk is struck dumb by his attractive French captive. For some thirty lines he soliloquises aside, while Margaret's repeated questions are ignored. As soon as he turns to speak to her, his questions are answered by the same theoretic 'silence' as *she* soliloquises aside, till they merge with 'I cry you mercy, 'tis but Quid for Quo.' This verbal mating-dance is simply the theatrical elaboration of Suffolk's first remark: 'Faine would I woe her, yet I dare not speake.'[17] Later presentation is mercifully more natural. One of the hyperarticulate Shaw's favourite lines was Claudio's 'Silence is the perfectest Herault of ioy', his first, stumbling reaction to Leonato's offer of his daughter. Hero, too, can only whisper in his ear, while Beatrice laughs at the tongue-tied lovers. Later Benedick, tricked into love for Beatrice, also suffers a whole scene of teasing in silence, his sole response a pathetic complaint of tooth-ache. The Prince can no longer say of him, 'he hath a heart as sound as a bell, and his tongue is the clapper, for what his heart thinkes, his tongue speakes.' His maturation into love is evident from his new reluctance for empty verbal banter. Orlando is similarly afflicted in a better sustained comic scene in which Rosalind and Celia congratulate him on his wrestling victory. He cannot even reply to Rosalind's gift of a favour, but as soon as the women turn to leave him, he asks himself, 'Can I not say, I thanke you?' As they turn back to him once more his courage deserts him again, leaving Rosalind looking silly as he still makes no response to her overtures.[18] Note, incidentally, the pause demanded by her two adjacent 'Sirs', while she waits in vain for an answer. Shakespeare is unostentatiously directing through the dialogue again:

Rosalind	He cals vs back: my pride fell with my fortunes,
	Ile aske him what he would: Did you call Sir?
[——]	Sir, you haue wrastled well, and ouerthrowne
	More then your enemies.
Celia	Will you goe Coze?
Rosalind	Haue with you: fare you well.

(*As You Like It* I.ii.418ff)

By the next scene, Rosalind is in the same state herself. Judging by its first lines, it should open, like the Temple Garden scene, with a pause, followed by:

Celia	Why Cosen, why Rosaline: Cupid haue mercie:
	Not a word?
Rosalind	Not one to throw at a dog.

(*As You Like It* I.iii.460–2)

Even in *All's Well*, Helena cannot answer the Countess's demands, whether she is in love or not, though her silent tears are sufficient affirmative for the experienced Countess. This unhappy modification of the platitude is typical of the problem plays, and is paralleled by a more difficult variant at the end of *Measure for Measure*.

Isabella's silence at the Duke's two proposals of marriage is opaque.[19] It would be easier to accept it as a wordless affirmation of love if it were commented on by the other characters, as is Shakespeare's practice elsewhere. As it stands, it allows the producer enviable liberties. In Jonathan Miller's production at Greenwich in 1975, it was used to clinch a cynical interpretation of the play, as the Duke waved the rest of the cast off-stage before making his proposition. Isabella's expression of settled loathing, her scuttling exit, made the parallel between this and Angelo's nauseous advances quite clear. But in fact Shakespeare has merely sidestepped an impasse. The Duke's proposal is required by the multiple marriages of the comic form, while Isabella's acceptance would be improper for a novice, and impossible for one of her fierce virginity, unless her earlier sincerity were undermined. At the same time, the Duke's offer is open and honourable in precisely the way Angelo's was not. Isabella's silence is in one sense a technical flaw, although it permits flexibility of interpretation.

In this last act similar, though lesser difficulties obtain in the wordless reunion of Claudio and Juliet – joyful, no doubt, but unnoted by the text. In the last plays this silence of reunion replaces the silent love at first sight of the comedies as a poignant and recurrent theme, and is always dwelt on by the dialogue. A clear progression is evident here. *Cymbeline*, probably the first in date, is the least adventurous, as dialogue directs action, and the joy of the silently embracing couple is lightly suggested by the bystanders' commentary. 'See, / Posthumus Anchors vpon Imogen; / And she (like harmlesse Lightning) throwes her eye / On him.'[20] In *Pericles*, Shakespeare is more daring, and the embrace is disarmingly interrupted by Marina, who interposes with childish insensitivity, just as her parents' kiss:

Pericles	O come, be buried a second time within these armes.
Marina	My heart leaps to be gone into my mothers bosome.
Pericles	Looke who kneeles here, flesh of thy flesh Thaisa . . .

(Pericles V.iii.Q:13)

Practice makes perfect, however. Marina's tactlessness is surprisingly hard to stage without being funny, and it is eliminated in the *Winter's Tale*. In this replica of the reunion-scene, Paulina politely leads up Perdita, and embarrassment is avoided. The silent embrace persists, however. The failure of speech is moving in each case. To see glad sights moves more than hear them told . . .

Leontes	Oh, she's warme:
	If this be Magick, let it be an Art
	Lawfull as Eating.
Polixenes	She embraces him.
Camillo	She hangs about his necke.
	If she pertaine to life, let her speake too.
Paulina	. . . it appeares she liues,
	Though yet she speake not. Marke a little while:
	Please you to interpose (faire Madam), kneele,

> And pray your Mothers blessing: turne good Lady
> Our Perdita is found.
>   (*Winter's Tale* V.iii.3318ff)

Against such a setting, Lear's crass reception of Cordelia's love-laden silence is all the more culpable. He values just those 'out-sides' Shakespeare has consistently repudiated, from the trashy show of royal power without authority, to the empty and verbose ostentation of love. France, on the other hand, chooses Cordelia for the very paradoxes epitomised in her loving silence: for him, she is 'most rich being poore, / Most choise forsaken, and most lou'd despis'd.' It is typical of Lear that at this point he is oblivious of his own use of paradox, since he understands only the outside, the obvious sense. He sneeringly calls Cordelia 'that little seeming substance' – she does not look much. Inadvertently though, he has expressed a greater truth: there is no pretence in her, and for this very reason she may seem nothing, but is of inestimable value. Similarly, when she answers his demand for love with 'Nothing', meaning all her love which is beyond expression, he replies, 'Nothing will come of nothing', whereas in reality everything – the subsequent tragedy – comes of this apparent nothing. There is no such thing as nothing, and what seems like nothing, silence, means most of all. In *Lear* this recurrent theme is presented as the initial, unapprehended truth on which the entire tragedy is founded.[21]

In terms of meaning, this is the *locus classicus* of silence. And yet it would be impossible for Cordelia to carry all the symbolic weight of Shakespeare's theme. Not only practical causes limit the use of silence. Its effect depends on rarity and surprise. Jonson's *Epicoene* inadvertently demonstrates the absurdity and tedium of a character persisting in speechlessness from scene to scene, and Shakespeare appears to have learnt his own lesson long before, in the questionable felicities of Lavinia's extended silence. Consequently, perhaps, Cordelia is packed off to France, and the implications of her loaded silence are further deployed in its more versatile theatrical correlative: the language of lunacy. As John Clare wrote, in his madness:[22]

> Language has not the power to speak what love indites:
> The Soul lies buried in the ink that writes.

But madness, gibberish, fooling, songs, rhymes and riddles are all spoken alternatives to silence, in that they too can convey the truths beyond the scope of normal speech. Like a composer passing his theme from instrument to instrument, Shakespeare employs all these for his truth-telling in Kent, Edgar, and the Fool. All counterbalance the deceit staged in the rich dress and pretentious language of the play's seemers, while at its heart lies the simplicity of Lear's speeches on his awakening. But Cordelia is the quiet absolute: greater than Virgilia, her very silence is the still centre of this turning world.

'Speech in their dumbnesse, Language in their very gesture'

So Shakespeare endows silence with absolute value. Silence tells no lies; love speaks in silence; in silence grief finds its profoundest expression. Yet, for all its metaphysical content, in practical theatrical terms it is a veritable 'O without a figure', a nothing, till a digit is added to it – either some gesture that takes the place of words, or the pointing finger of the dialogue to pick it out. Shakespeare draws his audience's attention to the silences that are meaningful, either by the comments of the onlookers (Beatrice to Claudio: 'Speake Counte, tis your Qu'), or by the bewilderment of the speechless himself (Orlando: 'What passion hangs these waights vpon my toong?'). Above all, action takes the place of words, and gesture becomes the language of silence. As Tolstoy grudgingly allowed:[23]

Shakespeare, himself an actor and a clever man, knew not only by speeches, but by exclamations, gestures, and the repetition of words, how to express the state of mind and changes of feeling occurring in the persons represented. So that in many places Shakespeare's characters instead of speaking, merely exclaim, or weep, or in the midst of a monologue indicate the pain of their position by a gesture . . .

Such gestures have been incidentally illustrated often enough already: Salisbury's beckoning and smiling, Kate's trampling her cap, Lavinia's wordless kiss. In conclusion, I would like to consider what lies behind Shakespeare's unique direction specifically to call for silence as well as gesture: Coriolanus's capitulation to his mother outside the walls of Rome, as he *Holds her by the hand silent*.

Typically, the gesture is historic, but the silence is Shakespeare's.[24] It is remarkable in that it is the climax of a long struggle – a climax all the more overpowering in its silence, which contrasts so sharply with the colossal uproar (insisted on by the plentiful authorial stage directions) of Coriolanus's preceding encounters, from his victory over Corioli and his tempestuous welcome to Rome, to the turbulence of his exile. Furthermore, this silent peak triply contradicts everything that we have come to expect of Coriolanus. He of all men is irrepressibly outspoken: as Menenius said, 'His Heart's his Mouth: / What his Brest forges, that his Tongue must vent.' He, too, is most incapable of the silent gesture that can mean so much more than speech, and, in spite of his mother's persuasions, never stands before the plebeians, cap in hand, knee kissing the stones, 'humble as the ripest Mulberry, / That will not hold the handling.' Above all, Coriolanus severs all the bonds linking him not only with his society, but with his own loved family and proper nature, gathering himself up to stand, like many another Shakespearean villain, 'As if a Man were Author of himself, and knew no other kin.' Such a resolve is culpable enough, according to the Shakespearean and Elizabethan moral code, but its enormity is all the greater in a play whose controlling image is Menenius's fable of the body of the common-wealth, with its 'Incorporate Friends', the many members of society.[25] But in this supreme moment all three characteristics are overturned, as Coriolanus recognises his kinship to family and thus to state in the wordless humility of silent gesture. The greatest victory, and defeat, of the play, is achieved without a sound.

Pliny described a painting by Timanthes, showing the sacrifice of Iphigeneia. She stands by the altar, Odysseus, Calchas and Menelaus around her, each in deeper distress. But Agamemnon's grief was beyond the artist, and Timanthes veiled his face from sight.[26] Shakespeare, like Timanthes, portrays the profoundest feelings by the negation of his own medium, by silence. But, like Timanthes, he too hides his actors' faces. Coriolanus, overwhelmed by the eloquence of his mother's pleas, turns away from her, so that neither she not the audience can tell what effect her words are having. And when Macduff is told of his family's slaughter, he covers his eyes without a word:

Ross   Your Castle is surpriz'd: your Wife, and Babes
          Sauagely slaughter'd: To relate the manner
          Were on the Quarry of these murther'd Deere
          To adde the death of you.
Malcolm   Mercifull Heauen:
          What man, ne're pull your hat vpon your browes:
          Giue sorrow words; the griefe that do's not speake,
          Whispers the o're-fraught heart, and bids it breake.
Macduff   My Children too?
                         (*Macbeth* IV.iii.2050ff)

    Ill suits conceit with passion, woe with wit.
    Here passion prompts each short, expressive speech;
    Or silence paints what words can never reach.

Appendix

Curae leves loquuntur, ingentes stupent is quoted direct in *The Book of Sir Thomas More* (S), l. 1600; it is misquoted in Tourneur's *Revenger's Tragedy* I.iv.23 ('We have grief too, that yet walks without tongue, / *Curae leves loquuntur, maiores stupent*'); and quoted in a French accent in *2 Return from Parnassus* for comic effect, which is some indication of its familiarity, at least to a university audience ('O, *Courae leues loquuntur, ingantes stoupent*, it is an Aphorisme in Galen'. The speaker thinks it means taking a suppository). Tilley quotes variations from Kyd, Dekker, Webster, Fletcher, and many others. In addition, I have come across these among other variants on the idea that grief, love, joy, or any deep feeling is dumb. Donne: 'Language thou art too narrow, and too weake / To ease us now; great sorrow cannot speake; / If we could sigh out accents, and weepe words, / Griefe weares, and lessens, that tears breath affords. / Sad hearts, the lesse they seeme the more they are' ('Elegie : Death', ll.1–5). Sidney: 'Dumbe Swannes, not chatring Pies, do Lovers prove, / They love indeed, who quake to say they love', and 'Wise silence is best musicke unto blisse' (*Astrophel and Stella* 54 and 70). Ford: 'They are the silent griefs which cut the heart-strings' (*The Broken Heart* V.iii.75). Samuel Daniel: 'Who can shewe all his loue, doth loue but lightly' (*Delia* 1), and 'Sorrow makes silence her best oratore' (*The Civil Wars* II.97 – part of an extended and effective presentation of the theme). Jane Austen: 'her happiness was of a quiet, deep, heart-swelling sort; and though never a great talker, she was always more inclined to silence when feeling most strongly' (*Mansfield Park* III.vi.), and Lizzie: 'You might have talked to me more when you came to dinner'; Darcy: 'A man who had felt less, might' (*Pride and Prejudice* III.xviii). Tennyson: 'I sometimes hold it half a sin / To put in words the grief I feel; / For words, like Nature, half reveal, / And half conceal the Soul within' (*In Memoriam* V.1–4). Conrad: 'His heart dilated within him so, when he saw the Goulds on the deck of the *Hermes*, that his greetings were reduced to a casual mutter' (*Nostromo* III. XI). Rossetti: ''Tis visible silence, still as the hour-glass . . . Oh! clasp we to our hearts, for deathless dower / This close-companioned inarticulate hour / When twofold silence was the song of love' ('Silent Noon'). Emily Dickinson: 'Confirming All who analyze / In the Opinion fair / That Eloquence is when the Heart / Has not a Voice to spare' (*Complete Poems* (1970), n. 1268). Marianne Moore: 'The deepest feeling always shows itself in silence; / not in silence, but restraint' ('Silence'). Ezra Pound: 'Objectivity and again objectivity, and expression: no hindside-before-ness, no straddled adjectives (as 'addled mosses dank'), no Tennysonianness of speech; nothing – nothing that you couldn't, in some circumstance, in the stress of some emotion, actually say. Every literaryism, every book word, fritters away some scrap of the reader's patience, a scrap of his sense of your sincerity'. When one really feels and thinks, one stammers with simple speech' (Letter to Harriet Monroe, January, 1915). Other undramatised variants in Shakespeare include: 'What my tong dares not, that my heart shal say' (*Richard II* V.v.Q:K); 'Be checkt for silence, / But neuer tax'd for speech' (*All's Well* I.i.69–70); 'giue thy thoughts no tongue' (Polonius giving advice! – *Hamlet* I.iii.Q2:C4); 'trueth should be silent' (Enobarbus telling truths and hence silenced in *Antony and Cleopatra* II.ii.803); 'The silence often of pure innocence / Perswades, when speaking failes' (*Winter's Tale* II.ii.867–8). The persistence of the theme through the centuries testifies to its inherent verisimilitude, rather than the literary erudition of its authors.

CHAPTER 8

Costume

'The great Lord Burleigh, when he put off his gown at night, used to say, "Lie there, Lord Treasurer".'[1]

– Signior Lucio, did not you say you knew that Frier Lodowick to be a dishonest person?
– *Cucullus non facit Monachum*, honest in nothing but in his Clothes.
(*Measure for Measure* V.i.2638ff)

The recurrent theme of seeming, which underlies much of Shakespeare's theatrical employment of silence, is equally prevalent in his use of costume. For in costume both opposing quantities can be visually epitomised – the appearance, and the reality; the essence as well as the outward form. Clothes can stand for part of the man, just as Burleigh in his gown became Lord Treasurer. But they may equally well belie the true man: proverbially, a rogue can hide under the monk's cowl. Yet, finally, instead of deceiving, Shakespearean disguise can often point to the truth: so, in *Measure for Measure*, Shakespeare's good and holy Duke is justly disguised in the habit of a Friar. Dress, then, can stand as an emblem of rank or character; it can disguise and deceive; disguise can itself lead to a hidden truth.

Introductory

Costume is by nature symbolic. Particularly in the days of manual trades, a man's dress inevitably betrayed his occupation. 'Where is thy Leather Apron, and thy Rule?' could be asked of Roman and Elizabethan carpenter with equal justification. Custom merely elaborates such natural symbolism. Effie Deans, on trial for her illegitimate child's murder in the mid-eighteenth century, had to appear before the court with her hair pathetically unbound and uncovered, since the snood implied virginity, a covered head the married state, and neither was her due. Even in the Second World War, the *Derby Evening Telegraph* carried the following report on its fashion page:

The coiffure seen in the accompanying picture was designed to represent the 'warring nations'. The bold upward sweep on the side of the head typified Britain's sturdy resistance and recovery; on the opposite side a long falling roll illustrated German decline. The United States was symbolized in the design, and curls represented the smaller Allied nations.

Hardly less intricate was the symbolism prevalent in Shakespeare's time, and his audiences were more alive than we to the emblematic significance of dress. It is ubiquitous in their literature. So in Lodge's *Rosalynde* Montanus, the disappointed shepherd, comes to the wedding dressed in tawny, 'to signifie that he was forsaken', a willow garland on his head (compare, for instance, Desdemona's willow song). 'His bottle hanged by his side wheron was painted despaire, and on his sheephooke hung two sonnets as labels of his loves and fortunes.' Fifteen years earlier, Elizabeth had been entertained by a burlesque marriage at Kenilworth, arranged by the local parishioners, in which the groom appeared with 'a fayr strawn hat . . . on hiz hed: a payr of harvest glovez on hiz hands, az a sign of good husbandry: a pen and inkorn at his bak. For he woold be knowen to be bookish.' Montanus' dress is a literary sophistication of such natural symbolism, and the parishioners' simple emblems are merely elaborated, but not changed in essence, in the intricate impreses of the triumphs and entertainments of the court. The drama uses these drearily enough, for instance in Marlowe's *Edward II*, or the lists in *Pericles*, but they are delightfully satirised in Nashe's description of Surrey's Florentine lists, and particularly in the appearance of his hero's own patron. Rather like Tweedledum or Tweedledee, he rode out with a 'well counterfeit water-pot on his head', its 'small thrids of water, like citterne strings', the tears of his brain, appearing to water the roses and briars of his mistress's beauty and disdain, depicted on his armour. More modified symbolic clothes-horses appeared in the drama also. Holinshed reports that Hal visited his father 'apparelled in a gowne of blew satten, full of small oilet holes, at everie hole the needle hanging by a silke thred', and in the popular dramatisation of the chronicle, *The Famous Victories*, this weird costume is reproduced and duly interpreted:

Tom   I pray you my Lord, what may be the meaning thereof?
Henry 5 Why man, tis a signe that I stand upon thorns, til the Crowne be
        on my head.
                    (Bullough IV.313)

Significantly, the moment does not recur in Shakespeare's version, just as Montanus' dress is forgotten in *As You Like It*, and the knights' impreses in *Pericles* are of questionable authority. Shakespeare tends to avoid the elaborate costumes of his sources, and ridicules the whole technique in the absurdities of the mechanicals' play in *A Midsummer Night's Dream*, where Starveling, in order to represent the moon, must enter loaded down with the thornbush, dog and lantern traditionally associated with the man in the moon.[2]

Shakespeare shows a clear preference for symbolic simplicity in his use of costume, as well as properties (to be illustrated in chapter 9). One cannot, of course, deny the notorious richness of Elizabethan stage costume, which is abundantly evident from Henslowe's accounts (he paid as much for taffeta and tinsel for the bodice of a woman's gown, as he lent to Jonson for the composition of a play!), and which is predictable from the fact that the actors were notorious for their use of their masters' cast-off wardrobes. Such sartorial ostentation is particularly prominent in the wearisome catalogues of dress dominating the stage directions to *Henry VIII*, a play which was indeed untypical of Shakespeare in its lavish realism, and was criticised for it.[3] Yet Shakespeare appears to share Joyce's pleasure in the jargon of the votaries of Dame Fashion; 'you would thinke a Smocke were a shee-Angell, he so chauntes to the sleeue-hand, and the worke about the square on't'. Through his characters he can both mock ('Whats this? a sleeue? 'tis like a demi cannon, / What, vp and downe caru'd like an apple Tart?'), and praise, with breathless enthusiasm – 'cloth a gold and cuts, and lac'd with siluer, set with pearles, downe sleeues, side sleeues, and skirts, round vnderborne with a blewish tinsell . . .' Such eulogies must indicate a stage reality. Beatrice has to have material grounds for her rejection of the Duke's flippant proposal of marriage, when she says 'No my lord, vnles I might haue another for working-daies, your grace is too costly to weare euery day.' Marina's rich dress is one of the assets rudely appreciated by the brothel-keepers in Mytilene, but Stratford's deaf producer some years ago still romantically dressed her in rags.[4]

Nevertheless, while costumes may be rich, their symbolism is simple. The traditional symbolic figures, Rumour *painted full of Tongues*, or Time with his wings and glass in *The Winter's Tale*, are rare exceptions, the limp off-shoots of Tudor tradition. As often as not, Shakespeare's tongue is in his cheek when he calls them on the stage, and the armed Prologue to *Troilus and Cressida* is as satirical as Starveling's Moon.[5] Above all, Shakespeare uses *ordinary* dress for

dramatic ends. So Coriolanus's changing fortunes are simply mirrored by his changes of costume, from his blood-stained emergence
from battle, *his Arme in a Scarfe*, to his triumphal return home
crown'd with an Oaken Garland, his candidateship *in a gowne of
Humility*, and his exile *in meane Apparrell, Disguisd, and muffled* (all
these stage directions are most probably authorial). Antony's conspicuous nakedness, stripped *for the Course* at the beginning of *Julius
Caesar*, should be very striking in performance; it obviously isolates
him from the rest of Caesar's train, and visually supports the scene's
suggestions elsewhere of his 'Gamesom' and 'quicke Spirit'. *All's
Well*, a black comedy if ever there was one, flamboyantly proclaims
its nature in its gloomy opening scene where, in the authorial stage
direction, Shakespeare instructs the characters to enter *all in blacke*. It
is an uneasy suggestion of the traditional black-draped stage and
funereally dressed cast of tragedy, and sets a melancholy note that will
persist. In *Richard II* a succession of messengers reporting Bolingbroke's martial landing on English shores, and the rush of supporters
to his side, culminates in York's entry 'With signes of war about his
aged necke', which brings the grim imminence of war straight on the
stage.[6]

Realism underlies and strengthens Shakespeare's practice here, as
in all other apsects of his theatrical technique. Desdemona interrupts
her song to have her dress unpinned; Fluellen, shrewdly kind,
presses his money on Williams – 'I can tell you it will serue you to
mend your shooes: come, wherefore should you be so pashfull, your
shooes is not so good . . .' In the nervous tension before his last battle
Macbeth has his armour put on him, and then irritably takes it off
again ('Pull't off I say'); Lear in his madness pulls off his boots. It is
easy to identify the change of dress conventionally marking spiritual
change, a stage symbol inherited from Tudor drama.[7] But such
change of dress would cease to be effective if it were not more than
merely symbolic. When Lear wakes from his healing sleep, he is,
sure enough, in fresh robes. But these have a different significance
for him, simply as one of the many unfamiliar things confronting
him. His bewilderment, and its real cause, are what give the moment
its strength:

> Me thinkes I should know you, and know this man,
> Yet I am doubtful: For I am mainely ignorant
> What place this is: and all the skill I haue
> Remembers not these garments: nor I know not
> Where I did lodge last night . . .
>   (*King Lear* IV.vii.2819ff)

In Shakespeare's hands the natural and the real is imbued with meaning. But in itself it is simple, and the symbolism of costume depends on nothing more than a changed gown, or a nightshirt.

The symbolism of costume

Thus it is often the plainest apparel that proclaims the man. Polonius's aphorism neatly describes the familiar stage technique. At his first appearance, Zenocrate calls Tamburlaine a shepherd, going by his dress ('If as thou seem'st, thou art so meane a man'), but at his proud reply changes to 'my Lord' ('for so you do import'). Tamburlaine proceeds ceremonially to discard his mean attire, and dress as a soldier, this staged change of costume marking the emergence of the martial hero. Marlowe stages several such well-marked, emblematic changes of dress, in this and his other plays.[8] Inevitably, Shakespeare uses the technique more subtly, playing on, and disappointing, conventional audience expectation in a way we have come to recognise in his maturer work. For instance, when Ophelia describes Hamlet's appearance in her closet, 'his doublet all vnbrac'd, / No hat vpon his head, his stockins fouled, / Vngartred, and downe gyued to his ancle, / Pale as his shirt', Polonius jumps to the natural conclusion – 'Mad for thy loue?' For, as many editors have pointed out, Ophelia has described the conventional dress of the distracted lover, just as Shakespeare satirically sketched it in his comedies. But Polonius's attitude to Hamlet's disarray is as superficial as the Queen's to his mourning at the beginning of the play. For the audience, however, who have just witnessed Hamlet's meeting with the ghost in the preceding scene, it is clear that 'his affections doe not that way tend', and that Ophelia, rather than her silly father, has involuntarily hit on the real reason for Hamlet's wild attire. She describes him 'As if he had been loosed out of hell / To speake of horrors.' This is exactly what the ghost had done, and Hamlet's apparently traditional dress has a graver cause than despised love – his knowledge of the horrible tale his father was released from hell to tell him.[9]

Similarly, Hamlet's 'customary suites of solembe blacke' in which he makes his first appearance are not merely the obstinate garb of mourning, that so clearly distinguishes him from the rest of Claudius's court. As he warned his mother, his true grief lies within. The *dramatic* significance of his black dress emerges as he tries to prompt the player:

Hamlet . . . let me see, let me see, the rugged Pirhus like Th'ircanian beast,
tis not so, it beginnes with Pirrhus, the rugged Pirrhus, he whose
sable Armes,
Black as his purpose did the night resemble . . .
(*Hamlet* II.ii. Q2:F3–F3ᵛ)

Hamlet, like Pyrrhus, is dressed in the black costume of the avenger.
It is not the only link between them. When the player takes over, his
description of Pyrrhus's hesitation in killing the prostrate Priam,
properly acted, should present a sharp visual premonition of Hamlet, sword in raised hand, about to strike, hesitating over the praying
Claudius. That Shakespeare intended an emphatic pause here, incidentally, is strongly suggested by his crucially placed incomplete
line:

Player . . . for loe his sword
Which was declining on the milkie head
Of reuerent Priam, seem'd i'th ayre to stick,
So as a painted tirant Pirrhus stood
Like a newtrall to his will and matter,
Did nothing:
(*Hamlet* II.ii. Q2:F3ᵛ. My italics)

Just as Lucrece's picture of the siege of Troy introduced a traditional
parallel between her fate as a raped woman and that of the besieged
town, so this player's speech introduces a specifically *theatrical*,
stylistically dated and quaint image of Hamlet's role. In each case
Shakespeare turns to the greater iconographic clarity of a more
formal, pictorial mode in order to provide his emblem, the explanatory stage image.[10]

Similarly deceptively simple, but significant, is the fact mentioned
earlier – that, in his scene with the Doctor, Macbeth calls for his
armour, is armed while the conversation progresses, but unexpectedly has it removed again at the scene's end. This sequence is
evident from his inconspicuous asides as he consults the Doctor:
'Giue me my Armor . . . Ile put it on . . . Come, put mine Armour
on: giue me my Staffe . . . Come sir, dispatch . . . *Pull't off I say* . . .
Bring it after me.' It is most clearly suggested at the very beginning of
the scene, in the ominously named Seyton's omniscience at this, his
first appearance:

Macbeth Ile fight, till from my bones, my flesh be hackt.
Giue me my Armor.
Seyton 'Tis not needed yet.
(*Macbeth* V.iii. 2251ff)

Just as, in the last scenes of his tragedy, Antony repeatedly calls on Eros, the god of love as well as his soldier, so in these last scenes Macbeth calls again and again for *Seyton*. And why should this *satanic* figure know that Macbeth needs no armour as yet? Because, as Macbeth himself realises, while his witches' prophecies hold, he needs no further protection. So this bizarre arming scene begins with 'Till Byrnane wood remoue to Dunsinane, / I cannot taint with Feare', and ends, significantly, thus:

Macbeth   Bring it after me:
            I will not be affraid of Death and Bane,
            Till Birnane Forrest come to Dunsinane.
                        (*Macbeth* V.iii.2282ff)

To make the point theatrically obvious, as the dialogue demands, not only Macbeth but perhaps even his entire army should enter in their next scene conspicuously *un*armed, although the enemy are already all around them. For it is only with the messenger's terrified report of 'a mouing Groue', that Macbeth finally cries:

            . . . Feare not, till Byrnane Wood
            Do come to Dunsinane, and now a Wood
            Comes toward Dunsinane. *Arme, Arme, and out* . . .
                        (*Macbeth* V.v.2368ff. My italics)[11]

Curiously, even Macbeth's distinct directions to his armourer (let alone the potential follow-up of the later scene) are ignored in production, like so many other Shakespearean stage directions. The fault is that we tend to read them metaphorically, rather than as straightforward indications of stage action. This is partly due to Shakespeare's increasingly allusive direction of action in the later plays, as well as to his increasingly indirect suggestion of the visual symbol the stage action implies. Metaphor, in fact, becomes more evenly shared between action and dialogue, but our tendency is generally to concentrate more on its literary manifestations, and not to imagine, or put into practice, its physical embodiment.

The Shakespearean development is neatly illustrated, for example, by the following sequence. In an unusually powerful scene in *King John*, Constance leaves a scene of lamentation for Arthur's imprisonment with her hair torn loose, in the theatrically traditional disarray of lunacy ('I will not keepe this forme vpon my head, / When there is such disorder in my witte')[12] But in the body of the scene she had turned her hair into an elaborate image of her son's state, binding it up as her son is bound prisoner, tearing it free as she would have him liberated. Stage action is turned into an image, but this image depends on Constance's explicit commentary for its existence:

France	Binde vp your haires.
Constance	Yes that I will: and wherefore will I do it?
	I tore them from their bonds, and cride aloud,
	O, that these hands could so redeeme my sonne,
	As they haue giuen these hayres their libertie:
	But now I enuie at their libertie,
	And will againe commit them to their bonds,
	Because my poore childe is a prisoner.
	(*King John* III.iv.1453ff)

Later, a similar series of actions needs no explanatory commentary: Northumberland enters *2 Henry IV* 'crafty sicke', the conventional invalid's coif on head and crutch in hand. At the news of his son Hotspur's death, he graphically discards these signs of sickness to arm himself for revenge, and even if the audience were not listening to his rather bad, bombastic speech, they could not fail to see, and understand, his enacted change of mind.[13] In *Julius Caesar* Shakespeare draws on this scene in his usual, economical manner, in order to translate an incident from Plutarch into theatrical terms, but goes on to turn the stage action into a visual image of larger import. Here the treatment is altogether more implicit. Plutarch tells how Brutus visited Caius Ligarius, an ailing sympathiser,

and sayed unto him: O Ligarius, in what a time art thou sicke! Ligarius risinge uppe in his bedde . . . sayed unto him . . . if thou hast any great enterprise in hande worthie of thy selfe, I am whole.

(Bullough V.96)

Shakespeare makes *Ligarius* visit *Brutus*, sick and muffled up in a kerchief, preserves Plutarch's exchange almost exactly, and translates Ligarius's sudden recovery into visual terms by making him, like Northumberland, graphically rip off his kerchief with the words, 'I heere discard my sicknesse.'[14] This admitted metaphor simultaneously demands stage action (if we are to do any justice to the dialogue), and, furthermore, introduces a more philosophical image to be continued in the rest of their exchange:

Ligarius	. . . What's to do?
Brutus	A peece of worke,
	That will make sicke men whole.

Ligarius   But are not some whole that we must make sicke?
Brutus   That must we also.
                    (*Julius Caesar* II.i.971ff)

Thus the internal stage direction is implicit, and could be overlooked by a careless producer. But the continuing verbal metaphor turns the necessary stage action into a further visual image of the cure to be worked by Caesar's assassination. Typically, the source has not only been translated into visual, theatrical terms, but has been turned into a stage symbol with implications undreamt of in Plutarch's straight-forward account.

A similar example of the symbolism of costume being deployed further by verbal imagery presents itself in *Macbeth*. Here again critical response came first to the linguistic image, and only later to its visual source. For, as David Jones has suggested, the pervasive imagery of the Last Judgement at Duncan's murder is supported by the flocking of the household onto the stage in their nightshirts. 'They present a visual resemblance to the spirits rising from their graves on the Last Day, and the theatrical image complements the verbal image.'[15] The arming and disarming scenes in *Antony and Cleopatra* are an interesting extended example of such closely co-ordinated verbal and visual imagery.

In *Antony and Cleopatra* Shakespeare briskly revitalises a drooping literary platitude – the conventional use of war imagery for love[16] – by making it fact. This lover *is* a warrior, whose tragedy springs from the conflict between his two roles. When Antony tells Cleopatra, 'I go from hence / Thy Souldier, Seruant, making Peace or Warre, / As thou affects', his apparently empty lover's compliment turns out to be disastrous, literal truth. If Cleopatra insists on fighting by sea, against all better judgement Antony obeys; if Cleopatra turns tail and flees, Antony flies after her. In this play, the literary platitude is for real. Moreover, Antony the warrior is subordinate to Antony the lover, and this reversal of roles is express-ed in the imagery of arms from the play's opening lines.

Philo   . . . His Captaines heart,
            Which in the scuffles of great Fights hath burst
            The Buckles on his brest, reneages all temper,
            And is become the Bellowes and the Fan
            To coole a Gypsies Lust.
                    (*Antony and Cleopatra* I.i.10ff)

However, at the high points of victory and defeat, the merely literal image becomes stage fact: the image is physically acted out.

Antony's promise to Cleopatra that he is 'thy Soldier . . .' is acted
out in an intimate scene, in which Cleopatra insists on arming him.
Significantly, this arming scene is Shakespeare's invention (it does
not occur in Plutarch), and Antony goes out from it to his only
military victory. This victory is also Shakespeare's pointed modification of Plutarch, where it is a mere 'saly' of slight importance.[17]
Shakespeare, however, substitutes it for Plutarch's lengthy but
irrelevant accounts of Antony's successful Parthian campaigns,
which were fought *while Antony was away from Cleopatra.*

Shakespeare does not merely tamper with Plutarch in this invented scene; he also alters his own wording of it. By singular good
fortune, the Folio has preserved for us the apparent arrangement of
the authorial manuscript, from which it was probably set up.
Shakespeare's symbolic intentions are all the more obvious from his
marginal addition, ringed in the following quotation:

Cleopatra   Nay, Ile helpe too, | *Antony.* |
               What's this for? | Ah let be, let be, thou art
               | The Armourer of my heart: False, false: This, this, |
               Sooth-law Ile helpe: Thus it must bee.
Antony   Well, well, we shall thriue now.
                              (*Antony and Cleopatra* IV.iv.2510ff)

To make his symbolic point clear, Shakespeare has squeezed in
Antony's remark down the right-hand margin and inbetween
Cleopatra's lines. As the audience can see, she is the armourer of his
heart – and body. *But* (as she gets the buckles wrong), Antony's wry
aside inadvertently identifies another aspect of their relationship –
she is 'False, false', and betrays him on numerous occasions.[18]

So the vicissitudes of war, be they success or defeat, are all seen in
terms of Cleopatra. Armed by her, Antony sweeps out to victory.
But at his triumphant return, it is she who is hailed as victor, and,
significantly, Shakespeare once again elaborates Plutarch in order to
give the audience a visual and verbal image of the lovers' relationship. According to Plutarch, Antony

came againe to the pallace, greatly boasting of this victorie, and sweetely
kissed Cleopatra, armed as he was . . .

                              (Bullough V.307)

Shakespeare elaborates Plutarch's fact, since the staged embrace is
simultaneously described like the shackling of the conquered enemy,
and the act of love itself:[19]

Antony   . . . Oh thou day o' th'world,
        Chaine mine arm'd necke, leape thou, Attyre and all
        Through proofe of Harnesse to my heart, and there
        Ride on the pants triumphing.
           (*Antony and Cleopatra* IV.viii.2663ff)

No wonder that Cleopatra's happy recollections earlier should have foretold such a reversal of roles – 'That time? Oh times . . . I drunke him to his bed: / Then put my Tires and Mantles on him, whilst / I wore his Sword Phillippan.' At such exultant moments, Antony may rejoice that she alone can leap through proof of harness to his heart. But Cleopatra is Antony's great adversary. When her navy's flight causes his second defeat at Caesar's hands, this is nothing to the war he feels between himself and her: 'my heart / Makes onely Warres on thee . . .' And when Mardian brings him the false news of Cleopatra's 'death', *this* is the wound from which no armour can save him. The exultation of 'leape thou, Attyre and all . . .' is remembered now, as his armour is discarded, for 'The seuen-fold shield of Aiax cannot keepe / The battery from my heart'.[20] No armour can defend him from Cleopatra, once his joyfully accepted victor, now the bringer of his death-wound. So Philo's opening image, from which we began, is completed now, as his lover's, not his Captain's heart, breaks the buckles on his breast and struggles to burst free:

        Off, plucke off . . .
        . . . Oh cleaue my sides,
        Heart, once be stronger then thy Continent,
        Cracke thy fraile Case. Apace, Eros, apace;
        No more a Soldier: bruised peeces go,
        You haue bin Nobly borne.
           (*Antony and Cleopatra* IV.xiv.2870ff)

Philo's verbal image is finally acted out at this, the real moment of defeat, as Eros, who but Eros, takes Antony's arms from him, and his life as warrior and lover comes to an end.

It is perhaps to be expected that the theatrical image so fully exploited here had its origins in the merely verbal intimation of an earlier play. *Troilus and Cressida* begins with Troilus's lines: 'Call heere my varlet, Ile vnarme againe, / Why should I warre without the walls of Troy: / That finde such cruell battell here within.' But no varlet appears, and the image is not staged. Its theatrical embodiment is successfully achieved in the later play, and from *Antony and Cleopatra*'s opening lines, Antony's reversal of roles from warrior to lover is expressed in the imagery of arms. Cleopatra arms him for battle and chains him as her captive on his return; her feigned death is his mortal wound. A 'cruell battell here within', the battle of the heart, usurps the stage. The inevitable theatrical corollary is the secondary presentation of the actual battles between Antony and Caesar, which are merely an off-stage tumult to this all-engulfing personal tragedy.[21]

Disguise

Theatrical disguise fulfils many minor functions. It is, perhaps primarily, fun for the audience, which takes a primitive pleasure in being allowed behind the scenes, participating in the rehearsals for Pyramus and Thisbe; sniggering with the disguised Hal and Poins as they eavesdrop on Falstaff with Doll perched on his knee; judiciously observing Feste slip on the false beard and gown of Sir Thopas in order to bait the distracted Malvolio. The last example in particular betrays the absolute otiose futility of such disguise; as Maria belatedly admits, 'Thou mightst haue done this without thy berd and gowne, he sees thee not.' But *The Spanish Tragedy* drew on this innocent pleasure also, as Hieronimo knocked up a curtain and Balthazar wandered in with props – 'what is your beard on?' 'Halfe on, the other is in my hand . . .' Failed disguises are a continual source of comedy ('Here comes the Lord Lysimachus disguised'!), particularly when the deceiver is as incompetent as Antonio in the masked ball of *Much Ado*, promptly recognised by his feeble wit and waggling head. Such masked balls and masques (*Love's Labour's Lost, Romeo and Juliet, Henry VIII*) reproduce contemporary fashions that much of the audience could not have indulged in. Then again, the fairies and tapers closing *Merry Wives* are pretty as well as funny (even with Mistress Quickly as their queen). And in purely practical terms, the heroines' boy-disguises of the comedies automatically extended the limited number of actors in the Elizabethan players' companies – more parts for as many actors – and intensified the complications of the plot accordingly.

Curiously, though, disguise is rarely used for evil ends in Shakespeare. Richard and Buckingham dutifully go through their historical paces, appearing on the Tower in *rotten Armour, maruellous ill-fauoured* for an elaborate and authentic stratagem, but usually such evil disguise is one of nature rather than dress, the second being definitely subsidiary. So both Iago and Macbeth deceive by their honest and smooth exteriors, and only fleetingly resort to sartorial tricks. The ruse is the same in each case (perhaps another example of Shakespearean re-cycling): both Iago and Macbeth return to the stage, after the murders they have engineered, with all the surprise of innocents awoken, in their nightgowns or nightshirts.[22]

Above all, however, Shakespearean disguise is used to foster the truth. This may be a spiritual and symbolic one: so one could parallel *Measure for Measure*'s Duke, justly muffled in his Friar's cowl, with Bottom, asinine and unaware, sporting his ass's head. It seems a little ponderous to see in Titania's infatuation with this lovable donkey an image of the animality of love. But J. M. Steadman has convincingly shown that in *Merry Wives* Falstaff's appearance disguised as Herne the Hunter evokes a familiar emblem of fleshly lust – that is, Actaeon, devoured by the hounds of his desire (as in Orsino's image). Falstaff is not only dressed like Actaeon, a man in hunter's garb with the head of a stag; he also adopts Actaeon's conventional pose in mid-metamorphosis, on all fours (so Falstaff: 'Ile winke, and couch'). The joke lies in the humiliatingly unheroic fairies, rather than hounds, which do not devour him, merely pinch and torment him with their tapers, singing: 'Fie on sinnefull phantasie: Fie on Lust, and Luxurie . . .'[23]

In broader, psychological terms, masks also encourage truth-telling, and several of the masked balls are used for these ends. So the visored Benedick has a chance to slip Beatrice a few nasty home-truths, but gets some in return, even though Beatrice may not know who she is talking to. Romeo attends the Capulets' ball masked like the other guests, and Juliet should probably be masked also, since a servant of the Capulet household is unable to tell Romeo who she is.[24] However, these masks merely obliterate the unhappy and fortuitous incompatibilities the lovers inherit from their families, while allowing nature to recognise its true match. So, masked, they can fall in love with the real person, and ignore irrelevancies of name. This masked encounter consequently provides the perfect illustration of Helena's aphorism in *All's Well*:

> The mightiest space in fortune, Nature brings
> To ioyne like likes, and kisse like natiue things.
> (*All's Well* I.i.229–30)

The heroines' boy-disguises have the same function, allowing for intimacy where it would otherwise have been impossible. Viola, dressed as Cesario, can defend women's love to Orsino, without admitting that she is thinking of them both; Rosalind can teach

Orlando to court her as Ganymede, with a freedom and honesty denied to her proper self; even in the early *Two Gentlemen*, Julia, disguised as a page, first witnesses Proteus's infidelity to her. Such conventions are not confined to the comedies; in *Henry V* Hal, disguised in Erpingham's cloak, walks among the common soldiers on the eve of Agincourt, and learns for the first time the extent of the responsibilities popularly laid on him.

It might seem then that Shakespeare's practice is the converse of that described by Emily Dickinson:

> A Charm invests a face
> Imperfectly beheld –
> The Lady dare not lift her Veil
> For fear it be dispelled –
>
> But peers beyond her mesh –
> And wishes – and denies –
> Lest Interview – annul a want
> That Image – satisfies –

Ulysses may agree ('Degree being visarded / Th'vnworthiest shewes as fairly in the maske'), but in practice only Cressida is capable of such titillation, and wishes – and denies – till Pandarus herds her and Troilus together, and roughly unveils her: 'Come draw this curtaine, and lets see your picture; alasse the day? How loath you are to offend day light.' Earlier, she had said she depended on her mask to defend her beauty and her secrecy to defend her honesty, but neither defence is needed by the true heroines. Her coquetry is characteristic of her alone. The other women are forthright with those they love, even Olivia breaking her vow, and promptly unveiling for Cesario – 'Ist not well done?' 'Excellently done, if God did all.'[25]

Yet Shakespeare also emphasises precisely the distinction made by Emily Dickinson, between the fictional 'Image', and the real confrontation of the 'Interview', face to face. Disguise, paradoxically, makes the *second* possible. So Orsino's fantasy love for the invisible (and indeed veiled) Olivia modulates into real interest in Cesario/Viola, with whom he can talk frankly and honestly about men's love; so Orlando's literary effusions over the heavenly Rosalind are brought down to earth by his lessons with Ganymede/Rosalind and her unromantic truths about womankind. So, indeed, Romeo's copy-book love for the never-seen, phantom Rosaline is ousted by his first Interview with Juliet. It is the shaky lovers of the problem plays who are taken in precisely by the 'face / Imperfectly beheld'.

Angelo and Bertram both fall for the bed-trick. In *All's Well* this stale theatrical ruse is psychologically more convincing: Bertram's adolescent superficiality is early demonstrated by his rejection of Helena. He is ready instead to fall in love with a woman he's hardly seen (Diana, glimpsed in a window), and is therefore less likely to notice that it is not her he sleeps with. In *Measure for Measure*, on the other hand, the bed-trick is used for the thematic purposes of plot, in order to make Angelo commit the equivalent of Claudio's crime, so that the playwright's motivation in using it is structural and thematic, rather than psychological. Moreover, Angelo has good reason to love Isabella, has seen her many times, and is less likely to be taken in by the substitution of Mariana (whom he also knows well). The device is therefore structurally better integrated but weaker in psychological terms. The defence in each case is, however, that both heroes are motivated by blind lust rather than love – hence, in each case, their lust is amply and ironically satisfied by the woman supposedly most abhorrent to them.

I have been concerned up till now with the more general implications of disguise. In the last act of *Measure for Measure* it has a more intricate, emblematic function. It is one of several traditional comic devices that are here neatly adapted to the moral theme. So, for instance, the marriages conventionally closing comedy are here harnessed to the central theme of justice. The play's moral is 'Judge not, that ye be not judged'; in the shrewd combination of justice and mercy with which the play ends, all the main characters are given their just rewards in the marriages allotted to them. To see Claudio reunited with Juliet is fair and happy enough; the submerged element of punishment becomes more apparent when we think of Angelo, denied death and forced into union with Mariana, a woman he evidently never loved. It is most obvious in Lucio's case, which is the give-away for the rest: his punishment is marriage to the whore he had wronged, *because* 'Marrying a punke . . . is pressing to death, / Whipping and hanging', as he dolefully protests, but 'Slandering a Prince deserues it', as the Duke retorts.[26]

Lucio's crime of slandering the Duke raises another aspect of the central topic which is given concreté embodiment in the last act. It is perhaps not often enough recognised that the play's secondary theme, that of reputation, is a natural extension of the central concept of the dangers of *judgement*. The play's main story is that of Angelo – a man of unjustified good reputation who turns out to be bad. He is figuratively unmasked in the last act, in which his crimes are made known. Parallel to him are the Duke and Mariana, who are both maligned in the body of the play, and literally unveiled (or un-muffled) in the last act, for their true reputations to be restored. (Such a dual use of unmasking, on the literal and metaphorical planes, is incidentally also used at the end of *All's Well* – a detail discussed on p. 191 below.) Thus the Duke's soliloquy on 'Place, and greatnes', and its vulnerability to false report, however clumsily introduced, is not a mere stop-gap while Isabella and Mariana arrange the bed-trick off stage. It is a formal meditation on the play's second most important theme. [27]

Just as enthronement in the seat of justice, and demotion from it, are used in the last act to illustrate the aphorism, 'Judge not, that ye be not judged' (as chapter 2 has shown), so unveiling and unmuffling are used to stress this theme, and its corollary of maligned reputation.

Mariana was originally slandered by Angelo, as a pretext for breaking off the engagement after her brother was drowned and her dowry lost. In his own words, 'her reputation was dis-valued / In leuitie'. According to the Duke, Angelo abandoned her, '*pretending* in her, discoueries of dishonor'. In the trial of the last act, Angelo is seated by the Duke to judge his own cause. Significantly, the first witness to be brought in is his victim Mariana, heavily veiled. She pointedly refuses the Duke's request that she should show her face: 'I will not shew my face / Vntill my husband bid me.' The moment is even a little unnatural, and apparently pointless, until its symbolic rationale becomes clear. Mariana's unveiling will be her way of identifying Angelo, and simultaneously accusing him as the man who was her betrothed husband, and who slept with her rather than Isabel. So it is only when *Angelo* loses patience and demands to see her face that she unveils ('My husband bids me, now I will vnmaske'). Now he is faced with the woman he wronged, who becomes his accuser. Even her fault is as neatly transferred to him, as its parallel was in the body of the play, when Angelo committed Claudio's crime. For Mariana can justly claim, in her turn, that the precise Angelo's reputation is disvalued for levity, since he has forced a woman into a clandestine sexual encounter. [28]

Precisely the same reversal of roles recurs later, when the Duke, disguised as the 'medling Fryer', is taxed by Escalus, Angelo, and, above all, Lucio, for the very libels Lucio had himself earlier made against the Duke, to his unrecognised face. Like Mariana, the Duke is judged by the man who originally maligned him, and who is himself guilty of the crime he is attributing to his victim:

Angelo	What can you vouch against him Signior Lucio?
	Is this the man that you did tell vs of?
Lucio	'Tis he, my Lord: come hither goodman baldpate, doe you know
	me? . . . and do you remember what you said of the Duke? . . .
	And was the Duke a flesh-monger, a foole, and a coward, as you
	then reported him to be?

(Measure for Measure V.i.2705ff)

The Duke's reply makes the purpose of the incident abundantly clear: 'You must (Sir) change persons with me, ere you make that my report.' Like Angelo, in his turn Lucio then unmasks what will be his accuser:

Lucio	Come sir, come sir, come sir: foh sir, why you bald-pated lying
	rascall: you must be hooded must you? show your knaues visage
	with a poxe to you . . . will't not off?
Duke	Thou art the first knaue, that ere mad'st a Duke.

(Measure for Measure V.i.2732ff)

By this parallel set of reversals the play's central theme is given multiple illustration. In each case the moment *acts out* in graphic, visual terms, the play's central theme. The 'judge' discovers his own prosecutor, the accuser becomes the accused and the judge is judged. As in *Lear*, 'Change places, and handy-dandy, which is the Iustice, which is the theefe?'[29]

Rich dress and nakedness

Shakespeare is not visibly interested in the elaborate disguises of evil, since his chief concern is the common disguise of man – ordinary dress. 'It yernes me not, if men my Garments weare', says Hal; 'Such outward things dwell not in my desires.' In Shakespeare's practice, costume is *the* dominant image (both verbal and visual) of the deceptive 'outward things' by which man tries to hide his own nature from himself, and others.

This practice has its roots in Tudor drama, where innocence was naked, vices like prodigality were extravagantly dressed, and a character's changes of state were evident from his ritualistic changes of costume. But Shakespeare's practice differs materially from that of his predecessors. The norm could be epitomised by Chaucer's Monk, who touches unexpected eloquence in his description of the conquered Cenobia:

> Allas, Fortune! she that whilom was
> Dredeful to kynges and to emperoures,
> Now gaureth al the peple on hire, allas!
> And she that helmed was in starke stoures,
> And wan by force townes stronge and toures,
> Shal on hir heed now were a vitremyte;
> And she that bar the ceptre ful of floures
> Shal bere a distaf, hire cost for to quyte.

For the Monk, the fall is a tragic one. But for Shakespeare, there is no indignity in such a state. Thus man appears as he really is, without gross, foolish pretensions, 'the thing it selfe'. This, the theme that is to dominate *King Lear*, is intermittently staged from the earliest plays.[30]

Even in Dame Eleanor's neat little *Mirror for Magistrates*-style tragedy, in *2 Henry VI*, the characteristic Shakespearean addition is made. Her fall follows the traditional pattern, from her first arrogant appearances, so richly dressed that Margaret complains 'Strangers in Court, doe take her for the Queene', to her last exit in the robe of a penitent, *bare-foote, and a white sheete about her, with a waxe candle in her hand, and verses written on her backe and pind on.*[31] The typical Shakespearean rider is her reason for refusing to change once her penance is done:

Elianor   My shame will not be shifted with my Sheet:
         No, it will hang vpon my richest Robes,
         And shew it selfe, attyre me how I can.
                   (*2 Henry VI* II.iv. 1288ff)

Like the many characters who learn after her, Eleanor recognises the discrepancy between spirit and dress. Yet, paradoxically, by her rejection of dress she restores its original meaning to it, since she leaves the stage a penitent both in mind and form.

Later, Petruchio echoes Eleanor in his grave distinction between dress and the man, as he goes to his wedding abominably attired, answering his friends' remonstrance with:

Petruchio   To me she's married, not vnto my cloathes:
          Could I repaire what she will weare in me,
          As I can change these poore accoutrements,
          'Twere well for Kate, and better for my selfe.
                 (*Taming of the Shrew* III.ii. 1500ff)

It is typical of the actors, that they should remain irrepressibly materialist in their version, in which Petruchio blandly explains that he is saving his finery from Kate's bad-tempered attacks. Once again the actors have failed to grasp Shakespeare's symbolic point.[32]

Eleanor and Petruchio's sober insistence on the irrelevance of outward form has its evil counterpart in Aaron and Richard III, both of whom embark on their lives of crime with the voiced determination to 'be bright and shine in pearle and golde', their rich dress being a stage reflection both of their ambition, and the glittering deception of evil ('Thorough tatter'd cloathes great Vices do appeare: Robes, and Furr'd gownes hide all'). This theatrical signpost was probably more easily grasped, since it was traditional; later variants on the same vice-convention are less obviously stated but the implications are still the same. We are perhaps partly blinded by the play's naturalism, and by indulgent memories of what he was like before, and fail to realise that an altogether less sympathetic Falstaff walks into the second part of *Henry IV*, pox-ridden, in debt, tricked out in borrowed silks and satins, a page dolled up like a little ape at his heels. No explicit stage direction demands the change. But that Falstaff should have become noticeably more showy and nasty since *1 Henry IV* is made clear from the text's continual references to his diseases, his debts, his attempts to get satin on credit, his dining with Mr Smooth, the silkman (what for?) . . . His behaviour in this play is also noticeably less attractive and less forgiveable. Shakespeare is consciously preparing us for his imminent rejection.[33]

Similarly, in *All's Well*, the dialogue makes it clear that Bertram should be extravagantly patched and plumed, particularly after his return from the Florentine wars. In both dress, and dealings with his wife, he thus sadly approves his father's account of the younger generation, 'whose iudgements are / Meere fathers of their garments: whose constancies / Expire before their fashions.' But Bertram is as it were the natural and unostentatious manifestation of the theatrical corollary between rich dress and false nature. It is more emblematically and flamboyantly marked by his parallel in Parolles, who is the archetypal embodiment of all false show. Bertram's callow superficiality is all the more evident from his association with Parolles, who is not only loud-mouthed and garrulous, but is draped in the 'strange suites' of the traveller (a common butt for Elizabethan satire). This ludicrous attire is continually mocked at: 'a snipt taffata fellow', 'that red-tail'd humble Bee', 'That Iacke an-apes with scarfes'. 'Why dooest thou garter vp thy armes a this fashion?' Lafeu demands of him, 'Dost make hose of thy sleeues? Do other seruants so?' Lafeu is the first to see through all these fluttering pretensions: 'the scarffes and the bannerets about thee, did manifoldlie disswade

me from beleeuing thee a vessell of too great a burthen. I haue now
found thee . . .' And he warns Bertram in a reverberant phrase:

beleeue this of me, there can be no kernell in this light Nut: *the soule of this
man is his cloathes*.

(*All's Well* II.iv. 1313ff. My italics)

However, after his humiliating public discomfiture as a liar,
Parolles decides to give up all pretence, and the interesting thing is
that he is approved and supported in his honest degradation. At
his next appearance he is so pathetically down-at-heel, so poorly
dressed, bedraggled, and stinking, that at first Lafeu does not even
recognise him. 'He lookes like a poore decayed, ingenious, foolish,
rascally knaue', Lavache reports, and for the first time he looks like
what he is. But in this state Lafeu takes pity on him, and supports
him precisely for being what he is: 'Sirrah, inquire further after me, I
had talke of you last night, though you are a foole and a knaue, you
shall eate.' Lafeu's kindness approves Parolles's brave choice of
honesty in degradation; 'Simply the thing I am / Shall make me liue'
is shown to be true, and not a philosophy to be despised. In this
sense, Lafeu's recognition and maintenance of Parolles should be
paralleled by Prospero's recognition of Caliban ('this Thing of
darkenesse, I / Acknowledge mine'), and his insistence that Alonso
in his turn should 'know, and owne' the drunken Stephano and
Trinculo.[34]

Curiously, Parolles's discovery is repeated by Timon, in more
extreme terms. One would not think of them as similar, but Timon,
like Parolles, begins his stage life in the 'Gilt, and . . . Perfume' of a
self-deceptive prosperity; at his betrayal by his Athenian friends, he
takes to nakedness and the woods. But, in this bestial state, nature
herself supports and feeds him. The point is dramatically made in a
superb speech, in which Timon is meditating on Nature, that
'Teemes and feeds all', from man in his arrogance, to the lowest
reptile. Stooping to dig, he begins to curse mankind with a venom
that makes him positively reptilian, and scarcely interrupts his curses
as he discovers food:

> That Nature being sicke of mans vnkindnesse
> Should yet be hungry: Common Mother, thou
> Whose wombe vnmeasureable, and infinite brest
> Teemes and feeds all: whose selfsame Mettle
> Whereof thy proud Childe (arrogant man) is puft,
> Engenders the blacke Toad, and Adder blew,

> The gilded Newt, and eyelesse venom'd Worme . . .
> Yeeld him, who all the humane Sonnes do hate,
> From foorth thy plenteous bosome, one poore roote:
> Enseare thy Fertile and Conceptious wombe,
> Let it no more bring out ingratefull man.
> Goe great with Tygers, Dragons, Wolues, and Beares,
> Teeme with new Monsters . . .
> . . . O, a Root, deare thankes:
> Dry vp thy Marrowes, Vines, and Plough-torne Leas . . .
>   (*Timon* IV.iii. 1796ff)

Impassively, Nature nourishes Timon, just as it feeds the newt and worm to whom, by his curses, he makes himself kin. 'Our dungie earth alike / Feeds Beast as Man',[35] and to realise the small distinction between man and beast is to achieve essential understanding. *Timon* leads directly to *Lear*.

Disguise, dress and nakedness in *King Lear*

The various theatrical implications of rich dress, undress, and disguise are most comprehensively explored in *Lear*, where they are the visual manifestation of the play's central theme, the rift between essential truth, and outward show. The mantle of the theme is worn (or discarded) pre-eminently by Goneril, Regan, Edgar, Kent, and, of course, Lear himself.

Simplest to identify are Goneril and Regan, who are an almost pantomime embodiment of evil, rich in lying speech and extravagant *décolletage*. They are the first to make Lear recognise man's gross pretensions:

> *Lear*   . . . Thou art a Lady:
>   If onely to go warme were gorgeous,
>   Why Nature needs not what thou gorgeous wear'st,
>   Which scarcely keepes thee warme . . .
>   (*King Lear* II.iv. 1567ff)

As Lear's speech suggests, Goneril and Regan should be richly if revealingly dressed. Their gorgeous and patently inadequate dress is a just and static emblem of their natures. Lear, on the other hand, goes through many costume changes as his understanding develops. In the first two acts of the play he should cling to the ostentations of regal paraphernalia even as he delegates its power. As Gloucester says, and the theatre should show, he has 'Prescrib'd his powre, /

Confin'd to exhibition'.[36] In the exile of the storm, that great leveller, such ostentations are lost; twice, here, Lear's miserable state is unfavourably compared to that of any animal, and once, in a moving image, Cordelia compares him to a watchman in a lonely post ('poore Perdu'), his naked skull his only helmet against the elements. Were we as accustomed as the original audience to seeing men always hatted, Lear's barehead, bedraggled appearances in the storm should have some impact:

Kent   This night wherein the cub-drawne Beare would couch,
          The Lyon, and the belly pinched Wolfe
          Keepe their furre dry, vnbonneted he runnes . . .
                    (*King Lear* III.i.Q:F3ᵛ; not in F)

Cordelia In the most terrible and nimble stroke
          Of quick crosse lightning to watch, poore Perdu,
          With this thin helme; mine [Enemies] dogge,
          Though he had bit me, should haue stood that night
          Against my fire . . .
                    (*King Lear* IV.vii.Q:K2, F:2784)

As understanding dawns, Lear sees the naked Edgar, and voluntarily undresses himself to man's real, now recognised state. In his madness he is crowned with garlands; waking from his healing sleep he finds himself in fresh clothes whose simplicity should match the new and naked dignity of his speech.

Such changes of dress are easy to chart; more turbid and troubled are the eddying currents of understanding to which they relate. They are, indeed, the simplifying stage emblem for a more complex mental development.

When Lear rejects Goneril's gorgeous dress, in the passage quoted earlier, he raises the question of need, which is crucial to the play. It echoes Timon's expostulation of the Banditti: 'Why should you want? . . . The bounteous Huswife Nature, on each bush, / Layes her full Messe before you. Want? why Want?'[37] But at this early stage in the play, Lear does not have Timon's bitterly acquired wisdom; he mistakenly believes that to reduce man to his essential needs would *degrade* him to the status of an animal:

                    O reason not the need: our basest Beggers
                    Are in the poorest things superfluous;
                    Allow not Nature, more then Nature needs.
                    Mans life is cheape as Beastes.
                              (*King Lear* II.iv.1564ff)

Outcast in the storm, however, his state is worse than that of an animal; fur drenched, 'vnbonneted he runnes . . .' Kent and Cordelia's images are in pointed antithesis to this speech. Nor is there degradation in such a state. Reduced to the simplest, animal needs, Lear can discover the miraculous transformations effected by such humbling necessity. And note that here Lear suffers not from the relatively sophisticated need of patience, but of simple warmth – just as Timon recognised his basic humanity in hunger ('That Nature being sicke of mans vnkindnesse / Should yet be hungry'). Outside the hovel, Lear speaks to the Fool:

> My wits begin to turne.
> Come on my boy. How dost my boy? Art cold?
> I am cold my selfe. Where is this straw, my Fellow?
> The Art of our Necessities is strange,
> And can make vilde things precious.
>   (*King Lear* III.ii.1722ff)

As the meditative simplicity of his speech suggests, Lear's wits have indeed begun to turn – to understanding, and altruistic sympathy. Fellow to the fool, Lear goes as gratefully to his straw as an ox to the stable. And once in the hovel, the strange art of our necessities allows him to see, in the muddied, bleeding, naked Edgar, a most precious image of his own nature. For him the lunatic is a Theban philosopher who teaches him what he really is. In his essential state, man the animal *needs* nothing:

Is man no more then this? Consider him well. Thou ow'st the Worme no Silke; the Beast, no Hide; the Sheepe, no Wooll; the Cat, no perfume . . .
     (*King Lear* III.iv.1882ff)

Though Lear's sanity is to pass through many further vicissitudes, here, and at the moment of death, he tries to put his new-found knowledge into practice, by stripping the false sophistications of borrowed dress ('you Lendings') off him. He should surely stand in the blaze of nakedness, even if only momentarily, for the Fool's painful joke to have its full impact: 'Prythee Nunckle be contented, 'tis a naughtie night to swimme in . . .'[38]

Beside him stands Edgar, at the very centre of the play, the embodiment of man in his essence: 'the thing it selfe', nothing more than 'a poore, bare, forked *Animall*'. He is the theatrical personification of that 'Nothing' that is everything, the human equivalent of Cordelia's love-laden silence.[39] In him, indeed, the play's moral antitheses find their simplifying stage image, for his bleak nakedness stands in direct opposition to the luxurious undress, the false sophistication of Goneril and Regan. Even Gloucester echoes Lear's vision of Edgar ('bare, forked'), without Lear's understanding, when the old man who is leading him points out the Bedlam in the distance, and Gloucester says, 'I'th'last nights storme, I such a fellow saw; / *Which made me thinke a Man, a Worme.* My Sonne / Came then into my minde . . .' But this worm is also the play's most precious object. The wholly debased Edgar appears at exactly the same moment to Lear and to Gloucester. When each of them realises that 'The Art of our Necessities is strange, / And can make vilde things precious', or, in Gloucester's parallel realisation, 'Full oft 'tis seene, / Our meanes secure vs, and our meere defects / Proue our Commodities', then Edgar, the basest of all creatures, appears, and becomes for one a moral, and for the other, an actual guide. Once again Lear's metaphysical plot finds a physical equivalent in Gloucester's parallel.[40]

Edgar is not merely the play's central symbol of the nothing that is everything, the human nature that we must accept. His meeting with his freshly blinded father also introduces another, more traditional aspect of the symbolism of dress. Gloucester dwells on Edgar's nakedness at this meeting: 'Is that the naked Fellow? . . . Sirrah, naked Fellow . . .' His first request is that the old man should get clothes for him: 'bring some couering for this naked Soule.' Gloucester is, in fact, unconsciously *redressing* his wrongs to his son, by reclothing the unrecognised Bedlam. Such a suggestion is not, indeed, irrelevantly punning: Skelton's Magnificence is raised up and reclothed by a character who introduces himself as Redress:[41]

> Redress   Then stand vp, syr, in Goddys name . . .
>   Take now vpon you this abylment,
>   And to that I say gyue good aduysement.
>   *Magnyfycence accipiat indumentum* . . .
>   Determyne to amende all your wanton excesse,
>   And be ruled by me, whiche am called Redresse . . .

Edgar, finally, not only stands as the visible embodiment of man's essential nature, but is also a striking instance of the irrelevancies of outward form. Its deceptive nature is seen in Goneril and Regan; its negligible importance in Edgar. He goes through a bewildering (and practically quite unnecessary) variety of disguises, but the true core remains unchanged. Our gloss is the moment when Edgar pretends to lead his father up Dover cliff. Gloucester shrewdly complains, not only that the ground seems no steeper, but that his guide's accent and sense both have improved. Edgar's reply is pointed: 'In nothing am I chang'd / But in my Garments.' He may go through a variety of bizarre disguises, but he remains steadfast to his father throughout. Dress and disguise are irrelevant; he is changed in nothing but his clothes.

Thus he passes from Edgar to Poor Tom ('That's *something* yet: Edgar I *nothing* am'); from Poor Tom to his dismissal of that figure as a fiend glimpsed on the top of Dover Cliff, while at the cliff's bottom he picks up Gloucester in his new, and more absolute incarnation as a 'most poore man, made tame to Fortunes blows / Who, by the Art of knowne, and feeling sorrowes, / Am pregnant to good pitty' (the credentials, if clumsy, are at least accurate). As a Cornish clown, he kills Oswald. In the final reduction of all these metamorphoses, he appears as a total cipher, the helmeted and nameless adversary who will fight with Edmund. Edmund should appear for these lists in actuality as he is described metaphorically – Edmund, Earl of Gloucester, in all the false and glittering arms of 'strength, place, youth, and eminence . . . victor-Sword, and fire new Fortune'; Edward, surely, in arms as rusty as Pericles's are to be later, to suit his self-description: 'Know my name is lost / By Treasons tooth bare-gnawne, and Canker-bit . . .' In a moment of heraldic, Arcadian simplicity, the conflict between false show and hidden worth is fought and won.[42]

Thus *King Lear* draws on an elaborate texture of costume symbolism for the staged, theatrical embodiment of its central theme. This extends from the simplicity of the traditional, Tudor costume-symbols, the rich dress of evil in Goneril, Regan and Edmund, Earl of Gloucester, or the enacted redressing of Edgar's wrongs, to the more complex Shakespearean extensions of such traditional correlatives – the irrelevancies of the merely external changes of dress in Edgar; the embodiment of essential man in Edgar as Poor Tom, and in Lear as he strips in the hovel, and unbuttons at the point of death. Edgar is pre-eminently the central stage symbol of the play in his nakedness, as the personification of what man really is, stripped of all sophisticating pretensions.

Kent is what might be called the metaphysical parallel to his physical symbol. Kent, like Edgar, is forced to take refuge in disguise in order to serve the man who has outcast him. In practical stage fact, he merely removes his beard ('I raiz'd my likenesse').[43] But in effect, his disguise is to retreat beyond the irrelevancies of rank and name to what he is essentially – the faithful servant, just as Edgar remained the faithful son, whatever bizarre new shapes his outward form might take. Edgar's self-description, in which he reduces himself to the absolutes that identify his nature, the 'most poore man, made tame to Fortunes blows', and so on, recalls the terms in which the disguised Kent offered his services to Lear. Kent's replies here are pointed in their insistence on qualities and essentials, and their dogged refusal to speak of externals like rank or name. Lear is no King; for Kent, he is simply what a king must have. And what is Kent?

Lear	. . . what art thou?
Kent	A man Sir.
Lear	What dost thou professe? What would'st thou with vs? . . .
Kent	Seruice.
Lear	Who wouldst thou serue?
Kent	You.
Lear	Do'st thou know me fellow?
Kent	No Sir, but you haue that in your countenance, which I would faine call Master.
Lear	What's that?
Kent	Authority.

(*King Lear* I.iv.540ff)

In Kent's case, such 'disguise' in the essentials can have no costume equivalent, except an absolute ordinariness of dress. Instead, the theatrical deployment of the theme comes through plot – the complications of Lear's partial recognition of Kent at the end of the play.

It might seem one of the play's gratuitous harshnesses that Lear should fail to recognise, in the Kent that introduces himself at the play's end, the Caius that served him throughout. Lear certainly recognises *Kent*, in a moment whose absurdity Tolstoy was quick to ridicule: 'Next he says that his eyes see badly, and thereupon recognises Kent whom all along he had not recognised':[44]

Lear	. . . Who are you?
	Mine eyes are not o'th'best, Ile tell you straight . . .
	This is a dull sight, are you not Kent?
Kent	The same . . .

(*King Lear* V.iii.3244ff)

Tolstoy's logic is impeccable; his ridicule misplaced. This moment is one of the play's many instances of the imperfections of the senses, particularly sanity and sight. It is Lear's equivalent of Gloucester's 'I stumbled when I saw'. Enlightenment came to Gloucester in his blindness; understanding to Lear in his madness. Both act out Montaigne's paradoxes:[45]

We must be besotted ere we can become wise, and dazled before we can be led . . . The weaknesse of our judgement, helps us more than our strength to compasse the same, and our blindnesse more than our cleare-sighted eyes. It is more by the meanes of our ignorance, than of our skill, that we are wise in heavenly knowledge.

Dim-sighted, Lear recognises Kent at last. But why should he not recognise that Kent is also Caius, the man who served him faithfully throughout the play?

Here we come to the nub of Kent's role. By choosing to serve Lear incognito, Kent embodies the saying that 'deeds speak louder than words', or, to put it into the play's terms, it is he who actually puts Cordelia's early boast into practice;

Cordelia   . . . I want that glib and oylie Art,
To speake and purpose not, since what I will intend,
Ile do't before I speake.
(*King Lear* I.i.246ff)

This is exactly what Kent does: as the faithful Caius, he acts first, and only speaks much later. In Act IV Cordelia fails to persuade him to drop his disguise, although it has no further practical purpose. This is another of those odd, faintly embarrassing Shakespearean moments (like Mariana's refusal to unveil for the Duke in *Measure for Measure*) that appear clumsy and unnatural, until their symbolic rationale emerges. For Kent must postpone relinquishing his disguise until it is too late. So, when he finally comes to speak, he is no longer heard:

Lear   This is a dull sight, are you not Kent?
Kent   The same: your Seruant Kent,
Where is your Seruant Caius?
Lear   He's a good fellow, I can tell you that,
He'le strike and quickly too, he's dead and rotten.
Kent   No my good Lord, I am the very man.
Lear   Ile see that straight.
Kent   That from your first of difference and decay,
Haue follow'd your sad steps.
Lear   You are welcome hither . . .
Albany He knowes not what he saies, and vaine is it
That we present vs to him.
(*King Lear* V.iii.3247ff)

Thus 'Caius' leaves Lear's service on the same absolute terms as he entered it. Although the man has gone unrecognised, his services are known and valued – 'He's a good fellow, I can tell you that, / He'le strike and quickly too . . .' Lear has recognised the essence, and it is not forgotten.

Kent's end is a definitive illustration of what has been miscellaneously noted already. The sliding scale from falsehood to truth is equally marked by the inches and centimetres of the theatre, costume and speech. The correlation is obvious in the staged personae of Shakespeare's villains – the glib, dandyfied Richard III, the bragging, beribboned Parolles (whose name is warning enough), Lear's elegant and eloquent daughters. But the two are so closely associated that they are interchangeable. Dress and speech can change places in linguistic metaphor; so Berowne's famous speech rejecting the language of courtly love is expressed wholly in terms of dress. 'Taffata phrases, silken tearmes precise, / Three pilde Hiperboles' are abandoned for 'russet yeas, and honest kersie noes'. Other linguistic variants on the same theme abound.[46] Timon, for instance, rebukes the hypocritical Poet's protestations of linguistic poverty with costume's powerful converse:

> Poet   . . . I am rapt, and cannot couer
>   The monstrous bulke of this Ingratitude
>   With any size of words.
> Timon   Let it go naked;
>   Men may see't the better.
>   (*Timon* V.i.2273ff)

But in Kent this interchange between costume and language is not merely metaphorical, it is physical fact. In *King Lear*, stark truth makes itself known in nakedness, and in silence. Edgar embodies the one; Kent and Cordelia the other. In the painful confusions of this last, failed recognition scene, we see that Kent's disguise has been, effectively, silence. When he finally comes to speak, Lear can no longer hear.

The last plays

The last plays continue Shakespeare's rich and fascinating use of costume in every aspect, from the decorative and delightful to the intricate and loaded.

Pericles is, most obviously, an echo of *Lear* in this particular respect. Shipwrecked at Pentapolis, like Lear in the storm, Pericles realises his essential nature in his nakedness: 'What I haue been, I haue forgot to know; / But what I am, want teaches me to thinke on: / A man throng'd vp with cold.' In his case as in Lear's, 'want', 'need', the necessities of clothes, warmth, shelter and food bring home the fact of their vulnerable mortality: 'they told me, I was euery thing: 'Tis a Lye, I am not Agu-proofe.' In his need Pericles, like Lear, discovers the miracles of necessity and gladly goes to Simonides' tournament in rusty armour rescued from the sea. Jousting success- fully in such poor equipment turns him into another, Edgar-like personification of nameless worth. The explanatory aphorism is perverted here, as another had been in *A Shrew*, by the corruption of the text: 'Opinion's but a foole, that makes vs scan / The outward habit, by [edd. 'for'] the inward man.' Yet for all the real passion and power of Pericles' reunion with Marina, I find his statutory change of dress at the end of this scene a little disappointing. It is too simply the standard symbol of spiritual regeneration, and the dia- logue introducing it lacks interest ('Giue me fresh garments . . . giue me my robes'), especially by comparison with Lear's confusion with his unfamiliar dress. Perhaps the text is at fault; perhaps Shakespeare had lost interest in the modification of such traditional symbolism; or perhaps, finally, such naturalistic modification would have been out of place in play such as *Pericles*, with its dumb shows and frank stage ritual.[47]

Where *Pericles* relates most closely to *Lear, The Winter's Tale* draws freely on the expertise of the rest of the canon. Autolycus's admirable versatility in disguise is chiefly a simple source of comedy. Never- theless, when he has assumed Florizel's rich Doricles-disguise and meets the Clown and Shepherd, it allows for the usual distinction between dress and the man to be made:

Clown	This cannot be but a great Courtier.
Shepherd	His Garments are rich, but he weares them not handsomely.
Clown	He seemes to be the more Noble, in being fantasticall: A great man, Ile warrant; I know by the picking on's Teeth.

(*Winter's Tale* IV.iv.263off)

The Clown is sadly provincial and out-of-date: as long ago as *King John*, the Bastard had satirised the affectation of tooth-picking.[48] Shakespeare repeats the distinction between the Clown's lovable superficiality, and the Shepherd's shrewdness, in the last act, when the two meet Autolycus again. He is out of luck, while they are now 'in the blossomes of their Fortune', honoured by both royal houses, nobly dressed, in acknowledgement of their preservation of Perdita. The Clown cannot resist crowing: 'you deny'd to fight with mee this other day, because I was no Gentleman borne. See you these

Clothes? say you see them not, and thinke me still no Gentleman borne.' But the Shepherd does not deduce nobility from his dress, wisely reversing his son's logic and trying to assume in his own nature the inherent virtues of nobility: 'Prethee Sonne . . . we must be gentle, now we are Gentlemen.'

In the sheep-shearing Perdita's costume as Queen of the feast is a pretty minor instance of costume symbolising essential nature (compare the asinine Bottom or Actaeon-Falstaff). She takes to queening it so naturally that she wonders at herself: 'Sure this Robe of mine / Do's change my disposition.' But her dress does not change, it simply brings out her inherent nobility. As such she is the antithesis of the Clown, who will never be noble (however amiable), whatever he wears. Finally, Polixenes' disguised appearance at the sheep-shearing lays him open to unwelcome home truths in the comic manner, since Florizel, not recognising his father, can tell him freely that he has no intentions of consulting his father about his marriage. Thus the play draws lightly on costume's traditional moral associations, or employs disguise in the manner of the comedies, without undue emphasis.[49]

Cymbeline, by contrast, is much more intricate and curious. Probably the earlier play, it shows Shakespeare ambitiously experimenting with a complicated use of costume symbolism, which had attracted much adverse criticism from outspoken critics like Johnson and Shaw. Yet the device rewards scrutiny, and the experiment is a bold one.

Cloten is a late brother to Parolles. He is over-dressed and loud-mouthed, but even in his earliest scenes smells as high as Parolles fallen on evil days – all his show cannot obscure the brute reality of his physical nature. But Cloten is 'all out-side'[50] in perceptions as well as manner. His scorn for Posthumus is tellingly expressed in terms of dress: 'A Hilding for a Liuorie, a Squires Cloth.' Imogen's retort is effective since it is couched in the terms Cloten understands: 'His mean'st Garment . . . is dearer / In my respect, then all the Heires aboue thee.' This 'penetrates', as Cloten would say, and his revenge is the supremely simple-minded one of dressing himself in Posthumus's clothes in order to rape Imogen. According to his reasoning, since the clothes fit him so well, the woman should too. The highly improbable, and (according to Shaw) unactable scene in which Imogen wakes by his headless trunk, and takes it for her husband's, may appear – in Johnson's words – 'unresisting imbecillity', but it is, in fact, a beautifully logical continuation of the same theme.[51]

For Cloten's superficiality governs his view of himself as well as others. When he encounters Guiderius in the Welsh mountains, he expects to be recognised by those old externals, dress and name. And just as the latter is meaningless ('Whats in a name?'), so the former should be. His exchange with Guiderius betrays his assumptions:

Cloten	Thou Villaine base,
	Know'st me not by my Cloathes?
Guiderius	No, nor thy Taylor, Rascall:
	Who is thy Grandfather? He made those cloathes,
	Which (as it seemes) make thee.

(Cymbeline IV.ii.2349ff)

Cloten has, in fact, forgotten that he is dressed in Posthumus's clothes, rather than his own. But Guiderius is right: Cloten is indeed made by his clothes; essentially, he is nothing. This idea is repeated in a conventional image when Guiderius fights him off-stage and returns with his head, saying, 'This Cloten was a Foole, an empty purse, / There was no money in't.'[52] Consequently, when Imogen wakes beside the headless corpse that is dressed in her husband's clothes, it is hardly surprising that she should take it for her husband. For there is no kernel in this light nut, no money in this empty purse; 'the soule of this man is his cloathes', as Lafeu said of Parolles. Headless, and in Posthumus's clothes, Cloten *is* Posthumus.

It may be that in this bizarre scene Shakespeare has over-reached himself in much the same way as he courted unease in the other quirks of plot that served symbolic ends, noted in this chapter (such as Kent's and Mariana's delay in making themselves known). The rest of the play is certainly more circumspect. Once again, all the old theatrical usages of costume recur. The low-born, but noble Posthumus is simply Cloten's opposite, being all inside. The point is epigrammatically made when he disguises himself as a British peasant, saying, 'To shame the guize o'th'world, I will begin / The fashion, lesse without, and more within.'[53] His conscious disguise is paralleled by the unconscious disguise of Guiderius and Arviragus: for all their wild upbringing, their nobility (like Perdita's) cannot be hidden. Imogen is a late sister to the heroines of the comedies, in a fraternal rather than amorous relationship, since her boy's disguise also brings her to an unknown truth – the instinctive affection that springs up between her and her unrecognised brothers, Guiderius and Arviragus. Like Romeo and Juliet, sister and brothers fulfil Helen's dictum, and 'kisse like natiue things', before they even know that this is what they are.

In *The Tempest*, finally, every aspect of costume recurs in its last, clearest form. Its prime function, visual delight, is amply exploited in the wedding-masque, with its reapers and goddesses, all *properly habited*, Ariel's flickering transmutations, from *water-Nymph* to *Harpey*, and the first and last display (we assume) of the King's men's equivalent of Henslowe's 'robe for to goo invisibell' at Prospero's appearance *on the top* (*inuisible*).[54] The perpetual Shakespearean theme of man's self-disguise, 'man, proud man, / Drest in a little briefe authoritie' – an authority which is often ill-fitting – is picked up for the last time in a verbal image clearly deriving from *Macbeth*:

Sebastian	I remember
	You did supplant your Brother Prospero.
Antonio	True:
	And looke how well my Garments sit vpon me.
	(*Tempest* II.i.968ff)

And the shoddy triviality of temporal ambition is given its last and most devastating stage image in the decoying of Stephano and Trinculo by armfulls of *glistering apparell*. It is a carrot Caliban dismisses as trash, but Trinculo worships like every foolish civilised man: 'Oh, ho, Monster: wee know what belongs to a frippery, O King Stephano.' Is kingship no more than this? we might ask, echoing Henry in his lonely responsibility before Agincourt.[55]

Finally, robes as the frank symbol of a function are staged in Prospero's donning and shedding of his magician's dress, both at the end of the play, and at its beginning. The purpose of this early scene is interesting. Before telling Miranda the play's prehistory, Prospero divests himself: 'Lend thy hand / And plucke my Magick garment from me: So, / Lye there my Art.' His subsequent account is not merely surprisingly prosaic and long-drawn-out for this late stage in Shakespeare's writing. Shakespeare pointedly prompts and emphasises our weariness by Prospero's repeated insistence on Miranda's sleepiness ('(Do'st thou attend me?) . . . Thou attend'st not? . . . Do'st thou heare?'), till she succumbs and dozes off.[56] Furthermore, the scene contrasts sharply with the storm and shipwreck of the preceding scene, and that triumphant staging of the unstageable. The violence of the contrast, and the stressed flatness of Prospero's retrospective narrative, suggest that the two in conjunction are a display of the magician's skill, be he Prospero or Shakespeare. He begins by conjuring up a prodigious illusory storm, then sheds his robes to speak without art – as Prospero's long speeches really are. A contrast is thus made between the dramatist-magician's embodied creation, and the layman's stilted prose narrative whose tense is past, not present. Costume points the change of role; Prospero lays aside his art and speaks as he will after the end of the play, when

> . . . my Charmes are all ore-throwne,
> And what strength I haue's mine owne,
> Which is most faint.
> (*Tempest* Epilogue 2322ff)

Prospero's final exit in the 'Hat, and Rapier' of the ordinary man is in no way pedestrian. The theme first introduced in *King Lear*, and increasingly prominent in the last plays, is the celebration of ordinary things. In each case misfortune makes the norm, ordinary life to which the characters may finally return, both precious and miraculous. It is the theme already discussed at the end of chapter 6 (p. 119): 'Nothing almost sees miracles / But miserie . . .' On the sinking ship, Gonzalo cries in despair:

> Now would I giue a thousand furlongs of Sea, for an Acre of barren ground:
> Long heath, Browne firrs, any thing . . .
> (*Tempest* I.i.76ff)

Safe on dry land, he still sees with the rapture of a rescued man, although his joy is counterpointed by the cynicism of others:

Gonzalo	How lush and lusty the grasse lookes?
	How greene?
Antonio	The ground indeed is tawny.
Sebastian	With an eye of greene in't.

> (*Tempest* II.i.727ff)

All the last plays end with a restitution of what they began with, but loss has made the objects dear. These plays act out the debate begun in *Troilus and Cressida*, 'Whats aughts but as tis valued?' Hermione and Imogen do not change, but their value does. Maligned, they are lost; loss makes them precious again. Like Antony of Fulvia, Posthumus and Leontes could both say of their wives, 'she's good being gon'. Restored to them, they have become inestimably dear, and yet Imogen is still Imogen, Hermione Hermione. The Duke of *Measure for Measure* had told Claudio, 'Happie thou art not, / For what thou hast not, still thou striu'st to get, / And what thou hast forgetst'; the theme recurs repeatedly elsewhere.[57] The last plays correct this very real instinct. As they end, everything has become new, even the perpetual commonplace of breath and motion – the miracle of nature most brilliantly brought home to us in Hermione's living statue. Of many other instances, let me quote only Miranda's wonder at the very ordinary Ferdinand:

Miranda   What is't a Spirit?
          Lord, how it lookes about: Beleeue me sir,
          It carries a braue forme. But 'tis a spirit.
Prospero No wench, it eats, and sleeps, and hath such senses
          As we haue: such.
                              (*Tempest* I.ii.553ff)

'Lord, how it lookes about'! pinpoints the charm. Even the rabble of malefactors at the play's end amazes Miranda: the whole world becomes a miracle when seen with her inexperienced eyes. In every one of the last plays satiety is driven out by freshness and wonder, but it is still the norm that has become wonderful.

It should not surprise us, then, that in the last of these plays, Shakespeare should make even ordinary dress a cause for admiration. We may think nothing of the dry clothes we put on daily, but for men just snatched from the sea even dry clothes are incredible:

Gonzalo   But the rariety of it is, which is indeed almost beyond credit.
Sebastian As many voucht rarieties are.
Gonzalo   That our Garments being (as they were) drencht in the Sea, hold
           notwithstanding their freshnesse and glosses, being rather new
           dy'de then stain'd with salte water.
                              (*Tempest* II.i.733ff)

It takes the wise old Gonzalo to see the miraculous in the commonplace right from the start of the play.

CHAPTER 9

Properties

Now to my tragic business; look you, brother,
I have not fashioned this only for show
And unless property; no, it shall bear a part.
                              (*Revenger's Tragedy* III.v.99ff)

The theatre of every age is tempted to sacrifice plays to properties
and sense to spectacle. By an odd coincidence, Ben Jonson and
Dickens both picked on a pump to epitomise the perennial tendency:

Stage-Keeper   But these Master-Poets, they will ha' their owne absurd
courses; they will be inform'd of nothing! . . . would not a
fine Pumpe vpon the Stage ha' done well, for a property
now? and a Punque set vnder . . . hee will not heare o' this!
                              (*Bartholomew Fair*, Ind. ll.26ff)

'We'll have a new show-piece out directly,' said the manager. 'Let me see
– peculiar resources of the establishment – new and splendid scenery – you
must manage to introduce a real pump and two washing tubs . . . That's the
London plan. They look up some dresses and properties, and have a piece
written to fit 'em. Most of the theatres keep an author on purpose.'
                              (*Nicholas Nickleby*, ch. xxii)

Such was, indeed, the London plan – and not only in Victorian times.
Even in 1613 Sir Henry Wotton complained about the Globe
Theatre's richly pedantic production of *Henry VIII*, complete with
its Georges and Garters, its guards in embroidered coats, and 'many
extraordinary circumstances of pomp and majesty, even to the
matting of the stage' (rather than the usual bare boards, or straw). In
1856, Kean's playbill for *A Midsummer Night's Dream* proudly listed
scenes such as the 'Workshop of Quince the Carpenter . . . the
Furniture and Tools . . . are copied from Discoveries at Hercu-
laneum', and even Granville-Barker's relatively austere production
of the same play is remembered chiefly for its famous golden fairies.
The story of Antony and Cleopatra has always presented irresistible
temptations, from Beerbohm Tree's spectacular production of 1906
–7, which sacrificed gobbets of text to grandiose effects, down to 'a
dissolving vision of the Sphinx' opening and closing the play, to the

ill-fated film of *Cleopatra* in 1963. Its makers spent as much on her
barge alone as sufficed to budget the entire contemporary film of *The
Caretaker*, and for all that, the epic was a flop. 'I only came to see the
asp', was Charles Addams' comment.[1]

Properties for mere spectacle are degenerate drama, but at their
best they have an important function. In the title-quotation above,
Vindice voices the exemplary dramatic theory, as he cradles his dead
mistress's skull. It has both a symbolic, and, later, a tactical role.
Vindice's flamboyant first entry, skull in hand, promptly labels him
a melancholic avenger in the Hamlet tradition. Later, chaps smeared
with poison, it will bear an even more important part in his revenge.[2]

Tourneur identified the theory, but applied it with crude gusto.
Other dramatists were more ingenious, and there is a particular
satisfaction in identifying their emblems. Jonson, Master-Poet extraordinary, had every reason to be proud of the propriety with
which his properties bore their part, especially in the elaborate
allegories of his masques and entertainments. But one wonders
whether his unlettered audiences, like T. S. Eliot, might not have
had the experience but missed the meaning, enjoying his heraldic
squirrels and cats without a second thought for their supposed ethical
connotations.[3] A less sophisticated habit of allegory and symbol was
evident in the minor civic pageants prepared for Elizabeth and James,
and was carried over into the theatre also. Thus Nashe, in pageant
fashion, brings on Solstitium *carrying a payre of ballances, with an
houre-glasse in eyther of them: one houre-glasse white, the other blacke*,
symbol of the exactly balanced night and day of the summer solstice,
and prop and figure together are then made to illustrate a brief
homily on moderation. *Arden of Feversham* uses more familiar properties less directly. After their murder of her husband, Alice tellingly
seats her lover, Mosby, in the only backed chair, the proper seat of
the master of the house. And in an earlier scene she rips out the pages
from her prayer-book, replacing them by Mosby's love-letters, and
forcing him to witness this graphic image of her idolatrous love.
Arden is not a sophisticated play; such techniques are merely natural
to the theatre of the time.[4]

Inevitably, Shakespearean examples abound (their selection has
been one of the chief difficulties in this chapter). For Shakespeare
does not only *invent* the properties that concretise a play's abstrac-
tions – for instance, giving the Wars of the Roses an unhistoric origin
in the Temple Garden scene, where rival Yorkists and Lancastrians
pick the roses that symbolise their faction. He also habitually slips his
function as director to his characters, and just as Launce seizes on the

props about him to illustrate his pathetic parting from home – 'this shooe with the hole in it, is my mother . . . this hat is Nan our maid' – so Hamlet calls for recorders and Othello turns his candle into a guttering image of life.[5]

For the instinct to symbolism is as natural in life as it is to the theatre. It is most obvious in superstition, from private obsessions (avoiding the cracks in paving stones) to religious ritual. In the Jewish wedding service the groom smashes a glass beneath his feet, in coincidental enactment of the image from *Pericles*, 'crack the glasse of her virginitie, and make the rest maliable'. It is pervasive from day to day. The connotations of Arden's chair are paralleled in *Sons and Lovers* where 'Morel, as master of the house, sat in his arm-chair' to share out the colliers' weekly takings. Or the gist of *Lear* could be seen in this clumsy little anecdote George Eliot transcribes from Riehl:[6]

Among rustic moral tales and parables, not one is more universal than the story of the ungrateful children, who made their grey-headed father, dependent on them for a maintenance, eat at a wooden trough because he shook the food out of his trembling hands. Then these same ungrateful children observed one day that their own little boy was making a tiny wooden trough; and when they asked him what it was for, he answered – that his father and mother might eat out of it, when he was a man and had to keep them.

Inevitably, then, such symbolism persists, even if in an attenuated form, in modern drama. Take Ibsen's *Wild Duck*, or Chekov's *Seagull* (a dead duck every time), or Albee's contrived punning. Here George is distributing metaphoric finger-snaps to his wife, Martha, and her latest lover, Nick:

George   (*flourishing the flowers*): SNAP WENT THE DRAGONS!! . . . (*taking a snap-dragon, throwing it, spear-like, stem-first at Martha*): SNAP! . . . (*throws one at Nick*): SNAP! . . . *you disgust me.*

Martha   Does it matter to you, George!?

George   (*throws one at her*): SNAP! No, actually, it doesn't . . .

Martha   (*a little afraid*) Truth or illusion, George. Doesn't it matter to you . . . at all?

George   (*without throwing anything*): SNAP! (*Silence.*) You got your answer baby?

Martha   (*sadly*) Got it.

                        (*Who's Afraid of Virginia Woolf*, Act III)

This is even worse than Falstaff, offering Hal his pistol-case: 'theres that will sacke a Citie' (*The Prince drawes it out, and finds it to be a bottle of Sacke*). Such punning on idea and thing is often better suited to the cinema, like the shot in *True Grit* of some children leisurely swinging – taken through the legs of the men about to be hanged. But the essential point persists. Properties have an important role, from the merely spectacular to the meaningful. The range from age to age is neatly spanned by Vindice's quintessentially Jacobean skull, and Osborne's pedestrian ironing board, which, he has said, plays as important a part as any of the characters in *Look Back in Anger*.[7]

Shakespeare's properties: range and development

The elaborate spectacle of *Henry VIII* which so offended Sir Henry Wotton was not, in fact, characteristic of Shakespeare. Like Jonson, he resisted the attractions of frivolous pumps and punks, and a survey of all the properties he demands (whether in explicit directions or through the implicit assumptions of the text) is striking for its modesty. No special large structures are called for; household furnishings are most common. This is true to the fashions of the time, and Arden's only backed chair is a vivid reminder of the comparative poverty of furnishings in a normal Elizabethan home (the rest of the house sat on forms or stools).[8]

   Tables, chairs and stools create a council chamber, with candles by night; with meat and dishes they make a banquet. More detailed directions add flagons of wine, serving men with napkins, logs, coals, spits and baskets, cushions for comfort or state, *Bason and Ewer, and other appurtenances*.[9] Comic scenes tend to rely more heavily on their properties – a buckbasket, dirty linen, a buck's head, or a stool, whips, drums, staves and sandbags – while histories specialise in standard army hardware: crossbows, gauntlets, crowns, corpses, coffins and tents.[10] Properties often mark a character's trade, as Wordsworth later observed in his improbable London scene:

> Now homeward through the thickening hubbub, where
> See, among less distinguishable shapes,
> The Italian, with his frame of images
> Upon his head; with basket at his waist
> The Jew; the stately and slow-moving Turk,
> With freight of slippers piled beneath his arm!
> (*The Prelude* VII.227ff)

Shakespeare concurs, however (*Enter old Gobbo with a Basket*). In both ancient Rome and Elizabethan Venice the poor petitioner carries a basket of doves or pigeons. Rebels carry swords, bucklers, *Staues, Clubs, and other weapons*. Messengers bring papers, lovers tear letters, men read books, women sew or play with flowers, and everyone (bar the women) drinks.[11]

Often the Bad Quartos are more informative. The players in *A Shrew*, for instance, are recognisable by the *packs at their backs*, and Kate is teased by meat that is first withheld from her and then rudely served *vppon [a] daggers point* (a common stage insult). Occasionally the props are unexpected: Timon may bear 'Nothing . . . But nakednesse' from Athens, but in the woods he is miraculously provided with a spade. Some plays have specialised needs, like the tun of tennis balls in *Henry V* or the tagged arrows of *Titus*. But in general the principle seems to have been that of *Henry V*'s Prologue, and poor props were recognised ciphers to a great accompt. Falstaff's regal pantomime could figuratively epitomise the general mode:

Falstaff This chaire shall be my state, this dagger my scepter, and this cushion my crowne.
Prince Thy state is taken for a ioynd stoole, thy golden scepter for a leaden dagger, and thy precious rich crowne for a pittifull bald crowne.

(1 Henry IV II.iv. Q:E2)

Yet even this apparently innocuous comic moment points us back to the emblematic function of properties. For, as J. M. Steadman has pointed out, a pillowed head was a recognised image of Sloth. In his parody of the King, Falstaff unwittingly crowns himself as Accidie personified.[12]

The most obvious function of properties is to suggest a scene. Henslowe's men boasted 'j Hell mought . . . ij marchepanes & the sittie of Rome' among their possessions,[13] but Shakespeare was much less ambitious. Formal scenic properties appear only occasionally, and even in the early, or corrupt plays, Shakespeare uses scenic props not merely for local effect but for thematic ends. The hawks and falconers hallooing that are required by the authorial stage directions to the hunting scene in *2 Henry VI* prompt a sequence of hunting images in the subsequent veiled discussion of ambition; the fishermen dragging a net in *Pericles* are visually apt for the preceding homily on man's fishy morality ('Maister, I maruell how the Fishes liue in the Sea?' 'Why, a Men doe a-land . . .'). In the middle plays, properties dwindle as dialogue takes over. In *Twelfth Night* Olivia turns the stage into her orchard merely by the command, 'Let the Garden doore be shut'; later references consolidate the impression and no prop but the stage door has been used. In a night scene in *Much Ado* Shakespeare sets the Watch to eavesdrop on Conrade and Borachio, using nothing more than a form and the stage door in the tiring house to set the urban scene. It is assumed, instead, in the vivid glances of the text.

Watch	Well masters, we heare our charge, let vs goe sitte here vppon the church bench till twoo . . .
Dogberry	One word more, honest neighbors, I pray you watch about signior Leonatoes doore . . .
	Enter Borachio and Conrade.
Borachio	Stand thee close then vnder this penthouse, for it drissells raine, and I will, like a true drunkard, vtter all to thee . . . Didst thou not heare some body?
Conrade	No, twas the vane on the house.

(Much Ado III.iii. Q:E4–E4ᵛ)

Shakespeare's increasing fatigue with the business of staging is best epitomised by a telling contrast in *Cymbeline*. When actually *in situ*, Iachimo's description of Imogen's bedroom makes feeble poetry but allows the theatre ample potential latitude:

> . . . But my designe
> To note the Chamber, I will write all downe,
> Such, and such pictures: There the window, such
> Th'adornement of her Bed; the Arras, Figures,
> Why such, and such . . .
> (*Cymbeline* II.ii.930ff)

Immediacy is suggested instead by details easy to stage or invisible to the audience – the book she is reading, the candle-flame bending towards her, the mole on her breast. Only later does the bedroom come to life, as Iachimo dwells on it to Posthumus in wicked, erotic detail, down the very Andirons '(I had forgot them) . . . two winking Cupids / Of Siluer, each on one foote standing . . .'[14]

Above all, the characteristic Shakespearean trend, from convention to its rejection or complication, still obtains. The traditionally black-draped tragic stage is used quite straightforwardly at the beginning of *1 Henry VI*, with its funereal hanging and black-dressed cast. But in *All's Well* Shakespeare reverses the expected norms and the ostensible comedy opens with an exactly parallel entry, *'all in blacke'*. The original audiences must have been profoundly disoriented by Shakespeare's ploy: they went to a play whose title proclaimed a comedy, and were faced with the opening of a tragedy.

But the mixture of modes establishes the nature of the play to come. By *Macbeth* the traditional 'Blacke stage for tragedies, and murthers fell' is created by the language alone, and here, instead, there is a possible ironic variant on this convention at the end of the tragedy. For, before the last battle, Macbeth commands: 'Hang out our Banners on the outward walls.' If this implicit stage direction were obeyed, the stage could be colourfully draped for his death and Macduff's victory over the powers of darkness.[15]

The same trend obtains in Shakespeare's use of properties to mark a character's status. These are generally as simple as the changes of costume detailed in the preceding chapter, and the interest lies instead in the Shakespearean inversions and extensions of the traditional symbols of rank.

Often enough these have their origins in civic convention. In *Henry VIII*, for instance, Buckingham is escorted to the scaffold, *the Axe with the edge towards him* – an historical detail lifted from Holinshed rather than a mere theatrical fiction. Audiences who understood the grim significance of such a slight detail, and who were also familiar with the allegorical figures of civic pageantry, are likely to have had no difficulty recognising in Shylock the conventional figure of Justice, knife and scales in either hand, as the dialogue clearly demands ('are there ballance here to weigh the flesh?'; Shylock: 'I haue them ready' . . . Bassanio: 'Why doost thou whet thy knife so earnestly?'), and as Kean, Kemble and Macklin are all recorded as presenting him. They may not, though, have recognised the irony. For Shylock stands as the personification of rigorous justice – without mercy. Staging thus picks up a dominant theme.[16]

In *Lear* there is a more interesting, and less well-known transference of convention, when the Fool catches Lear tipping the disguised Kent for tripping up Oswald, and insists on 'hiring' Kent too, by pressing his coxcombe on him. The dialogue makes it clear that Kent thrice silently resists the offer, and that the Fool finally puts it on his head, willy-nilly, before turning back to address the King:

Fool   Let me hire him too, *here's my Coxcombe.*
Lear   How now my pretty knaue, how dost thou?
Fool   *Sirrah, you were best take my Coxcombe.*
Lear   Why my Boy?
Fool   Why? for taking ones part that's out of fauour, nay, and thou canst not smile as the wind sits, thou'lt catch colde shortly, *there take my Coxcombe*; why this fellow ha's banished two on's Daughters, and did the third a blessing against his will, if thou follow him, *thou must needs weare my Coxcombe.* How now Nunckle? would I had two Cox-

combes and two Daughters . . . If I gaue them all my liuing, I'ld keepe my Coxcombes my selfe, *there's mine*, beg another of thy Daughters.

(*King Lear* I.iv.625ff. My italics)

It is fitting livery for the fool's service both are about to share, and for the point to be theatrically effective, it must be staged.

In such extensions of a prop's thematic point, the interrelation of verbal and visual imagery is constantly evident, as even a simple example from *2 Henry VI* can illustrate. For here Duke Humphrey's formal surrender of his staff of office is *staged* in a little ritual, but the larger implications of this conventional rite are re-emphasised by Humphrey's later *verbal* image, as he is delivered prisoner into Cardinal Beaufort's custody: 'Ah, thus King Henry throwes away his Crutch, / Before his Legges be firme to beare his Body.'[17] As we have seen before, such interplay between staged and linguistic versions of the same image can span the entire canon, and there is an interesting example of this in *The Tempest*.

Here Ferdinand and Caliban enter to two consecutive scenes, each, according to the stage directions, bearing logs – a burden which not only visually marks them both as Prospero's slaves, but is the starting-point to a contrast between them. For in effect both act out Hamlet's image of life (an image that recurs verbally elsewhere in the canon). 'Who would fardels beare, / To grunt and sweat vnder a wearie life?' Each answers Hamlet's question in turn as, grunting and sweating under their loads, they enter to voice their particular philosophies of malediction or acceptance:

Enter Caliban, with a burthen of Wood (a noyse of Thunder heard).
Caliban   All the infections that the Sunne suckes vp
           From Bogs, Fens, Flats, on Prosper fall . . .
           (*Tempest* II.ii.1038ff)

Enter Ferdinand (bearing a Log).
Ferdinand There be some Sports are painful; and their labor
           ~~Delight in them [sets] off: Some kindes of basenesse~~
           Are nobly vndergon; and most poore matters
           Point to rich ends.
           (*Tempest* III.i.1235ff)

So a philosophic image is turned into a stage picture. Such a delicately allusive, recapitulatory use of old images is incidentally typical of this play.[18]

Thematic and structural use of properties

It is never difficult to trace the Shakespearean patterns of development. But this study of his properties must lack the thematic structure naturally evolving in some earlier chapters, such as those on kneeling or costume. For there is no single symbolic point ordering Shakespeare's use of properties; it is necessarily random, varying from property to property and play to play. Indeed, not all properties even demonstrate Shakespeare's conscious control of his material. A study of his use of letters, for instance, fulfils the opposite and equally interesting function of betraying some embarrassing Shakespearean lapses.

Characters reading or tearing papers was a common explanatory dumb show which Shakespeare exploited with increasing deftness. The development of presentation has already been glanced at in an earlier chapter (see pp. 23–4 above); more telling is the unexpected insight a tally of such letters can give us into poor plotting. In several plays a number of letters are hard worked keeping the plot and its scattered characters together. But in the extremest cases they betray Shakespeare's low cunning as he tries to rub out his tracks: he camouflages the influx of letters vital to the plot by making his characters distribute many others whose function and contents are never revealed and are, of course, non-existent. In this respect *Lear* is statistically outstanding; letters appear twelve times functionally and three times as mere camouflage. It says something for Shakespeare's skill that we tend not to notice; much more painful is his readiness to pull explanatory letters out of the air in the hurried conclusions of both comedy and tragedy. No chronological development is evident here: Shakespeare is inveterately slipshod over narrative organisation.[19]

At the end of *The Merchant*, for instance, Portia blandly declares:

> . . . Anthonio you are welcome,
> And I haue better newes in store for you
> Than you expect: vnseale this letter soone,
> There you shall finde three of your Argosies
> Are richly come to harbour sodainly.
> You shall not know by what strange accident
> I chaunced on this letter.
> *Antonio* I am dumb.
>
> (*Merchant of Venice* V.i.Q:K^v)

Like Antonio, we are dumb, and can only admire Shakespeare's impertinence. We 'shall not know', either, what easy morality overtook Portia, prompting her to read a letter not addressed to her (and then to seal it again), let alone how she came to pick it up, or why Antonio's fortunes should so opportunely be mended. Rymer, in his turn, was justly incensed by the ending of *Othello*, where the dead Roderigo is pressed into posthumus postal service. Not only does Cassio tell us that 'euen but now he spake, / After long seeming dead' (mercifully, off-stage – but even so a risky enough reprise of Desdemona's resuscitation to clear Othello). Piling insult on injury, Shakespeare conjures then not one but two letters from Roderigo's pockets, to corroborate his and Iago's crimes. As Rymer says, 'Never was old deputy Recorder in a Country Town, with his spectacles in summoning up the evidence, at such a puzzle: so blunder'd, and bedoultefied: as is our Poet, to have a good riddance: And get the Catastrophe off his hands!'[20]

Yet this cavalier attitude to the mere mechanics of plot is balanced by Shakespeare's equally consistent concern for thematic point. Thus the staging of letters is rarely interesting, while their wording is often pointed. For instance, the love-letter Hamlet wrote to Ophelia in the old days of their courtship is not merely a parody of the conventional love lyric, but betrays a crucial trait – Hamlet's habitual academic scepticism, that evidently existed before the play began. One could compare the unimportant exchange from *Coriolanus*, 'Friend, art thou certaine this is true?' . . . 'As certaine as I know the Sun is fire', with Hamlet's little rhyme:

> *Doubt* thou the starres are fire,
> *Doubt* that the Sunne doth moue,
> *Doubt* truth to be a lyer,
> But neuer doubt I loue.
> (*Hamlet* II.ii.Q2:E4. My italics)

By the same token the Ghost's truth is questioned and the tragedy begins. Similarly, in *Julius Caesar*, Shakespeare goes out of his way to add to Plutarch's wording of the letters thrown in at Brutus's window: 'Brutus thou sleep'st; awake, *and see thy selfe.*' The last phrase evidently betrays the hand of Cassius, the anonymous author: shortly before, he had asked Brutus: 'Tell me good Brutus, Can you see your face?' So either Shakespeare or Cassius is at pains to suggest that his persuasions have a general currency. A shared moment in *Richard II* and *Lear* illustrates Shakespeare's prudent re-cycling of useful material in the same context. For, as Matthew Black has pointed out, a trivial joke in *Richard II* (Shakespeare's addition to a straight dramatisation of Holinshed) is turned to thematic ends in *Lear*. York had seized the treacherous letter from Aumerle's bosom with the following exchange: Aumerle: 'My Lord, tis nothing'; York: 'No matter then who see it'.[21] In *Lear* the same episode is repeated as a put-up job by Edmund, when Gloucester catches sight of the false letter of Edgar's treachery. Now, however, the dialogue is extended to reintroduce two ideas thematic to the play – the dreadful and paradoxical importance of an apparent 'nothing', and the questionable validity of sight:

Gloucester	What Paper were you reading?
Bastard	Nothing my Lord.
Gloucester	No? what needed then that terrible dispatch of it into your Pocket? The quality of nothing hath not such need to hide it selfe. Let's see: come, if it bee nothing, I shall not neede Spectacles . . .

(King Lear I.ii.365ff)

Shakespeare's structural use of properties inevitably leads us to a closer scrutiny of the plays in which they appear, for they are rarely as straightforward as they seem. Hamlet, for instance, may appear to be merely typified as the conventional melancholic when he holds Yorick's skull in his hands, much as the sight of Cleopatra with her asps vividly visualises Antony's old pet-name for her as 'my Serpent of old Nyle' (although subtler readings for this image have been offered). But the skull's function is larger than this, just as the gravediggers' interlude is far more than Bradley's moment of comic relief before the strenuous last scene. This skull is no mere emblem; it is a real skull, and as Hamlet turns it in his hands, sniffs it ('pah'), and responds to it ('my gorge rises at it'), he can be seen literally coming to grips with death, previously an academic abstraction that had obsessed him from the play's beginning. This physical confrontation with the reality is climactic and pivotal; once Hamlet has come to terms with death, he can, and does grapple with all the other problems that he had dallied with hitherto. Hence follow his struggle with Laertes, his admission of love for Ophelia, above all his new-found and liberating resignation ('if it be, tis not to come'), his revenge of his father's murder, and his own release into the felicity of death.[22]

Hamlet with Yorick's skull is a flamboyant stage image that has epitomised our mental picture of him for centuries. In *Romeo and Juliet* a far less obtrusive prop does not mark a structural turning-point, but epitomises in miniature the play's total structural mode.

Why, one wonders, should Shakespeare direct so carefully the Nurse's entry to tell Juliet of Tybalt's death, and Romeo's banishment, the day before their wedding was to be consummated? *Enter Nurse with cords*. And yet this apparently innocuous entry is symptomatic. *Romeo and Juliet* is built on a sharply marked pattern of progression and reversal – a pattern which is not only evident in the see-saw motion of the plot, but is continually stressed by the dialogue. Witness the Friar's resumé ('I married them, and their stolne marriage day / Was Tibalts doomesday'), or Capulet's extended antitheses at Juliet's 'death' ('Our instruments to melancholy bells, / Our wedding cheare to a sad buriall feast: / Our solemne himnes to sullen dyrges change . . .'). It dominates whole speeches, like the Friar's consolation of Romeo (III.iii.); it recurs in minor images ('Afore mee, it is so very late that wee may call it early by and by', and again, 'Is she not downe so late or vp so early?'). Staging re-echoes the total mode. So the Nurse's entry *with cords* (implicit token of Romeo's approach and the marriage's happy consummation) is followed by her incoherent laments, 'A weraday, hees dead, hees dead.' Yet, for all her and Juliet's subsequent grieving, the ropes remain a silent, ironical reminder of the scene's ultimately gratifying issue. Later a larger, human property is made to fulfil the same dualistic function, as Juliet drinks her potion and *fals vpon her bed within the Curtaines*, ostensibly dead, while on the main stage the happy bustle for her wedding to County Paris begins. This particular staged juxtaposition neatly illustrates Johnson's praise, that Shakespeare's plays exhibit 'the real state of sublunary nature . . . in which the loss of one is the gain of another; in which, at the same time, the reveller is hasting to his wine, and the mourner burying his friend.' At the same time, Johnson's general encomium inadvertently identifies *Rome and Juliet*'s particular structural mode. It informs both narrative whole, and minor stage and verbal images alike, so that, with Coleridge, 'still we can only say, our tongues defrauding our eyes, this is another oak leaf.'[23]

It is hardly surprising that *Richard II*, *Romeo and Juliet*'s close rival and contemporary, should vie with it in such controlled use of properties. Nor have the play's producers been blind to their silent potential. John Barton's well-known production of the play (Stratford 1973–4) was criticised as 'litera'-minded, blackboard-scratching', since he provided a tub of earth at stage front for the actors to finger at every reference (and there are many) to England's soil. But such theatrical intrusion was perhaps particularly unnecessary in a play whose hero takes on himself the role of producer, and, like Duke Senior, 'Findes tongues in trees, bookes in the running brookes, / Sermons in stones', and an image of his own cause in everything.[24] His development in his use of illustrative properties is significant, since he uses them to mark his own fall, and his increasingly economical use of them also mirrors his own growth in spiritual stature.

At his resignation of the crown, Richard carefully arranges himself and Bolingbroke, the crown held between them. This is not merely a static, graphic tableau for the play's climax, but also the starting-point for a pivotal stage image which is deployed at length in Richard's poetic commentary. For Richard compares himself and Bolingbroke to two buckets in a well. His is the heavier, 'downe, vnseene, and full of Water', while Bolingbroke is 'The emptier euer dancing in the ayre.' The image ostensibly describes their contrasting fortunes, Bolingbroke at his height while Richard is at the nadir. Implicitly, however, it contrasts with the Gardener's image shortly before, where Richard and Bolingbroke had been compared to two scales, Richard's empty save for himself 'And some few vanities that make him light', while Bolingbroke's was weighted by his own greatness and the support of England's peers. Richard's increasing gravity in the latter part of the play is thus marked by the clear shift of balance between the two images, the second, and more important of the two, being *staged*. Richard's increasing gravity is incidentally also marked by another verbal parallel, for at his return to England he spoke lightly of his possible loss of the crown: 'Say, is my kingdome lost? why twas my care, / And what losse is it to be rid of care?' But when the loss is real, frivolity turns to responsibility and regal poise is gained as the crown is surrendered: 'The Cares I giue, I haue, though giuen away, / They 'tend the Crowne, yet still with me they stay.'[25]

The paradoxes of Richard's continuing loss of external power, and increase in internal gravity, are marked by yet another brilliant stage image, another bright focal point for the scene. His resignation of the crown is a series of negations, with the formal divestment at its centre:

> Now, marke me how I will vndoe my selfe . . .
> With mine owne Teares I wash away my Balme,
> With mine owne Hands I giue away my Crowne,
> With mine owne Tongue denie my sacred State . . .
> (*Richard II* IV.i.2124ff)

As Professor Mahood points out, Richard's first words proclaim the theme in an unstageable pun: 'I, no; no, I' ("Aye, no . . ." and "I know no I" – 'for', as Richard immediately adds, 'I must nothing bee'). It is dwelt on with increasing explicitness:

> No Lord of thine . . .
> No, nor no mans Lord: I haue no Name, no Title;
> No, not that Name was giuen me at the Font . . .
> Oh, that I were a Mockerie King of Snow,
> Standing before the Sunne of Bullingbrooke,
> To melt my selfe away in Water-drops . . .
>   (*Richard II* IV.i.2176ff)

When he calls for the mirror, and throws it to the ground, shattering his own reflection, he simply provides a stage image of all the verbal negations that had gone before. He literally undoes himself:

> A brittle Glory shineth in this Face,
> As brittle as the Glory, is the Face,
> For there it is, crackt in an hundred shiuers.
>   (*Richard II* IV.i.2210ff)

But here again stage image ostensibly marks the end of Richard's fall, whereas in fact it implies the beginning of his spiritual growth. For, as Bolingbroke sourly observes of this distasteful display, 'The shadow of your Sorrow hath destroy'd / The shadow of your Face' – a criticism Richard promptly turns to his own advantage, boasting, like Hamlet:

> 'Tis very true, my Griefe lyes all within,
> And these externall manner of Laments,
> Are meerely shadowes, to the vnseene Griefe,
> That swells with silence in the tortur'd Soule.
> There lyes the substance . . .
>   (*Richard II* IV.i.2219ff)

Much the same point had been made earlier, in his image of the bucket, 'vnseene, and full of Water'. As Richard loses all the outward forms of power, 'The name, and all th'addition to a King' that Lear mistakenly chose to retain, his inner substance increases, and nothing brings him all things. The paradox is exploited in both these crucial stage images. Further, the greater Richard becomes in himself, the less he needs external properties to illustrate and explain his own state. By his last soliloquy in the Tower, he can make his brain the female to his soul, and create a kingdom in his mind.[26]

CHAPTER 10

Sources, sub-plots and conclusions

Meer-Craft	By m'faith you are cunning i' the Chronicle, Sir.
Fitz-Dottrell	No, I confesse I ha't from the Play-bookes,
	And thinke they'are more authentique.
	(Ben Jonson: *The Devil is an Ass* II.iv.12–4)

Critics, more than other men, are apt to 'construe things after their fashion, / Cleane from the purpose of the things themselues.'[1] It may seem that a spurious significance has sometimes been wrung from innocent stage business in the foregoing study. Interpretation will always remain open to question. But a comparison of the plays with their sources conclusively demonstrates the conscious nature of Shakespeare's inclusion of theatrical effects. For it is these, above all, that turn a prose or verse narrative into the drama that is seen in action. To reconsider the material of the preceding chapters in terms of its relationship to the sources raises a number of interesting conclusions. Let us begin with the technique of source-translation.

The dramatisation of Shakespeare's sources

The span of independent invention covered in Shakespeare's translations of his sources into theatrical terms is neatly illustrated by three related moments in *1 Henry VI* – a fitting play to start from.

Dramatisation at its crudest simply transfers the action of the source onto the stage. At the surprise attack on Le Mans, Hall says some of the French 'rose out of their beddes in their shertes, and lepte over the walles'. So Shakespeare directs: *The French leape ore the walles in their shirts*.[2]

More inventive dramatisation gives its incidents theatrical reality by supporting dialogue; at its best, this dialogue can suggest a larger significance to the scene. So Hall continues that other Frenchmen fled 'naked . . . for saving of their lives, levyng behynde theim all their apparell'. But Shakespeare dovetails this with Hall's earlier assurance, that Talbot's 'only name was, and yet is dredful to the

Frenche nacion'. According to Shakespeare's stage directions, an English soldier enters *crying, a Talbot, a Talbot* and the French *flye, leauing their Clothes behind*. The soldier then scoops up his booty, commenting, 'The Cry of Talbot serues me for a Sword,'[3] and Talbot's dread power is epitomised.

Finally, the dramatist *invents* the action that presents the implications of his story in theatrical terms. So Shakespeare completes his portrayal of Talbot in a fictional scene where the Countess of Auvergne takes him captive. She boasts that just as she possessed his picture, now she has the substance, which she will take prisoner. He laughs:

> Talbot   No, no, I am but shadow of my selfe:
> You are deceiu'd, my substance is not here;
> For what you see is but the smallest part,
> And least proportion of Humanitie . . .
> *Winds his Horne, Drummes strike vp, a Peale of Ordenance:*
> *Enter Souldiors . . .*
> . . . Talbot is but shadow of himselfe.
> These are his substance, sinewes, armes and strength.
> (*1 Henry VI* II.iii.891ff. SD probably authorial)

And Shakespeare's Talbot, but not Hall's, dies when his reinforcements fail to reach him.[4]

In the Roman and English history plays there is a clear premium on accuracy, and much of the dramatisation is of the first kind, though it is by no means crude. The arrest of Hastings in *Richard III*, the complex manoeuvres at Philippi and Corioli (whose accuracy only emerges on consultation of Plutarch), the scene confronting the guards in Cleopatra's monument, even Charmion's last words – all these are impressive instances of Shakespeare's care and discretion in bringing history back to life on the stage.[5] But even in this, the simplest stage of narrative-to-dramatic translation, Shakespeare's technique extends from the straightforward transference of Holinshed and Foxe into the elaborate stage directions for Queen Katharine's trial, Anne Boleyn's wedding, or Elizabeth's christening, in the flat veracity of *All is True (Henry VIII)*, to the unostentatious control of every known detail of Caesar's assassination – through dialogue alone.[6] At the technical mid-point between the two is the outspoken artifice of *Henry V*, where the representative symbolism continually forced on the dramatist is frankly admitted ('Into a thousand parts diuide one Man'), and Pistol's noisy triumph over one grovelling Frenchman epitomises Holinshed's account of the French rout at Agincourt. Egregious Cyphers to this great Accompt![7]

Such substitution of the individual for the general is the first independent step of dramatic translation. It is quickly utilised in the earliest plays, in both symbolic and realistic scenes. Hall's remark, that the battle of Towton was 'in maner unnaturall, for in it the sonne fought against the father, the brother against the brother', is represented by the emblematic entry and laments of *a Sonne that hath kill'd his Father, at one doore: and a Father that hath kill'd his Sonne at another doore*, each with the requisite corpse. Hall mentions Edward IV's habitual lamentations for the dead Clarence, 'for whose lyfe not one creature would make intercession', whenever he was sued for pardon for any criminal condemned to death. Shakespeare concretises the idea in the eloquent scene in which Edward grants Derby remission for his servant's capital offence, while accusing himself in Hall's terms. Elsewhere Hotspur's disappointing correspondence with many confederates is evoked by one letter read on stage.[8] In such representative scenes, not only individual actors and action replace general statement, but the incident often provides a partial commentary on the rest of the play. So, for instance, Hall describes Richard III's nightmare devils on the eve of Bosworth Field, sensibly attributing them to his guilty conscience. In the *True Tragedy* the devils turn into his victims' ghosts in a nightmare Richard *describes*. Shakespeare, utilising and surpassing both his sources, *personifies* Richard's guilt and Richmond's security, the ghosts appear in the flesh (as it were), and recapitulate the complex action of the play as effectively as the play's prehistory was given a personal life in the choric laments of the four queens. More subtly, later, Shakespeare combines pointed gesture and emphatic imagery to turn Ligarius's rejection of his sickness into a stage image of Brutus's healing revolution – the implication undreamt of in Plutarch's account.[9]

Even when the dramatisation is at its most servile and Shakespeare merely readjusts his prose source into blank verse (as in Katherine's defence, the list of French and English dead at Agincourt, or of Antony's royal allies in *Antony and Cleopatra*), he will demand the action that gives life to the dialogue. Volumnia's pleas to Coriolanus are accurately versified Plutarch, but for her anxious observation of her son's reactions: 'Nay, go not from vs thus.'[10] And these invented actions, which give the audience the necessary visual focus for its attention, are promptly turned to a larger purpose. In *Richard III* Shakespeare ignores Buckingham's splenetic absence from the coronation banquet, in order to show him emblematically handing Richard up into the throne he helped him steal. In *Measure for Measure* Shakespeare, not his sources, Cinthio or Whetstone, makes his Duke pointedly enter Vienna on the arms of his two supporting deputies. In *Antony and Cleopatra*, Shakespeare, not Plutarch, calls for the insignificant entry of *Anthony, Caesar, Octauia betweene them,* so embodying Caesar's later description of her as 'the peece of Vertue which is set / Betwixt vs, as the Cyment of our loue.' Shakespeare makes Antony significantly sit down when he has 'lost command', and rejects Caxton's touching scene, where 'Andromeda' (Andromache) kneels to Hector with her children in her arms, for Cassandra's ominous tableau, Priam leaning on Hector, 'and all Troy on thee, / Fall all together'.[11]

Such slight details of added action broaden into invented symbolic scenes like the Talbot–Auvergne scene. The shallow superficiality of Shakespeare's Proteus, and not Montemayor's Don Felix, is clinched by his acceptance of Sylvia's portrait in lieu of her person, 'since', as she says, 'your falsehood shall become you well / To worship shadowes, and adore false shapes.' By contrast Valentine, outlawed in the forest, realises with greater honesty that physical separation may destroy his love. Exploiting the hypnotic theme of the superficial image once more, Shakespeare substitutes for the prosaic ring Holinshed's Richard gave Bolingbroke at his deposition, the mirror he shatters in a flamboyant final annihilation of all the outward forms that had made up his nature as King.[12] Shakespeare introduces three caskets from the *Gesta Romanorum* into a story from *Il Pecorone* as the central symbol uniting both plots of *The Merchant of Venice*, having reversed the mottos of the *Gesta*'s first two caskets, altered the contents of the second and third, and invented his own motto for the leaden casket, which becomes the play's key.[13] In *Antony and Cleopatra* Shakespeare introduces the Bacchanalian dance, with its pointed arrangement (*Enobarbus places them hand in hand,* SD most probably authorial) and refrain ('Cup vs till the world go round'), clear image of the unsteady world and reeling world-sharers who hold it in their hands. Unveiling, and enthronement in the seat of justice, so precisely used in *Measure for Measure*, to the discomfiture of 'our proude Justlers of peace' (Whetstone's pun) is the theatrical symbolisation of Shakespeare's theme in this play, and both theme and illustrations have no part in Whetstone's work.[14] Shakespeare introduces Macbeth's significant refusal to arm, and the equally meaningful moment when Banquo's ghost (which is Shakespeare's invention) twice 'pushes' him from his stool, just as its line is to oust him from the throne. Insofar as his reminiscence of the play can be trusted, Forman's account of this scene suggests that the action was staged, and not merely metaphorical.[15] On a mere hint from Greene,

Shakespeare creates the sheep-shearing scene in *The Winter's Tale*, in which Perdita's flower-distribution is the dramatic vehicle for a crucial discussion of bastardy (rejected by Perdita, proof of her purity) and cross-breeding (approved by Polixenes, contradicting his later irritable rejection of Florizel and Perdita's union). Shakespeare introduces the recurrent rituals of *Lear* and the last romances: the symbolic deaths and revivals of Imogen and Hermione, the reunion after 'death' of Gloucester with Edgar, Lear with Cordelia, Hermione with Leontes, Imogen with Posthumus and Cymbeline, Ferdinand with Alonso, which all simply act out Leontes' punning promise that repentance 'Shall be my re*creation*.' By the fulfilment of repentance the father finds himself born again in his new-found children, and husband and wife, reunited, effect a mutual resurrection.[16] And the whole sequence of unreal deaths in *Cymbeline*, whereby Imogen 'dies' to each member of her family in turn (father and mother, husband and brothers), is summed up in the extraordinary, wholly ritualistic vignette preceding her final reconciliation with her husband. As often in such emblematic scenes, a commentary to elucidate it is provided. Imogen is still disguised as Fidele:

Posthumus	. . . Oh Imogen!
	My Queene, my life, my wife: oh Imogen,
	Imogen, Imogen.
Imogen	Peace my Lord, heare, heare.
Posthumus	Shall's haue a play of this?
	Thou scornfull Page, there lye thy part.
Pisanio	Oh Gentlemen, helpe,
	. . . Oh my Lord Posthumus,
	You ne're kill'd Imogen till now . . .
	(*Cymbeline* V.v.3507ff)

Inevitably, this death, like all her others, is Shakespeare's invention.[17]

The personified stage image: the human parallel

One of the most fascinating general characteristics of Shakespeare's theatrical translation of his sources in his habitual invention of a parallel sub-plot. At first its function is geometric, as it were: fun in *The Comedy of Errors* is simply compounded by Shakespeare's second set of servant-twins. This develops into a standard, recurrent pattern: the re-enactment of the main plot at a cruder level, which at once modifies and stresses the main theme. *Love's Labour's Lost* has no known narrative source; Shakespeare makes Armado impregnate Jaquenetta and dismisses him to win her at the plough, in base reflection of the more refined courtship of Navarre's lords and ladies. Shakespeare supplements Lodge's couples by Touchstone and Awdrey, whose frank lust is a commentary on the other loves of *As You Like It*. Sir Andrew's barren courtship (which has no source) ironically mirrors Orsino's self-deceiving infatuation in *Twelfth Night*. Shakespeare adds both Beatrice and Benedick (possibly on a hint from Castiglione's *Courtier*) and the Watch, to the main plot of *Much Ado*; eavesdropping activates all three plots and the Watch are the only set of characters not led astray by what they overhear. In *The Merchant of Venice* Shakespeare introduces the parallel between Antonio's and Portia's love for Bassanio; Gratiano; and imports and alters Jessica and Lorenzo from their embryos in Marlowe's *Jew of Malta*. Portia and Bassanio are thus doubled, *Errors*-fashion, in the light-hearted Nerissa and Gratiano, but the generous love of Portia and Antonio, both of whom are prepared to give and hazard all their wealth for Bassanio, finds a tarnished reflection in the more mercenary elopement of Jessica and Lorenzo. This technique, perfected in the comedies, governs the later history plays also, Falstaff's relevance to *Henry IV* depending on this principle. It is most obvious in Hal's interview with his father, and its mock enactment by him and Falstaff earlier in the play, but informs the sub-plot elsewhere also. The lack of faith among Hotspur's rebels, for instance, is paralleled by the staged fiasco at Gadshill, and Falstaff's complaint – 'a plague vpon it when theeues can not be true to one another' – serves as a commentary for both.[18]

These invented sub-plots present the enacted stage image in its most fully developed form. For, increasingly frequently, the intentional crudeness of these largely sourceless parallels is not merely ethical, but technical. Their structural function is to present the play's themes in simplified and enacted, physical terms. For instance, in *All's Well* Helena is essentially noble: as the Countess quickly tells us, 'she deriues her honestie' (from her father), 'and atcheeues her goodnesse' (by her deeds). For all her internal virtues, however, Bertram rejects her because she is unworthy of his inherited nobility – an outward grace that is his by form, and not by nature, and which is specifically forfeited by his ill deeds. Shakespeare, and not Painter, firmly establishes this in the symbolic moment when Bertram gives Diana the ring which is the 'honour longing to our house' and so trades his inherited honour for a night's infidelity.[19] But Shakespeare clarifies the contrast between Bertram and Helena even further by introducing Parolles, who simply echoes Bertram's inessential nobility in the two standard Shakespearean images of outward show – loud words and flamboyant dress. Bertram, like Parolles, is all outside; in Lafeu's words, there is no kernel in either of these light nuts. The trial scene in which Parolles is *literally* unblindfolded and made to face up to his own lies is thus the stage equivalent of Bertram's interrogation in the last act, when the scales *metaphorically* fall from his eyes, and he is forced to admit his own folly. Similarly, in *The Tempest*, Stephano and Trinculo are visibly muddied by their pursuit of glistering apparel, while Sebastian and Antonio are only morally sullied by their planned treachery. Stephano and Trinculo are drunk stupid while the rest of the cast, in turn, are more refinedly sunk in an enchanted daze.

Hamlet and *Lear* are particularly interesting in this context. *Hamlet* is outstanding for its large number of illustrative parallels, and for Hamlet's awareness of them. 'What doe you call the play?' Claudius demands. 'The Mousetrap, mary how: tropically' (or, in the First Quarto's accentuation of the pun, 'trapically'), is his reply. 'This play is the Image of a murther doone . . .' The larger play enclosing it contains a series of such illustrative tropes, or figures, and Hamlet dominates them all. 'How all occasions doe informe against me' is the play's structural motto, as Hamlet discovers his own cause in all things, from the Player's feigned grief to the mindless belligerence of Fortinbras's army, from Laertes ('by the image of my Cause, I see / The Portraiture of his'), to the popularity of the child-actors, whose usurpation of the City Tragedians' esteem is image for Hamlet of Claudius's ill-merited popularity at his accession.[20] But Hamlet is surrounded by further reflections of which he is himself unaware. Both King and Player King echo his meditations on the dulling of intentions by delay, while in his Pyrrhus speech the Player acts out the moment to come, when Hamlet's sword will hang above the prostrate king, and delay to strike. It is typical of *Hamlet*, most problematic of all problem plays, that in it alone Shakespeare's additions should be wholly unassessable (no Ur-Hamlet being extant). But, on the comedies' showing, it is at least a plausible guess that Shakespeare brought together the girl set to trap Hamlet, the courtier killed in the closet scene (both present in Saxo and Belleforest), and the young man who kills Hamlet, into the family that parallels Hamlet's own.[21] Equally characteristic of Shakespeare would be the pointed contrast between Ophelia's real madness at her father's death, and Hamlet's traditional feigned lunacy at his; be-

tween Laertes' unthinking vengefulness and Hamlet's nobler uncer-
tainty; between Laertes' treachery with the poisoned rapiers and the
justice of Hamlet's unplanned revenges, each enemy dying in the
trap of his own making.

In *Lear*, by contrast, both plots have well-established sources, and
Shakespeare's originality and skill lie in the effect achieved by their
juxtaposition. For the story of the Paphlagonian Prince becomes
symbolic *by* its paralleling Leir's tragedy. The bastard son of the
Arcadia is turned into Gloucester's natural son, the actual equivalent
of Lear's morally unnatural daughters; the blinding of the Paphlagonian Prince, staged in Gloucester's appalling torture, becomes the
visible physical equivalent of Lear's emotional torment (and
Shakespeare cuts the attempted murder of Leir in order to preserve
the distinction between his two plots). Gloucester's physical blindness is Lear's spiritual night (and Lear's madness too owes very little
to the Leir sources). Yet again, the Paphlagonian Prince's mere
longing for suicide is enacted in Gloucester's leap, and this frankly
symbolic death and resurrection are the stage image of Lear's healing
sleep and his awakening (also sourceless).[22] Just as Shakespeare
transforms the simple symbolism of his sources, in which thunder
warns of divine retribution, what else? – and poor clothes obviously
indicate shrunken fortunes,[23] so he imports a whole range of moral
significances unintimated by either of his sources. And much of the
play's complexity depends on the cross-currents between Gloucester
and Lear's stories, the harsh physical symbolism of the one simultaneously paralleling and contrasting with the broader metaphysical
content of the other.

'Tell me good Brutus', Cassius said, 'Can you see your face?' and
was answered: 'No Cassius, / For the eye sees not it selfe but by
reflection, / By some other things.' The stage images presented by
Shakespeare's parallel plots are a pointedly inadequate reflection of
their central object. We can understand Lear better by seeing his
similarities to Gloucester, and then how he differs from him; Hamlet's subtler virtues emerge on contrast with Laertes. Parolles betrays
Bertram's smooth vice in his own brash roguery. Timon's justifiable
loathing of man, a crescent conviction, is played off against the static
– Apemantus's mere habit of misanthropy. This 'poore vnmanly
Melancholly sprung / From change of [fortune]' (as Apemantus
sneeringly calls it) is learnt by experience and has all the cogency
Apemantus's railing lacks. As Fluellen concluded his meditation on
the unlikely similarities between Henry of Monmouth and Alexander of Macedon, 'there is figures in all things'. Shakespeare's habitual

creation of the illustrative theatrical image merely reaches its largest form in the mirror-action of his minor characters and parallel plots.[24]

Verbal and visual imagery

For Shakespeare, indeed, there are figures in all things, including his sources. One of the most suggestive aspects of his use of his sources is the interplay of verbal and visual imagery between the two. Occasionally an event in the source is merely echoed in an image in the play: for instance, behind Henry IV's famous 'Vneasie lies the head that weares a crowne' may lurk Hólinshed's disquisition on the King's sensational near-assassination by a spiked engine 'like a caltrop' that was hidden in his bed.[25] More far-reaching is Holinshed's account of the six-months' darkness descending on Scotland after the murder of King Duff, and the subsequent execution of Donwald and his wife 'before [they] saw anie sunne after the murder was committed'. Shakespeare utilises the fact and extends its consequence, introducing the Macbeths' repeated invocations of the night that is to fall on Duncan ('O neuer / Shall Sunne that Morrow see'), which, like all bloody instructions, here as in *Hamlet*, return 'To plague th'Inuenter', Lady Macbeth most obviously dying in the dark.[26]

Here a historical event is responsible both for a play's recurrent verbal imagery, and its stage embodiment (the sleepwalking scene). However, it is more common for a *phrase* in the source to suggest a visual effect in the play. If Shakespeare read Latin freely, then it is for instance possible that Richard's offer of his breast to the sword he puts in Anne's hands sprang from a rhetorical flourish in Legge's *Richardus Tertius*.[27] Less dubious is the barmicidal banquet in which Shakespeare's Timon 'sprinkles' (the word is twice repeated) water on his guests. Its original source is clearly the feasts of the dead attended by Plutarch's Timon, where, in North's words, 'they make sprincklings and sacrifices for the dead'. Lucian, and not Boiardo, describes Timon's flatterers in parasitic terms ('Even while the poor wretch was having his liver eaten by so many vultures, he thought they were his friends . . . When they had finally eaten him down to the bone, and sucked the marrow, they left him dry'). The image is not only recurrently echoed in the play's imagery ('Oh you Gods! What a number of men eats Timon?'), but is staged in the banquet that is Shakespeare's invention, and its inset emblem, the Masque of the Five Senses, all of which have been *fed* by Timon, according to the Masque's presenter. Like the arming scene in *Antony and Cleopatra*, this masque is evidently a Shakespearean after-thought, specifically introduced in order to present a central theme in theatrical terms.[28]

Yet again, Holinshed says Macbeth invited Banquo and Fleance 'to come to a supper that he had prepared for them, which was in deed, as he had devised, present death', and Shakespeare once again repeats the fact, but continues to twist it against Macbeth, who is forced to attend his own grim banquet of the dead. This invented scene becomes the epitome of Macbeth's reign, not only Macbeth recalling it in the metaphors of one of his last speeches ('I haue almost forgot the taste of Feares . . . I haue supt full with horrors'), but an innocent Lord echoing Macbeth in his hopes for a time when 'we may againe / Giue to our Tables meate, sleepe to our Nights: / Free from our Feasts, and Banquets bloody kniues.' As Rosencrantz tells Claudius, the state suffers with its King, and Scotland shares Macbeth's diseased rest and his uneasy meals, haunted by murder.[29]

As these examples show, the interplay from verbal to visual image between Shakespeare and his sources spills over into a larger and more signiıcant traffic within the Shakespearean play. Shakespeare's stage images are habitually supported by related linguistic images which combine to form a single metaphoric pattern. Richard's historic descent from Flint Castle walls is made symbolic by the recurrent preceding sun-king comparison, and clinched in Richard's final self-association with Phaeton as he descends. Froissart (whom Shakespeare probably had not read) reports that Richard handed his crown to Bolingbroke; in the play the two bucket-and-scales images which give the staged scene its pivotal significance are Shakespeare's own. Shakespeare introduces the thematic arming and disarming imagery scattered through *Antony and Cleopatra*, and its two theatrical foci when Cleopatra is seen to arm Antony for victorious battle, and when Antony disarms at Cleopatra's 'death'.[30] In Iago Shakespeare returns to his youthful description of Sinon, who

>   . . . like a constant and confirmed Deuill,
>   . . . entertain'd a show, so seeming iust,
> And therein so ensconc't his secret euill,
> That Iealousie it selfe could not mistrust,
> False creeping Craft, and Periurie should thrust
>   Into so bright a daie, such blackfac'd storms,
>   Or blot with Hell-born sin such Saint-like formes.
>   (*Rape of Lucrece* ll. 1513–1519)

Othello is thick with images of devilry, possession and the innocent soul, and their implications are strikingly confirmed by two stage images – Iago gloating over Othello's possessed body in its fit, and Othello and Iago's last encounter:

Othello	I looke downe towards his feet, but that's a fable.
	If thou beest a diuell, I cannot kill thee.
Lodovico	Wring his sword from him.
Iago	*I bleed sir, but not kil'd.*

(Othello V.ii. Q:N. My italics)

Needless to say, neither action, related imagery, nor their potent diabolic implications are intimated by Cinthio.[31]

In *Antony and Cleopatra* Philo's description of Antony as 'the Bellowes and the Fan / To coole a Gypsies Lust' is promptly echoed in the authorial stage direction, *Enter Anthony, Cleopatra . . . with Eunuchs fanning her.*[32] It is a slight instance of the continual traffic between the theatrical and linguistic in Shakespeare's work. But 'in such indexes', as Nestor says,

> (although small pricks
> To their subsequent volumes) there is seene
> The baby figure of the gyant masse . . .
> (*Troilus and Cressida* I.iii. Q:C3ᵛ)

Behind the rational combination of verbal and visual imagery in a single play there lies a larger sub-conscious cross-flow of metaphor, both visual and linguistic, throughout the canon. The imagery of the stanza from *Lucrece* foreshadows the theatrical paradox of *Othello*, in which the 'blackfac'd' naif is ensnared, body and soul, by the 'Saint-like' demi-devil, for no given reason. It is, indeed, extraordinary how many images from Shakespeare's two epyllions foreshadow themes and scenes in his later plays.[33] Again, Edward Armstrong notes that 'My sweete ou[n]ce of mans flesh, my in-conie Iew' in *Love's Labour's Lost* is a bizarre premonition of the main action of *The Merchant of Venice*, and Professor Wilson Knight observes that Lear's unusual preference, 'Thou'dst shun a Beare, / But if [thy] flight lay toward the roaring Sea, / Thou'dst meete the Beare i'th'mouth', accurately prefigures the two calamities governing the centre of *The Winter's Tale* – both, it might be added, having scant support from Greene's *Pandosto*.[34]

Such traffic can move from the early enactment of an image to its later verbal reminiscence. In the sourceless gardeners' scene in

Richard II the trite comparison of kingdom to garden is given an extended theatrical presentation; in *Henry V* the stage image reappears as a lengthy descriptive speech on 'this best Garden of the World, / Our fertile France', while in *Hamlet* it surfaces as a single image ('Fie on't, ah fie, tis an vnweeded garden / That growes to seede').[35] The shattered mirror of *Richard II* is remembered in a passing metaphor of *Measure for Measure*.[36] In *Hamlet*'s play-scene we twice see the old king die as poison is poured into his ear – a horrid sight recalled in Iago's malignant image, 'I'le poure this pestilence into his eare.' Not only the moral implications of all the villains' deaths in *Hamlet*, but the particular stage fact of Hamlet, forcing Claudius to drinkdown his poisoned cup, is literally summed up by Macbeth: 'This euen-handed Iustice / Commends th'Ingredience of our poyson'd Challice / To our owne lips'. Laertes drives the point home: 'He is iustly served, it is a poyson temperd by himselfe.' Othello hovering over Desdemona, candle in hand, meditating on her extinction, recurs in a verbal form in Macbeth's 'Out, out, breefe Candle', and the source of the pervasive unstaged clothes imagery in *Macbeth* is not Holinshed but the extensive history of costume symbolism, linguistic and actual, in the preceding plays.[37]

Such traffic can likewise move in reverse, from an image's early, verbal suggestion to its later enactment. In the Shakespearean fragment of *Sir Thomas More* the Sheriff warns his Londoners to do as they would be done by, or 'other ruffians as their fancies wrought / wth sealf same hand sealf reasons and sealf right / woold shark on yo^u and men lyke ravenous fishes / woold feed on on another', and this is given a similar stage reality as was endowed by Richard's gardeners, in *Pericles*, where the fishermen develop the same image ('Maister, I maruell how the Fishes liue in the Sea?' 'Why, as Men doe a-land; / The great ones eate vp the little ones').[38] In *Hamlet*, again, Claudius proposes a merely linguistic image ('what if this cursed hand / Were thicker then it selfe with brothers blood, / Is there not raine enough in the sweete Heauens / To wash it white as snowe'), whose fallacy is staged in the pathetic action of Lady Macbeth's sleepwalking scene. 'O faire affliction, peace' cries France, in *King John*; Constance replies: 'No, no, I will not, hauing breath to cry: O that my tongue were in the thunders mouth, / Then with a passion would I shake the world' – a longing Shakespeare only dares turn to stage reality in *Lear*. And the action of *Lear* is further foreshadowed in Hal's spoken confidence to Bates, Court and Williams:

though I speake it to you, I thinke the King is but a man, as I am: the Violet smells to him, as it doth to me; the Element shewes to him, as it doth to me; all his Sences haue but humane Conditions: his Ceremonies layd by, in his Nakednesse he appeares but a man.

(Henry V IV.i.1951ff)

Hal's simple antitheses are the prose gloss on Lear's madness ('all his Sences haue but humane Conditions'), and one of the storm's theatrical functions ('the Element shews to him, as it doth to me'). In his three attempts to undress, in the hovel, pulling off his boots, and at the point of death, Lear simply tries truly to lay his ceremonies by – as he had failed to do in his first attempt 'Vnburthen'd' to crawl toward death.[39]

But it would be to impose a false order to see such traffic as two-way and orderly. The parallels proliferate and modulate from play to play – as the earlier study of the cluster of associations connected with lovers' dying kisses has shown. In *2 Henry IV* 'Rumour is a pipe . . . of so easie, and so plaine a stop, / That the . . . wau'ring multitude / Can play vpon it.' The verbal image is briefly paralleled in Rosalind's forthright dismissal of Silvius's yearning for Phebe: 'wilt thou loue such a woman? what to make thee an instrument, and play false straines vpon thee? not to be endur'd . . .' Hamlet echoes it succinctly once again, in his praise of Horatio (who is 'not a pype for Fortunes finger / To sound what stop she please'). But it is *demonstrated* in full, with the requisite illustrative props, in his lengthy and embarrassing scene with Giuldenstern, Rosencrantz, and the recorders. Iago echoes the image once again as Desdemona and Othello are reunited in Cyprus ('O, you are well tun'd now, / But I'le set downe the pegs that make this musique'). But it is most subtly *enacted* in the image's continuation, Cassio's cacophonous aubade that heralds the disintegration of their relationship.[40] Desdemona and Othello are a pipe upon which Iago can play as he pleases, and his music is a very ugly one.

Again, the song in *As You Like It*, 'Blow, blow, thou winter winde, / Thou are not so vnkinde, as mans ingratitude', accurately prefigures its larger stage enactment in *Lear*, with Lear himself providing the same commentary on the storm ('I taxe you not, you Elements with vnkindnesse. I never gaue you Kingdome, call'd you children . . .'). But the ingratitudes the song merely named are most comprehensively embodied in *Timon*, where all friendship but Flavius's is mere feigning, friends and benefits are forgot, and ingratitude is the abiding theme. However, the contrast between man's inhumanity and nature's indifference, staged in *Lear*, is verbal-

ly explored here in the magnificent speeches of Apemantus and
Timon's disillusion:

Apemantus   . . . what think'st
            That the bleake ayre, thy boysterous Chamberlaine
            Will put thy shirt on warme? Will these moyst Trees,
            That haue out-liu'd the Eagle, page thy heeles
            And skip when thou point'st out?
                        (*Timon* IV.iii.1842ff)

Timon's exile has all the imaginative justification Duke Senior's
lacks, and it is he, rather than Duke Senior, who should reply:

            This is no flattery: these are counsellors
            That feelingly perswade me what I am.
                (*As You Like It* II.i.616–7)

A single theme thus surfaces in play after play, its dramatic expression growing from song and speech to turbulent stage image, and
finally to entire plot and extended harangue. Conversely, Timon's
outcry against his creditors – 'Cut my heart in summes . . . Tell out
my blood' is an abbreviated linguistic echo of the major scene in
which Shylock actually prepared to measure out Antonio's blood, in
exchange for the gold he owed. And this, the prime stage image, had
yet another verbal descendant in *Julius Caesar*, in the quarrel between
Brutus and Cassius:

Brutus   . . . I can raise no money by vile meanes:
          By Heauen, I had rather Coine my Heart,
          And drop my blood for Drachmaes . . .
Cassius . . . O I could weepe
          My Spirit from mine eyes. There is my Dagger,
          And heere my naked Breast: within, a Heart
          Deerer then Pluto's Mine, Richer then Gold:
          If that thou bee'st a Roman, take it foorth.
          I that deny'd thee Gold, will giue my Heart.
                    (*Julius Caesar* IV.iii.2048ff, 2078ff)

In *The Merchant* Shylock's imminent butchery of Antonio had a dual
function, staging the inhumanity of the creditor's demands, and the
quality of Antonio's love for Bassanio, for whom he was ready to
shed his blood. Both implications are raised again, purely metaphorically, in this quarrel as in *Timon*.[41]

As Eliot said, 'The whole of Shakespeare's work is *one* poem.'[42] Shakespeare is best elucidated by Shakespeare. His self-explanatory unity lies in the remarkable coherence of recurrent moral themes, and the imagery in which they are habitually expressed. But when we speak of Shakespeare's imagery, we cannot treat either linguistic, or theatrical, imagery in isolation, for the two are inextricably combined.

Of course Shakespeare is not unique in this. The Elizabethan and Jacobean dramatists in particular, with their fruitful proximity to the conventions of mediaeval drama, had a rich form of symbolic art ready to hand. Kyd and Marlowe frequently employ ritualistic action in the manner later adopted in Shakespeare's earliest scenes, as a visual focus for the dialogue. A particularly impressive, late Marlovian instance is the 'gloomie fellow in a meade belowe', the Mower who makes his appearance at Edward II's fall. Time with his scythe stands silent by, as those on the stage lament the vicissitudes of fate and the imminence of death, and the scene ends with the Mower's loaded demand: 'Your worship I trust will remember me?' 'Remember thee fellow? what else? . . .' He is a memento mori, no less.[43] Just as the stocking of Kent draws on the stocking of Justice, Reason, and other virtues in the Tudor moralities, so the stocking of Justice Overdo in *Bartholomew Fair* satirically echoes the same convention.

'Hog in sloth, Foxe in stealth, Wolfe in greedinesse . . .' Edgar intones, and *Volpone* later stages the Aesopean metamorphoses of greed in a variety of ways. Mosca's opening entertainment is a verse celebration of the theme, tracing as it does the transmigration of Pythagoras's soul, from Apollo to ox and ass, camel and brock; the characters are unequivocally branded by their names; their bestial behaviour further fits them for such simplifying labels. The play's basis in animal parable is finally clinched in the absurd stage image – Sir Politic's actual metamorphosis into a tortoise, as he hides under its shell, only black-gloved hands, capped head, and feet protruding. And this animal disguise is paralleled by Volpone's own less obviously foxy appearance as he lies in wait for his prey at the play's beginning ('Giue me my furres . . .'). No wonder, then, that Sir Politic's tortoise departure should be promptly capped by Volpone's entry, with the line, 'Am I then like him?'[44] Jonson integrates the verbal and staged image from his earliest plays: in *Every Man In His Humour*, Matthew praises the 'sparkes of wit' in his own poetry, and Wellbred comments aside, 'Would the sparkes would kindle once, and become a fire . . .' In the last act his verses are indeed set alight on the stage by Justice Clement, who moralises: 'See, see, how our *Poets* glorie shines! . . . and, now, it declines as fast . . . *Sic transit gloria mundi*', Knowall clinching the point with 'There's an *embleme* for you, sonne . . .'[45] In Heywood's *A Woman Killed with Kindness* the man who is later to be the adulterer appears in a costume that must be mud-bespattered from his journey ('His horse is booted / Up to the flank in mire, himself all *spotted* / And stain'd with plashing'). The moral implications of this striking theatrical appearance, at once emblematic and realistic, are made clear by repeated references later to his mistress as a 'spotted strumpet' with 'spotted body' and 'spotted sins'. Webster, in his turn, is also full of highly sophisticated interplay between stage action and its ironic echo in the verbal imagery accompanying it.[46] Even the least distinguished plays attempted such techniques. *Promos and Cassandra* – Whetstone's only play – has for its theme corruption by bribery, epitomised in financial terms in the sub-plot, and in the main plot embodied in the bad bargain between Promos (the Angelo-figure) and Cassandra. It is given its visual symbol when *The Mayor presentes the King, with a fayre Purse* at his return to Julio, in the traditional ritual of a royal entry, and – reversing normal civic convention – the King pointedly refuses it.[47] The corrupt text of *Arden of Feversham* would appear to enact Christ's parable, 'If the blind lead the blind, both shall fall into the ditch', as the two murderers, Black Will and Shakebag, grope through a 'misticall' mist:

Will   Come let vs go on lyke a couple of blind pilgrims.
        Then Shakebag falles into a ditch.
                    (*Arden of Feversham* ll. 1774–5)

Will's line suggests that the simile should be acted out, one morally blind malefactor leading the other to his downfall through the stage trap.

The representational poverty of much subsequent English drama seems to be partly due to its severing from this tradition, its apparent ignorance of the visual imagery of the stage. My impression is that it is particularly rare in comedy (as indeed it was relatively scarcer in Shakespeare's): Shaw's staged debates and much Restoration Comedy share a premium on verbalised wit. Even the ostensibly poetic drama of the Romantic poets singularly lacks this key element in the poetry of the Elizabethan stage, bar their lifting a few obvious, and generally identifiable Shakespearean stage symbols (for instance, in *The Cenci*, Macbeth's disrupted banquet at I.iii, Lear's thunder and

Othello's light for life at III.ii). But it seems to have been born again in the dramatic renaissance of the twentieth century, most obviously in the cinema, and also in the work of some dramatists. Tom Stoppard is positively Elizabethan in his inventiveness: *After Magritte* is a slight comic *jeu d'esprit* based on a series of visual ambiguities; the theme of *Jumpers*, mental acrobatics, is given its visual emblem in the teetering human pyramid with which the play begins. Even Eliot, with his generally academic and literary theatrical technique, appears to stage the saying that 'In the country of the blind, the one-eyed man is king' in *The Cocktail Party*, where the two Guardians are one-eyed, in comparison with the rest of the morally blind cast – Aunt Julia wearing a pair of spectacles in which one lens is broken, while Sir Henry Harcourt-Reilly rather more obviously proclaims his nature in his first exit, singing the 'One Eyed Riley'.

Rymer thought that Shakespeare's 'Words and Action are seldom akin, generally are inconsistent, at cross purposes, embarrass or destroy each other.'[48] I would make the contrary assertion: that, in Shakespeare's words,

> all this dumbe play had his acts made plain.

Notes

Introduction

1 See R. Berry: *On Directing Shakespeare* (1977), p. 30, and cf. M. Charney: 'Hamlet without Words', *ELH* 32 (1965), p. 459: 'I don't for a moment believe that we can really recover Shakespeare's intentions'; D. Mehl: 'Emblematic Theatre', *Anglia* (1977), p. 138: 'in many cases we shall never know whether a certain visual effect was ever intended'.

2 *Johnson on Shakespeare*, I.79.

3 See R. A. Foakes: 'Suggestions for a New Approach to Shakespeare's Imagery', *SS* 5 (1952), pp. 81–92. Later expanded by: W. D. Smith: 'Stage Business in Shakespeare's Dialogue', *SQ* (1953), pp. 311–16; Clifford Lyons: 'Stage Imagery in Shakespeare's Plays', *Essays on Shakespeare and Elizabethan Drama in honour of Hardin Craig*, ed. R. Hosley (1963), pp. 261–74; N. Coghill: *Shakespeare's Professional Skills* (Cambridge 1964), especially in the Preface and Ch. 1; M. C. Bradbrook: 'Shakespeare's Primitive Art', *Proceedings of the British Academy 1965* (1966), pp. 215–34; D. Mehl: 'Emblematik im englischen Drama der Shakespearezeit', *Anglia* (1969), pp. 126–46 (translated in *Ren. Dr.* (1969), pp. 39–58), also 'Visual and Rhetorical Imagery in Shakespeare's Plays', *E&S* (1972), pp. 83–100; I-S. Ewbank: '"More Pregnantly than Words": Some Uses and Limitations of Visual Symbolism', *SS* 24 (1971), pp. 13–18; D. Seltzer: 'The Actors and Staging', *A New Companion to Shakespeare Studies*, ed. K. Muir and S. Schoenbaum (Cambridge 1971), pp. 35–54. Charney's other works include the essay in *ELH* 32 quoted in n. 1 above, also reprinted in *Shakespeare's 'More Than Words Can Witness': Essays on Visual and Nonverbal Enactment in the Plays*, ed. S. Homan (Lewisburg. U.S.A. 1980), and 'Shakespeare's Unpoetic Poetry', *Studies in English Literature* (1973), pp. 199–207. These largely theoretic manifestos ran concurrently with a number of articles on isolated topics, such as R. B. Waddington: 'Antony and Cleopatra: "What Venus did with Mars"', *Shk. Studies* (1966), pp. 210–27; A. C. Dessen: 'Hamlet's Poisoned Sword: A Study in Dramatic Imagery', *Shk. Studies* (1969), pp. 53–69; W. Ingram: 'Enter Macduffe; with Macbeth's Head', *Theatre Notebook* (Oct. 1971), pp. 75–7. The visual element also continued to be canvassed, though with little interpretation, in sections of more wide-ranging works, notably: J. L. Styan: *Shakespeare's Stagecraft* (Cambridge 1967); J. Russell Brown: *Shakespeare's Plays in Performance* (Harmondsworth 1969), pp. 19–79; S. Wells: *Literature and*

Drama (1970). The whole approach heralded by Foakes's influential article had been broadly anticipated by W. Poel: *Shakespeare in the Theatre* (1913) and *Some Notes on Shakespeare's Stage and Players* (Manchester 1916); R. Flatter: *Shakespeare's Producing Hand* (1948).

At the end of the 1960s new impetus was brought to a flagging movement by the emergence of the iconographic approach. On the one hand this had its roots in the study of emblem books by Alciati, Whitney, and others, whose influence on Shakespeare's *verbal* imagery was first pointed out by the Rev. H. Green: *Shakespeare and the Emblem Writers* (1870). On the other it derived from a number of studies of pageantry and emblem on the Tudor stage, in particular A. S. Venezky: *Pageantry on the Shakespearean Stage* (NY 1951); T. W. Craik: *The Tudor Interlude* (Leicester 1958); D. Mehl: *The Elizabethan Dumb Show* (1965); D. M. Bergeron: 'The Emblematic Nature of English Civic Pageantry', *Ren. Dr.* (1968), pp. 167–98 and *English Civic Pageantry, 1558–1642* (1971); R. Southern: *The Staging of Plays before Shakespeare* (1973).

The grandmother of Shakespearean inconography would appear to be M. F. Thorp: 'Shakespeare and the Fine Arts', *PMLA* (1931), pp. 672–93, followed much later (this list is selective) by: L. J. Ross: 'The Meaning of Strawberries in Shakespeare', *Studies in the Renaissance* (1960), pp. 225–40, and 'Shakespeare's "Dull Clown" and Symbolic Music', *SQ* (1966), pp. 107–28; S. Schuman: 'Emblems and the English Renaissance Drama: A Checklist', *RORD* (1969), pp. 43–56; W. S. Heckscher: 'Shakespeare in His Relationship to the Visual Arts: A Study in Paradox', *RORD* (1970–1), pp. 5–71; J. M. Steadman: 'Iconography and Renaissance Drama: Ethical and Mythological Themes', *ibid*. pp. 73–122; A. Haaker: '*Non sine causa*: The Use of Emblematic Method and Iconology in the Thematic Structure of *Titus Andronicus*', *ibid,* pp. 143–68; B. Gellert: 'The Iconography of Melancholy in the Graveyard Scene of *Hamlet*', *S. Phil.* (1970), pp. 57–66, and (as B. G. Lyons) 'The Iconography of Ophelia', *ELH* 44 (1977), pp. 60–74; M. H. Golden (later Fleischer): 'The Iconography of the English History Play' (Ph.D. Columbia 1964), and 'stage imagery', *A Shakespeare Encyclopaedia*, ed. O. J. Campbell and E. G. Quinn (1974), pp. 819–20, and 'Stage Imagery in Shakespearean Studies', *SRO* (1965), pp. 10–20. All but one of these are articles on isolated topics. With reason in 1973 N. Alexander was commenting, 'it seems time for a more substantial demonstration' of the theatrical and iconographic approach to Shakespearean imagery (*SS 26* (1973), p. 176). For the criticisms of the original propagandists, see note 5; for some of the books see note 4.

4 M. Bluestone: *From Story to Stage* (The Hague, 1974) studies the theatrical translation of source-material but is uninformed about the standard use of stage action and its meaning. J. Hasler: *Shakespeare's Theatrical Notation* (Bern, 1974) has an extended study of the direction of action through dialogue, but suffers from the same shortcoming, being limited to the comedies. Both carry on from A. Gerstner-Hirzel: *The Economy of Action and Word in Shakespeare's Plays* (Bern, 1957), and R. Stamm: *Shakespeare's Word Scenery* (Zurich and St Galen, 1954), also 'Elizabethan

Stage Practice and the Transmutation of Source Material by the Dramatists', *SS* 12 (1959), pp. 64–70, and *The Shaping Powers at Work* (Heidelberg, 1967), pp. 11–84. My own approach is similar in principle to that proposed by R. Watkins and J. Lemmon: *The Poet's Method* (1974). Their subsequent volumes on individual plays have proved disappointing, suffering from some of the defects outlined above, and the limitations of line-by-line analysis honestly recognised by Hasler in his own work (*op. cit.* p. 204).

5　D. Mehl: 'Emblematic Theatre', *Anglia* (1977), p. 132 and *passim*; see also J. M. Steadman: 'Iconography and Methodology in Renaissance and Dramatic Study: Some Caveats', *SRO* (1972–4), pp. 38–52. Many of the criticisms raised by Steadman and Mehl could be illustrated by J. Doebler: *Shakespeare's Speaking Pictures, Studies in Iconic Imagery* (Albuquerque, 1974), which has, however, a full and informative bibliographic introduction.

Chapter 1: Action and expression

1　*Rape of Lucrece* ll. 1403–4. Epigraph from M. E. de Montaigne: *Essays*, tr. J. Florio (Everyman 1965), II.144.
2　*Coriolanus* III.ii.2176ff.
3　*Hamlet* I.ii.Q2:B4; *Winter's Tale* V.ii.3023–4; *Julius Caesar* III.i.1286. My italics.
4　*Hamlet* III.ii.Q2:G3ᵛ–G4 and II.ii.Q2:F4ᵛ.
5　M. C. Bradbrook: *Elizabethan Stage Conditions* (Cambridge 1932, repr. Hamden, Conn. 1962), pp. 109ff and *Themes and Conventions of Elizabethan Tragedy* (Cambridge 1935), pp. 20–3 (both rigorously formalist); A. Harbage: 'Elizabethan Acting', *PMLA* (1939), pp. 685–708 (a formalist whose views were later modified, e.g. in *SQ* II (1951), pp. 360–1); B. L. Joseph: *Elizabethan Acting* (Oxford 1951, 2nd ed. 1964: the formalist stance of the first edition is radically qualified in the second); S. L. Bethell: 'Shakespeare's Actors', *RES* (1950), pp. 193–205 (arguing for a mixture of styles). All supporting the naturalism of the Elizabethan stage: R. A. Foakes: 'The Player's Passion: Some Notes on Elizabethan Psychology and Acting', *E&S* (1954), pp. 62–77; M. Rosenberg: 'Elizabethan Actors: Men or Marionettes?', *PMLA* (1954), pp. 915–27; supported by D. Klein: 'Elizabethan Acting', *PMLA* (1956), pp. 280–2; A. J. Gurr: 'Who Strutted and Bellowed?' *SS* 16 (1963), pp, 95–102, 'Elizabethan Action', *S. Phil.* 63 (1966), pp. 144–56, and *The Shakespearean Stage 1574–1642* (Cambridge 1970), pp. 71–6, where some degree of formalism is admitted to be inevitable.
6　Ed. J. P. Collier (*Shakespeare Society*, 1841), p. 29.
7　*The Staple of News*, Induction l. 45, *Works* VI, p. 280.
8　*Troilus and Cressida* I.iii.Q:C. Many more instances of this kind are quoted in the articles listed above.
9　*Coriolanus* I.iii.361; *1 Henry IV* III.iii.Q:G3.

10 T. Rymer: *A Short View of Tragedy*, *The Critical Works of Thomas Rymer*, ed. C. A. Zymansky (New Haven 1956), pp. 85–6.

11 Quoted: *Hamlet* III.ii.Q2:G3ᵛ, and cf. 'the two houres trafficque of our Stage' (*Romeo and Juliet*, Prologue, Q2:A2).

12 *Winter's Tale* I.ii.196.

13 *Hamlet* V.i.3444 (not in Q2:M4ᵛ); *Julius Caesar* I.ii.285; Harbage, *PMLA* (1939), p. 696.

14 *Ibid.* p. 704.

15 *Henry VIII* III.ii.2080–1, V.iii.3181. Examples of this kind are quoted by M. C. Bradbrook: *Themes and Conventions of Elizabethan Tragedy*, pp. 21–2, as illustrative of a formal theatre. Harbage's point is also answered by Rosenberg, *op. cit.* p. 918–19.

16 e.g. by Foakes, *op. cit.* p. 76.

17 The rhyme about Ford is quoted by H. Gardner, ed. *J. Donne: The Elegies and The Songs and Sonnets* (Oxford 1965), p. 268 and n. 1. Other quotations from Nashe: *The Unfortunate Traveller*, *Works* II.301, 321, *The Praise of the Red Herring*, *Works* III.219.

18 *Love's Labour's Lost* III.i.Q:C3ᵛ.

19 See also *Two Gentlemen* II.i.414–5, *Tempest* I.ii.341, *Titus* III.ii.1456–9 for the folded arms of melancholy (only the last, the earliest in date, is acted); *Troilus and Cressida* III.iii.2108–9 for tiptoe strutting; *Love's Labour's Lost* V.ii.2001, *1 Henry IV* V.i.2714 for itching elbows; and *Richard III* III.v.2091 for wagging straws.

20 Joseph, *op. cit.* (1964), p. 16.

21 Quoted: *King Lear* V.iii.3280; *Hamlet* II.ii.Q2:F2. S. L. Bethell is still overcategorical: 'It therefore seems likely that (a) the longer verse passages were delivered as formal rhetoric . . . (b) This rhetorical manner was presumably shaded off into something more like naturalism in the shorter exchanges of dialogue and in conversational prose' *RES* (1950), p. 204. Later chapters will show formal effects in informal dialogue and vice versa.

22 *1 Henry IV* IV.ii.Q:H3; *Troilus and Cressida* III.iii.Q:G3ᵛ; *Merchant of Venice* II.viii.Q:D4–D4ᵛ; *Timon* I.i.44ff. My italics.

23 *Rape of Lucrece* ll. 1415–16.

24 Leonardo da Vinci: *The Literary Works*, ed. J. P. Richter (1970), l. 345, §594; *The Prelude* (1805), IX. 160ff; *Tristram Shandy* V.iii; *Kim*, ch. IV.

25 *The Letters of John Keats*, ed. M. Buxton Forman (Oxford 1948), p. 418. Note Keats's instinctive quotation of Shakespeare in the context of gesture.

26 *Winter's Tale* II.i.673–4; *Hamlet* I.v.Q2:D4ᵛ; *Merchant of Venice* II.ii.Q:C3ᵛ; *Twelfth Night* II.v.1062ff. My italics.

27 *Julius Caesar* I.ii.324ff; *Hamlet* II.i.Q2:E2; *Coriolanus* V.i.3226ff. My italics. For the use of *thus* see also J. Hasler, *Shakespeare's Theatrical Notation* (Bern, 1974), pp. 88–90, and note 20.

28 *Hamlet* III.ii.Q2:H3ᵛ; Slender in *Merry Wives* I.i.142, 146, 153; *Othello* III.iii.Q:H3ᵛ; *As You Like It* V.iv.2644–5; *Pericles* IV.ii.Q:F4ᵛ.

29 Bradbrook: *Elizabethan Stage Conditions*, p. 109.

30 *Macbeth* III.iv.1335–6; *Othello* V.ii.Q:M^v; *Tempest* IV.i.1659–60. My italics.

31 *Hamlet* II.ii.Q2:F2, and cf. Q1:E2^v.

32 See Brooke's *Tragicall Historye of Romeus and Juliet*, Bullough I.313, ll. 1040–1.

33 *2 Henry IV* V.iv.Q:K3^v and see W. H. Matchett: 'Some Dramatic Techniques in *The Winter's Tale*', *SS* 22 (1969), p. 95.

34 *Hamlet* I.i.Q2:B^v. He also accuses the ghost of usurping the dead king's form.

35 *Hamlet* I.v.Q2:D3^v. The essence is, perhaps significantly, preserved in the Bad Quarto, Q1:C4^v–D.

36 *Rape of Lucrece* l. 359; *Venus and Adonis* ll. 421, 611, 709–10; S. T. Coleridge: *Biographia Literaria*, ed. G. Watson (Everyman 1962), ch. xv, p. 177.

37 *Julius Caesar* III.i.1329–31, III.ii.1723ff, V.i.2372ff (my italics), and for Calphurnia's dream, see II.ii.1069ff.

38 *True Tragedy* O:C3^v and Hall, Bullough III.181–2, cf. *3 Henry VI* II.vii281; *True Tragedy* O:E4 and *3 Henry VI* V.iv–v.2970–2, cf. Hall, Bullough III. 166, 205. Cade's dialogue is more accurate in *Contention* Q:G2^v than *2 Henry VI* IV.vii.2741–3 (see Bullough III. 115, n. 6 and 116, n. 1). Bullough also notes an historical change of scene-order in *Time Tragedy* (Bullough III.163–4).

39 See T. J. B. Spencer: 'Shakespeare and the Elizabethan Romans', *SS* 10 (1957), p. 34. Earlier quotation from Nashe, from *Pierce Penilesse*, *Works* I.212.

40 *Julius Caesar* I.iii.434, 577, I.ii.280–1, 318–19. My italics.

41 Quoted in this paragraph: *Troilus and Cressida* V.ii.Q:K2^v; *Othello* IV.i.Q:I4^v–K; *Winter's Tale* I.ii.265–7.

42 *Measure for Measure* V.i.2535–6, 2609–11, 2893–4, 2751–2.

43 *Cymbeline* I.vi.605–6, 635, 649–50, and see l. 689ff.

44 *Othello* I.iii.Q:D2^v, II.i.Q:E3.

45 See *Richard III* II.i.1205–6, 1210, 1263ff.

46 *Merchant of Venice* IV.i.Q:G4^v.

47 *1 Henry IV* V.iv.Q:K2^v; *Othello* V.ii.Q:M4^v.

Chapter 2: Position on the stage

1 *The Poems of Sir Walter Raleigh, with those of Sir Henry Wotton*, ed. J. Hannah (1891), p. 29.

2 T. J. King: *Shakespearean Staging, 1599–1642* (Cambridge, Mass. 1971), pp. 2–3.

3 See R. Hosley: 'The Discovery-space in Shakespeare's Globe' *SS* 12 (1959), pp. 39–41. Quotations from *The World and the Child* C3^v, *2 Henry VI* I.i.187–8; *King Lear* I.i.291.

4 Doors as gates: e.g. *1 Henry VI* I.iii.363ff; *3 Henry VI* IV.vii.2500ff, V.i.2697ff; *2 Henry IV* I.i.47ff; *Henry V* III.iii.1309ff; *Timon* V.iv.2574ff.

As tomb-doors: *Titus* I.i.111ff; *Romeo and Juliet* V.iii.2898 (Q1:K: *Romeo opens the tombe*); *Much Ado* V.iii.2522ff. As cave-entrance: *Timon* V.i.2233, 2360 (probably authorial SDs); *Cymbeline* III.iii.1556ff. Doors left ajar at *2 Henry IV* IV.v.2582 and *Macbeth* II.ii.652, II.iii.797.

5 For the structure of the discovery-space see Hosley, *op. cit.* p. 46, and 'The playhouses and the stage', *A New Companion to Shakespeare Studies*, ed. K. Muir and S. Schoenbaum (Cambridge 1971), p. 32. For its distinction from the thrusting out of a curtained bed, as in *Romeo and Juliet* IV.iii–v and *Othello* V.ii, see Hosley: 'The Staging of Desdemona's Bed' *SQ* XIV (1963), pp. 57–65. Hosley's statistics in *SS* 12 cover the plays written for the first Globe only, where the discovery-space is demanded in *Merry Wives* I.iv.432–59; *Troilus and Cressida* III.iii.1888; *Pericles* V.i.Q:H2^v–3. I am aware of only the following elsewhere: *Merchant of Venice* II.vii.973–4, 1052, II.ix.1112, 1197; *Winter's Tale* V.iii.3206; *Tempest* V.i.2141–2; *Henry VIII* as quoted; concealment at *King John* IV.i.1572ff, *1 Henry IV* II.iv.1462–94; *Hamlet* III.iv.2379ff. Tents as in *Troilus and Cressida* III.iii.1888 at *Richard III* V.iii.3484, 3520, 3685–6 (all probably authorial SDs), and quotation from ll. 3438–9. G. Wickham: *Early English Stages II*, part I (1963), p. 319, compares this with the plot of *2 Seven Deadly Sins*: 'A tent being plast one the stage for Henry the sixt. he in it A sleepe . . .' (Greg: *Dramatic Documents from the Elizabethan Playhouses* (Oxford 1931), II, plate II, ll. 3–4). He erroneously assumes both tents to be pre-set, but the dialogue contradicts him ('Here pitch our Tent . . . Vp with my Tent . . . Vp with the Tent', ll. 3433, 3441, 3448).

6 See Hosley: 'The Gallery over the Stage', *SQ* VIII (1957), p. 21, n. 12 and p. 26, n. 24; 'Shakespeare's Use of a Gallery over the Stage' *SS* 10 (1957), pp. 88–9, n. 31; corroborated on ample textual evidence by King, *op. cit.*, pp. 46, 147.

7 See G. Wickham: *Early English Stages I* (1959), p. 89.

8 Quoted: Ecclesiastes 3:20; *Summer's Last Will* ll. 1773–7 (Nashe: *Works* III.289); *Spanish Tragedy* (1592), ll. 1934ff, imitating *2 Tamburlaine* II.iv.97ff; *1 Tamburlaine* IV.ii.32, 26–7; *Contention* Q:B4^v. For a parallel and a potential source for Marlowe's stage image see M. C. Bradbrook: 'Shakespeare's Primitive Art', *Proceedings of the British Academy 1965* (1966), p. 216, and Hallet D. Smith: 'Tamburlaine and the Renaissance', *Elizabethan and other Essays in Honour of G. F. Reynolds* (Univ. of Colorado Studies, Series B, Studies in the Humanities, II.4; Boulder, Colorado 1945), p. 129, n. 14. Final quotation from Dekker: *News from Hell, Non-Dramatic Works*, ed. A. B. Grosart (N.Y. 1963), II.92.

9 *Hamlet* I.v.845ff, V.i.3444ff; T. Lodge: *Wit's Miserie* (1596), p. 56: 'the Visard of ye ghost which cried so miserally at ye Theator like an oister wife, *Hamlet, reuenge*'. Trap for realism: *Timon* IV.iii.1625ff; possibly *Tempest* I.i.19 (with tackle dropped from the gallery, to suggest a ship). See R. Watkins: *On Producing Shakespeare* (1950), p. 52, and N. Coghill: 'The Basis of Shakespearian Comedy' *E&S* (1950), p. 24. For spirits see *2 Henry VI* I.iv.646–7 (SD probably authorial) and *Macbeth* IV.i.1604ff; for many non-Shakespearean examples see e.g. J. C. Adams: *The Globe*

Playhouse (Cambridge, Mass., 1943), pp. 113–31 (his conclusions on stage structure are fanciful).

10 E. K. Chambers: *The Elizabethan Stage* (Oxford 1923), III. 54–5, n. 5; Hosley: *SS* 10 (1957), pp. 77–8.

11 *2 Tamburlaine* V.i.147–56, and see the *Letters of Philip Gawdy*, ed. I. H. Jeayes (1906), p. 23: 'My L. Admyrall his men and players having a devyse in ther playe to tye one of their fellowes to a poste and so to shoote him to deathe, having borrowed their Callyvers one of the players handes swerved his peece being charged with bullett missed the fellowe he aymed at and killed a chyld, and a woman great with chyld forthwith, and hurt an other man in the head very soore . . .'

12 *1 Henry VI* I.iv.465ff and Bullough III. 55. See Cambridge ed. (1952), pp. 129, 131; new Arden ed. (1962), pp. 28–9; Hosley: *SQ* VIII (1957), p. 20, n. 10 and *SS* 10 (1957), p. 86, n. 4 (no reasons given).

13 *1 Henry VI* II.i.720 (cf. Hall, Bullough III.54), I.vi.639, III.ii.1451–2, 1471–2, cf. *Tempest* III.iii.1535 SD and ll. 1559–61, 1566, 1619ff. 'The top' cannot be Dover Wilson's 'music room above . . . the upper stage' (Cambridge ed. p. 160), or Chambers' unspecified room 'on a level with the upper row of [auditorium] galleries' (*W. Shk.* I.293), neither of which appear to have existed. See Hosley: *SS* 10 (1957), p. 86, n. 8, and 'Was there a Music-room in Shakespeare's Globe?' *SS* 13 (1960), pp. 113–23. For his solution of 'the top' as that of the tiring house, see *SS* 10, p. 86, n. 8.

14 *1 Henry VI* IV.ii.1952ff, V.iii.2570ff.

15 *Titus*, I.i.2, 25, 75, 264, 333, 375; quoted: *Titus* I.i.Q:B3ᵛ, II.i.Q:C2ᵛ.

16 *Romeo and Juliet* II.ii.Q2:Dᵛ, III.v.Q2:H3ᵛ.

17 *Richard II* III.iii.Q:F4ᵛ, G2. The descent is historic, the associated image Shakespeare's (see Holinshed, Bullough III.403). Both plays are tentatively dated 1595 although the order of priority is uncertain. See P. Ure, new Arden ed. *Richard II* (1956), pp. xxix, xliv, and *W. Shk.* I.345–6.

18 For the boxed-in sections of the gallery standing for windows, see Hosley: *SQ* VIII (1957), p. 19, n. 8. Windows at e.g. *Two Gentlemen* IV.ii.1706ff, cf. *Othello* I.i.89ff (Shakespeare is re-cycling again, but with a very different serenader out of sight this time); *Merchant of Venice* II.vi.925ff (stolen from the *Jew of Malta* II.i.19ff); *Henry VIII* V.ii.3014ff. Standard use of gallery for city walls: *King John* II.i.505, IV.iii.1996; *Henry V* III.i.1082 (SD probably authorial); *Coriolanus* I.iv.499ff; *Timon* V.iv.2512. Pulpit and hill: *Julius Caesar* III.ii.1528ff, V.iii.2500ff; monument in *Antony and Cleopatra* IV.xv.2996ff.

19 *Richard II* IV.i.Q:Hᵛ and *3 Henry VI* I.i.31ff. The origin of both scenes is Hall's account of Henry VI's reign, when 'the duke of Yorke with a bolde countenaunce, entered into the chamber of the peres, and sat downe in the trone royall, under the clothe of estate (which is the kynges peculiar seate) & in the presence aswel of the nobilitie, as of the spiritualitie', he traced his claim to the throne (Bullough III.173–5). Most historians stress Richard's appearance in full regal dress for the abdication.

20 *Henry VIII* II.iv.1343–5 SD, 1366 (my italics), cf. Holinshed, Bullough

IV.466–7; *Measure for Measure* V.i.2538–9, 2743, 2375, 2380–1, 2670–2.

21 *King Lear* III.vi.Q:G3ᵛ–4 and IV.iii.Q:I (neither in F).

22 Lovers: *A Midsummer Night's Dream* IV.i.1511ff; *1 Henry IV* III.i.1754–5, 1769–71; *Hamlet* III.ii.Q2:H. Domesticity: e.g. *Coriolanus* I.iii.361 SD most probably authorial (quoted); *Winter's Tale* II.i.614; *Henry VIII* III.i.1615ff: *Enter Queene and her Women as at worke* (SD most probably authorial), and 'Your Graces find me heere part of a Houswife' – hence probably staging Holinshed's vivid detail: 'the cardinals were come to speake with hir. With that she rose up, and with a skeine of white thred about hir necke, came into hir chamber of presence' (Bullough IV.470).

23 *Spanish Tragedy* (1592), ll. 524ff; *Pericles* II.iii.Q:Dᵛ; *Macbeth* III.iv.1256, 1398–9; *Spanish Tragedy* (1592), l. 321.

24 *Spanish Tragedy* (1592), ll. 314ff; *Edward II* IV.vii.53–4; T. Heywood: *A Woman Killed With Kindness*, ed. R. W. van Fossen (1961).

25 *Titus* III.i.Q:E3 (my italics), and see pp. 73, 110.

26 Bullough III.118, cf. Daniel 4.25 and 32, 5.21. The Biblical parallel is missed by the Cambridge and new Arden editors, and by Noble, who notes an echo of Daniel 3.22 in the next scene, V.i.3159 (see R. Noble: *Shakespeare's Biblical Knowledge* (1935), p. 126). For the laws on church attendance see R. Bayne: 'Religion', *Shakespeare's England* (Oxford 1916), I.75.

27 *Richard II* III.ii.Q:F2ᵛ, cf. *Edward II* IV.vii. For similar undercutting in the next scene of *Richard II*, see p. 103.

28 Plutarch from Bullough V.301–2; *Antony and Cleopatra* III.xi.2043–4 (my italics), III.x.2008–9, III.xi.2069; *Romeo and Juliet* III.iii.Q2:G4ᵛ.

29 *Henry VIII* III.ii.2258ff; *Bonduca* ll. 1683ff.

Chapter 3: Taking by the hand

1 Falstaff's catechism: *1 Henry IV* V.i.Q:13ᵛ; his outstandingly apt use of biblical allusions noted and tabulated by Noble: *Shakespeare's Biblical Knowledge*, pp. 169–74, who suggests a self-comparison to Adam and then Christ at *1 Henry IV* I.ii.201–3 (Cf. Mark 15.28).

2 M. Morgann: 'An Essay on the Dramatic Character of Sir John Falstaff', *Eighteenth Century Essays on Shakespeare*, ed. D. Nichol Smith (Oxford 1963), p. 279.

3 *Othello* IV.i.Q:13ᵛ, and for a competent account of the *linguistic* imagery, see S. L. Bethell: 'The Diabolic Images in *Othello*', *SS* 5 (1952), pp. 62–80; for the second stage image see p. 195.

4 There is no such interpretation in Plutarch, Bullough V.123–4. The discovery of Titinius's body, and the detail of his upward face, are Shakespeare's invention. The SD for sound effects also probably authorial.

5 J. Boswell: *Life of Samuel Johnson*, ed. G. B. Hill and L. F. Powell (1934), II.90; T. S. Eliot: 'The Function of Criticism', *Selected Essays* (1966), pp. 32–3.

6 Sir T. Elyot: *The Boke named The Gouernour*, ed. H. H. S. Croft (1880), I.xxi. pp. 235–6.

7 Quoted: *Timon* IV.ii.1552ff, IV.iii.1877–8, I.i.118–19, IV.ii.1561–2 (and Timon further seen to shake hands at I.i.184, 203); *Hamlet* I.v.Q2:E, II.ii.Q2:F2ᵛ; *A Midsummer Night's Dream* V.i.Q:H4ᵛ.

8 Referred to: *Lear* III.iv.1822 (Kent and the Fool), IV.i.2264, IV.vi.2461, V.ii.2928ff (Gloucester and Edgar), V.ii.Q:K3ᵛ (SD for Cordelia and Lear; not in F); *Macbeth* V.i.2158 (cf. II.ii.726ff). Taking the sleepwalking scene's hints, she could say the last lines of II.ii. gently: 'be not lost / So poorely in your thoughts', as she leads him off.

9 *Winter's Tale* V.ii.3147–50; *Coriolanus* V.iii.3539 and pp. 133–4.

10 *Duchess of Malfi* I.i.463ff. The only legal requirement was *verba de praesenti* – agreement before a witness. See A. Underhill: 'Law', *Shakespeare's England*, I.407.

11 See further pp. 130–1.

12 In *A Midsummer Night's Dream* Helena's hand is whiter than 'That pure conieaIed white, high Taurus snow, / Fand with the Easterne winde' (III.ii.Q:E2); Juliet is like 'a rich Iewel in an Ethiops eare' and 'a snowie Doue' (*Romeo and Juliet* I.v.Q2:C3ᵛ). 'Bolted' in *The Winter's Tale* introduces the idea of sifted white flour as well.

13 *Julius Caesar* IV.iii.2098–9.

14 *Ibid.* IV.i.1931–2, before the quarrel's resolution.

15 B. L. Joseph: *Elizabethan Acting* (Oxford 1951), pp. 64–6, e.g. at *Hamlet* III.ii.Q2:H3ᵛ ('by these pickers and stealers'), and *Winter's Tale* IV.iii.1694. A left-handed rogues' handshake equally suitable at, e.g., *1 Henry IV* II.i.726ff or *Antony and Cleopatra* II.vi.1292–4: 'giue mee your hand Menas, if our eyes had authority, heere they might take two Theeues kissing', on analogy with the 'Palmer's kiss' cliché (see pp. 84, and 214, n. 7). Next quotation from *Merry Wives* II.ii.1008ff, and for Cloten's literalism see p. 166.

16 *King John* III.iii.1324; *Othello* IV.ii.Q:Lᵛ.

17 Compare quoted passage from *1 Henry VI* III.i. with Hall, Bullough III.51. Other examples at *2 Henry VI* V.i.3049ff; *3 Henry VI* IV.ii.2196 –7, IV.vi.2419–20, V.i.2765; *Richard III* II.i.1130–98, dramatising the Hall quoted in text (Bullough III.254). Final quotation from *Othello* III.iv.Q:H4ᵛ.

18 *Hamlet*, II.ii.Q2:F2ᵛ–3, F:1420. Further comparable reversals at I.i.92, 94, I.ii.189–90, and see N. Coghill: 'Shakespeare as a Dramatist', *Talking of Shakespeare*, ed. J. Garrett (1954), p. 26. Last quotation from *Timon* I.ii.357ff.

19 Nashe: *Works* III.236–7, *Summer's Last Will* ll. 104, 126–7; A. S. Venezky (now A. V. Griffin): *Pageantry on the Shakespearean Stage* (New York 1951), p. 132.

20 Referred to: *3 Henry VI* IV.vi.2419ff; *Pericles* II.iv.Q:D3; *Merry Wives* III.i.1242ff; *Julius Caesar* III.i.1326–31. Shakespeare does not play such double-take tricks on his audience in plays like *Othello* or *Lear*, whose stories were *at the time* less familiar to the public, having their origins not in classic history but folk tradition or foreign novellas.

21 *Henry VIII* II.iii.1166–9, and see ll. 1187–9. An invented scene.

22 E. A. J. Honigmann, ed. new Arden *King John* (1965), pp. xix, liii–lviii,

argues for its precedence to the *Troublesome Raigne*; Bullough (IV.5) inclines to the older, reverse orthodoxy.

23 *King John* III.i.1253, 1157, 1170–3. Shakespeare replays Blanch's predicament later, in *Coriolanus* V.iii.3459ff (Volumnia to her son) and *Antony and Cleopatra* III.iv.1700 (Octavia to Antony), without the gesture.

24 Quoted: *Antony and Cleopatra* III.xiii.2293–4, IV.viii.2661–3, 2683 (my italics). All three hand kisses are Shakespeare's invention; the messenger scene is wholly fictional, and for the rest, see Plutarch's brisk account, Bullough V.306, 307.

Chapter 4: Kneeling

1 Quoted: *Thomas of Woodstock*, l. 1507 (dated c.1590–3); *Lear* III.ii.1723 –4, III.iv.1814–5. I assume Lear kneels since he says 'Ile pray'.

2 Examples: spirits to god: *Cymbeline* V.iv.3127–8; men to God: *King Lear* IV.vi.2473ff; on oath: *Titus* IV.i.1635ff. F *Othello* specifies kneeling for Othello's oath of vengeance and Desdemona's later oath of fidelity; both contrast with Iago's insincere echo (III.iii.2110–20, IV.ii.2864ff). King to country: most movingly in *Richard II* III.ii.1366ff. Subjects to king, *passim*; in humbleness, etc, see below. Wife to husband, *Taming of the Shrew* V.ii.2735 and Q:G˅ SD. Another pointed comparison between Portia's kneeling to Brutus for confidence (only granted when she was proved herself worthy), and Calphurnia to Caesar for influence (promptly granted and then retracted on the conspirators' ridicule). The two scenes are ironically juxtaposed and linked by the common action: *Julius Caesar* II.i.911ff, II.ii.1045ff. Children to parents: see below.

3 Quotations from *All's Well* I.iii.522ff; *1 Henry VI* III.iv.1702ff; *2 Henry IV* IV.v.Q:I˅–2 and cf. Bullough IV.318, ll. 659–70. The old Hamlet's loss of his crown, stolen from his sleeping side (*Hamlet* I.v.744ff, acted out at III.ii.1995ff) does not come from the known sources (see Bullough VII, 62, 87). Of course we do not know about the Ur-Hamlet, but Shakespeare may be recycling material from the earlier *2 Henry IV* here.

4 Quoted: *1 Henry VI* V.iv.2654–6, and cf. Hall and Holinshed, Bullough III.61, 76–7. For further examples of isolationism, see p. 219, n. 25. Richard kneeling to his mother: *Richard III* II.ii.1380ff.

5 *2 Henry VI* II.ii.1017, 1029–30, and cf. Bullough III.122, n. 1 and 119–20. My italics.

6 *1 Henry VI* III.i.1386ff (Richard made Duke of York), and *2 Henry VI* I.i.68ff (Suffolk endowed with its Duchy). Other knightings at *2 Henry VI* V.i.3072; *3 Henry VI* II.ii.932ff; *King John* I.i.170–1; and, rather late in the day, *Cymbeline* V.v.3273. For their popularity, cf. a comic knighting in *Summer's Last Will*, Nashe: *Works* III.267, l. 1071.

7 Quoted: *2 Henry VI* IV.ii.2509–10. Staged at *2 Henry IV* IV.ii.2199ff, where, as soon as treaty is agreed on, the rebel troops scatter 'Like youthfull Steeres, vnyok'd', while Prince John's refuse to move till dismissed by him in person. In Holinshed (Bullough IV.272–3) this is

part of royal 'policie' – while the rebel troops disperse, Westmorland secretly reinforces the King's men and no discharge is given them. Shakespeare abandons the regal slur for an emblematic point.

8 *Contention* Q:F4, cf. Fabyan, Bullough III.114, n.2; Jonson: *Part of the King's Entertainment*, ll. 264–7, *Works* VII.91. For further misunderstandings of stage symbols, see pp. 154–5, 165.

9 Quoted: *Richard II* I.iv.Q:C2ᵛ and Bullough III.427; compare the two kneelings with Bullough III.399, 404; *Julius Caesar* III.i.1341ff, 1364–5 (not in Plutarch, Bullough V.87. The whole of Antony's scene over Caesar's corpse is Shakespeare's invention).

10 'Quid vis facerem? an fratrum geminam necem / hac dextera effuso rependam sanguine? / faciam? paratis ensibus pectus dabo; / et si placet magis, moriar ulnis tuis' (Bullough III.307). For the invention of this scene, see Bullough III.236–7 and compare Hall, Bullough III.249.

11 *The Changeling* III.iv.167ff.

12 *2 Henry IV* IV.v.Q:Iᵛ.

13 Quoted: Nashe: *The Terrors of the Night*, *Works* I.347; *Hamlet* II.ii.Q2:G; *Othello* II.iii.Q:F3ᵛ; *Love's Labour's Lost* IV.iii.Q:F2; *Measure for Measure* II.ii.943–4 (cf also the opposite dilemma in *Macbeth* IV.iii.1838ff: 'Angels are bright still, though the brightest fell. / Though all things foule would wear the brows of grace / Yet Grace must still looke so'). Dover Wilson suggests emending 'not' to 'now', since Angelo is playing on his name. Johnson would emend to ''Tis yet'. Lever, in the new Arden, glosses 'write' as 'designate', 'Deuills horne' as 'the part unmistakeably revealing the devil's identity' (a cardinal error), and ''Tis' as referring to 'good Angell', giving us the staggering aphorism that 'Good Angel' is not the devil's crest! I do not see how an audience could jump from this to his paraphrase: 'Angelo will reveal the diabolical side of his nature, "the devil's horn", while designating it with his own name "angel", though this is not his real title' (Camb. ed. (1922), p. 132; new Arden ed. (1965), p. 55).

14 'This speech, in which Hamlet . . . is not content with taking blood for blood, but contrives damnation for the man that he would punish, is too horrible to be read or to be uttered.' (*Johnson on Shakespeare* II.990)

15 *Timon* III.v.1260; cf. *Romeo and Juliet* III.i.Q2:G: 'Mercie but murders, pardoning those that kill'; *Measure for Measure* II.i.727–8: 'Mercy is not it selfe, that oft lookes so, / Pardon is still the nurse of second woe', and II.ii.855ff: 'Yet shew some pittie'; 'I shew it most of all, when I show Iustice; / For then I pittie those I doe not know, / Which a dismis'd offence would after gaule'. Most fully argued in *Timon* III.v. Title quote from *Measure for Measure* II.ii.830–1.

16 Quoted: *Merchant of Venice* IV.i.Q:Hᵛ; *Tempest* V.i.1977ff. Cf. also *Measure for Measure* II.ii.809ff and 863ff: 'Oh, it is excellent / To haue a Giants strength: but it is tyrannous / To vse it like a Giant', and *Timon* III.v.1265–6: 'pitty is the vertue of the Law, / And none but Tyrants vse it cruelly'. Cf. also Jonson's *Timber*: 'No vertue is a *Princes* owne; or becomes him more, then his *Clemency*: And no glory is greater, then to be able to save with his power . . . The state of things is secur'd by

Clemency; severity represseth a few, but it irritates more' (*Works* VIII.599, ll. 1162ff). Exemplified by the lenient Justice Clement in *Every Man in his Humour*, and by the dinner party replacing the judgements of Justice Overdo in *Bartholomew Fair*.

17 Quoted: *Merchant of Venice* IV.i.Q:H^v; *King John* IV.i.1671ff; *Henry V* II.i.669ff and cf. Holinshed, Bullough IV.384–5.

18 Kneelings in *Titus* I.i.126, 188, 411, 433, 476ff (see 507ff), 526ff, II.iii.1047, III.i.1355ff, IV.i.1635, V.iii.2640. The same general point made by H. Gardner: *Religion and Literature* (1971), pp. 77–8.

19 *Richard III* II.i.1222ff, cf. Hall, Bullough III.250, and see N. Coghill: *Shakespeare's Professional Skills* (Cambridge, 1964), pp. 24–6, based on a production directed by Sir Lewis Casson with H. Granville-Barker in the Old Vic in 1940. Granville-Barker and Coghill both assume Lear recognises Gloucester but he does not do so till some eighty lines later. Such recognition of essential qualities, not persons, is characteristic of Shakespeare's enlightened lunatics; cf. *Titus* V.ii.2306–2352.

20 Kneeling and quotations from *Measure for Measure* V.i.2369ff, 2606, 2797, 2805–6, 2815–6, 2829ff, 2871–3, 2841ff, 2838. Johnson is stern: 'Angelo's crimes were such, as must sufficiently justify punishment . . . and I believe every reader feels some indignation when he finds him spared. From what extenuation of his crime can Isabel, who yet supposes her brother dead, form any plea in his favour[?] . . . I am afraid our Varlet Poet intended to inculcate, that women think ill of nothing that raises the credit of their beauty'! (*Johnson on Shakespeare* I.213). The embodiment of Isabella's image in Claudio's resurrection was pointed out to me by a student, Miss J. Davey.

21 Quoted: *Merchant of Venice* II.ii.Q:C^v–C2^v; *Pericles* V.i.Q:I (cf. *Merchant of Venice* II.ii.651–4), V.iii.Q:I3; *Cymbeline* V.v.3359–60, 3560ff; *Winter's Tale* V.iii.3333ff; *Tempest* V.i.2152, 2181ff, 2269ff. My italics.

22 Quoted or referred to: *Coriolanus* II.i.1075, cf Plutarch, Bullough V. 515; V.iii.3399ff, cf. Plutarch, Bullough V.539; final tableau at V.iii.3530ff as in Plutarch, Bullough V.540–1.

23 Quoted or referred to: *King Leir* ll. 2298ff (Bullough VII.393–4); *King Lear* V.iii.2950–2 (my italics). Compare this note of harmony with Hamlet's to Gertrude: 'when you are desirous to be blest, / Ile blessing beg of you'. (*Hamlet* III.iv.Q2:I4). In general terms, just as some sense of guilt is inherent in parenthood, so a part of filial love is a sense of infinite obligation. This theme, touched on in *Hamlet* and explored in *Lear*, dominates the last plays, e.g. Alonso to Miranda: 'I am hers. / But O, how odly will it sound, that I / Must aske my childe forgiuenesse?' (*Tempest* V.i.2175–7).

Chapter 5: Kissing and embracing

1 Quoted: Sidney: *Astrophel and Stella* 79, ll. 12–13; *King John* II.i.312–3. Staged kisses (sample only) of welcome: *Tempest* V.i.2067ff; parting: *Timon* IV.ii.1579 (SD most probably authorial: *Embrace and part*); war-

riors – e.g. *i Henry IV* V.ii.Q:I4^v, 'I will imbrace him with a souldiours arme, / That he shall shrinke vnder my curtesie'; in amity: *1 Henry VI* V.iii.2615; as seal of marriage: listed by Priest, *Twelfth Night* V.i. 2320; staged, *King John* II.i.854–5; by proxy, *3 Henry VI* III.iii.1793ff; explicitly stated, *Taming of the Shrew* III.ii.1505–6, *Merchant of Venice* III.ii.1485. It cannot be made the symbol of divorce (*Richard II* V.i.2336–7).

2 Quoted: title-quotation: *Love's Labour's Lost* IV.i.Q:D4; *Taming of the Shrew* IV.i.1719ff; *2 Henry VI* IV.i.2219ff; Touchstone in *As You Like It* III.ii.1246; Lavache in *All's Well* II.ii.833ff, and see *Hamlet* V.ii. 3597ff.

3 Quoted: *Othello* V.i.Q:L3^v; *Love's Labour's Lost* V.ii.Q:H2; *Othello* II.i.Q:E (F:947); *Love's Labour's Lost* V.ii.Q:H2.

4 Quoted: *Love's Labour's Lost* V.ii.Q:K^v (my italics); *Henry V* IV.i.2111– 2. 'When a young man came up to him in Zurich and said, "May I kiss the hand that wrote *Ulysses*?" Joyce replied, somewhat like King Lear, "No, it did lots of other things too." ' (R. Ellmann: *James Joyce* (1965) p. 114).

5 Judas kiss: as platitude, e.g. *Riche his Farewell to Militarie Profession* (1581): 'she gave him other Judas' kisse . . .' (Bullough II.37); specifically staged at *3 Henry VI* V.vii.3202ff, and also at *3 Henry VI* IV.viii.2627, *Richard III* II.i.1144. Quoted or described: *Richard II* I.iii.343–351, III.iii.1620 –3, 1690ff, Q:G2 (my italics), and cf. Bullough III, 385–6, 392–3, 403; see further p. 68 above.

6 Plutarch's *Life of Marcus Brutus*, Bullough V.102. My italics.

7 Quoted: *Hero and Leander* I.185. Other handshakes as kisses at *Love's Labour's Lost* V.ii.Q:I4^v ('by this Virgin palme now kissing thine, / I wilbe thine'), *Two Gentlemen* II.ii.575–6, where Julia asks for a 'holy kisse' to 'seale the bargaine' of their exchange of favours, and Proteus replies 'Here is my hand', and, probably, *Romeo and Juliet* IV.i.Q2:L2^v, where Paris parts from Juliet with 'this holy kisse'. It is a marriage handshake; cf. Donne's 'Extasie', ll. 5ff: 'Our hands were firmely cimented / With a fast balme, which thence did spring . . . So to' entergraft our hands, as yet / Was all the meanes to make us one.'

8 Cf. Suffolk to Margaret: 'Oh Fairest Beautie, do not feare, nor flye: / For I will touch thee but with reuerend hands, / *I kisse these fingers for eternall peace, / And lay them gently on thy tender side*' (*1 Henry VI* V.iii.2483ff. My italics). Ignorance of this elucidatory parallel makes the reading of Romeo's first quatrain appear problematic. Editors generally assume him to take Juliet's hand, apologising for the advance by promising a *future* kiss, but their reading is based on an unfounded correction of Q2's 'did readie' (followed by F:672) to Q1's 'ready'. Q2's reading is of the highest authority, being demonstrably set up from authorial copy; Q1 is a reported text and wholly without authority, although its reading here is metrically better. Q2's past tense implies past action. It was also common to emend 'sin' (Q1, Q2, F:671) to 'fine' (Warburton), or 'pain' (Dover Wilson) to support the unfounded interpretation of future absolution.

9 The assumption that the lovers kiss on the last line of the first sonnet is

supported by K. Muir: *Shakespeare the Professional* (1973), p. 100. Earlier quotation from Keats: *Isabella*, st.ix.

10 *Romeus and Juliet*, ll. 259ff. Bullough I.293.

11 Quoted: *Johnson on Shakespeare*, I.404; *All's Well* V.iii.3053–4 (and cf. II.iii.1070ff), V.iii.3070ff; W. Painter: *The Palace of Pleasure*, Novel 38, Bullough II.396.

12 Quoted: *Troilus and Cressida* III.ii.Q:F2; *Othello* III.ii.Q:H2.

13 Quoted: *Troilus and Cressida* IV.ii.Q:H2ᵛ, III.ii.Q:F3, IV.iv.Q:H4 (my italics).

14 Quoted: *Antony and Cleopatra* III.x.1985–6. The first scene between Antony and Cleopatra is entirely Shakespeare's invention (I.i.15–69), and for the kiss at III.xi.2101, cf. Plutarch, Bullough V.302, n. 1 (Bullough's act and scene references differ at this point from those of the Hinman First Folio).

15 Quoted: *Coriolanus* IV.v.2764ff, V.iii.3519. For the first embrace, see Plutarch, Bullough V.513; for the second, cf. Bullough V.528. R. Berry, in *The Shakespearean Metaphor* (1978), pp. 89, 99, notes the sexual imagery of the first embrace as 'a plain . . . statement that war is a quasi-sexual activity', but misses its later parallel.

16 Study of the Shakespearean image-cluster originates in Walter Whiter's *Specimen of a Commentary* (1794). It was reassumed (in ignorance of this predecessor) by Caroline Spurgeon in *Shakespeare's Imagery* (1935) informs most of Wilson Knight's work, and is the basis of such critical works as Edward Armstrong: *Shakespeare's Imagination* (1946) or Martin Green: *The Labyrinth of Shakespeare's Sonnets* (1974).

17 Other life-giving kisses at, e.g., *2 Tamburlaine* II.iv.69–71; *3 Henry VI* V.ii.2837ff; Tennyson: *In Memoriam* XVIII.14–16: 'I, falling on his faithful heart, / Would breathing through his lips impart / The life that almost dies in me'.

18 Quoted: Sir T. Browne: *Hydriotaphia, Works*, ed. S. Wilkin (1846), III.484; Castiglione: *The Book of the Courtier* (Everyman ed. 1959), Book IV, p. 315; Sidney: *Astrophel and Stella* 81, ll. 5–6; *Faustus* V.i.1771; Donne: 'The Expiration', ll. 1–2; J. Oldham: *The Lamentation of Adonis*: 'Kiss, while I watch thy swimming Eye-balls roul, / Watch thy last Gasp, and catch thy springing Soul. / I'll suck it in, I'll hoard it in my Heart . . .' (*Works* (6th ed, 1703), pp. 221–2). Pope's debt was pointed out by Warton.

19 A marked improvement on Brooke's 'A thousand times she kist his mouth as cold as stone' (l. 2731, Bullough I.356), and Shakespeare's own earlier conventionality: 'Oh take this warme kisse on thy pale cold lips' (*Titus* V.iii.Q:K4).

20 Echo noted by Steevens. *Hero and Leander* was first published in 1598; Shakespeare may have seen it in manuscript. The debt cannot be the other way round since Marlowe died in 1593, and *Romeo and Juliet* is generally dated 1595.

21 *King Lear* IV.vii.2776ff. My italics.

22 *Antony and Cleopatra* IV.xv.3088 (accepting Johnson's emendation of 'in'), V.ii.3561ff. In Plutarch the asp bites her arm (Bullough V.316), as

in other Roman authors' accounts. Shakespeare's variant can be traced to Nashe's *Christ's Tears, Works* II.140 ('At thy breasts (as at Cleopatras) Aspisses shall be put out to nurse'), and Peele's *Edward I* (1593), sc.xvi. If so, these clearly fused with a personal association.

23 *Antony and Cleopatra* V.ii.3544. For some of the wilder explanations, see Variorum ed. (1907), pp. 365–6.

24 *Antony and Cleopatra* IV.xv.3023, 3046–8 (my italics), 3063ff. Pope's emendation of 'when' to 'where', ignores Antony's lines, which Cleopatra answers, that he will importune death 'vntill' they have embraced.

25 *Romeo and Juliet* V.iii.Q2:L3; *Antony and Cleopatra* V.ii.3538.

26 Quoted: *Othello* V.ii.Q:M.

27 *Othello* III.iii.Q:G3ᵛ, III.iv.Q:I2.

28 *Othello* IV.i.Q:Kᵛ, V.ii.Q:M3.

29 | | |
|---|---|
| *Desdemona* | Talke you of killing? |
| *Othello* | I, I doe. |
| *Desdemona* | Then heauen haue mercy on me. |
| *Othello* | Amen, with all my heart. |
| *Desdemona* | If you say so, I hope you will not kill me. |
| *Othello* | Hum. |

(Othello V.ii.Q:Mᵛ)

Othello	. . . thou art to die.
Desdemona	The Lord haue mercy on me.
Othello	I say Amen.
Desdemona	And haue you mercy too.

(Othello V.ii.Q:M2)

A pointed alteration of the source: "The wretched Lady . . . called on Divine Justice to witness to her fidelity, since earthly justice failed' (Cinthio: *Gli Hecatommithi*, Bullough VII.251).

30 *Romeo and Juliet* V.iii.Q2:L3; *Othello* V.ii.Q:Mᵛ.

Chapter 6: Weeping

1 *Titus* III.i.1151ff, 1172ff, 1369ff, 1263ff.

2 *Romeo and Juliet* I.i.Q2:Bᵛ, Q2:A3ᵛ.

3 *Titus* III.i.Q:E3.

4 *Two Gentlemen* II.iii.623–5.

5 *Merchant of Venice* III.ii.Q:E4; A. Golding: *Ovid's Metamorphoses*, ed. W. H. D. Rouse (1904), XI.218–44.

6 *Richard II* III.iii.Q:G2.

7 *Winter's Tale* II.i.726; *Antony and Cleopatra* IV.xv.3097ff.

8 *3 Henry VI* I.iv.627ff.

9 *King John* IV.i.1601.

10 *King Lear* IV.vii.2827–8, 2807–8.

11 Bullough I.359, l. 2866.

12 *All's Well* IV.iii.2215–6, and see *Timon* IV.iii.2133ff; *Tempest* V.i.1964.

13 *King Lear* II.iv.1583, and see IV.vii.2796–7.

14 *3 Henry VI* II.i.735, recalled in *Richard III* I.ii.346–55. Aaron is proud of his negro inability to blush (*Titus* IV.ii.1798ff, V.i.2237–8); Warwick and Margaret (*3 Henry VI* III.iii.1832, I.iv.581ff) and Antiochus and his daughter (*Pericles* I.i.Q:A4ᵛ) none of them blush at their crimes.

15 *Richard III* I.iii.830–2; compliment returned at I.iv.1071–2, and cf. *King Lear* III.vii.2160–7. Clarence calls on Richard to save him; Gloucester, about to be blinded, on Edmund. Both are cruelly disabused.

16 *Two Gentlemen* II.iii.602–4.

17 *Merchant of Venice* II.viii.1069, echoing *The Jew of Malta* II.i.47–54.

18 *Hamlet* I.ii.Q2:B4ᵛ, and for false use of religious argument see Satan's perversion of holy texts in the wilderness, Matthew 4.1–11; Shylock at *Merchant of Venice* I.iii.398ff; *Richard III* I.iii.812ff; for Iago see R. Noble, *Shakespeare's Biblical Knowledge*, p. 216.

19 *Cymbeline* I.v.545ff.

20 See C. J. Carlisle: *Shakespeare from the Greenroom* (Chapel Hill 1969), p. 179.

21 *Titus* I.i.Q:B. Titus's crime is shared by his sons, Lucius suggesting the sacrifice and performing it with his brothers' help.

22 H. Gardner: *Religion and Literature* (1971), pp. 77–8, and see p. 73 above.

23 A. Copley: *Wits fittes and fancies* (1595), C4, and see Bullough VI.43 for the source's treatment, where the shooting of arrows to heaven is merely a revenger's ruse to feign lunacy.

24 *Rape of Lucrece* l.1508; *2 Henry VI* III.ii.1756ff; *3 Henry VI* III.ii.1706ff; *Richard III* III.v.2085ff and I.ii.344, 357.

25 *As You Like It* I.i.149–51; *King John* IV.ii.1946–7, 1981–4, IV.iii.2106 –11.

26 *A Midsummer Night's Dream* III.ii.1149, 1180–4; *Two Gentlemen* III.ii.1513–20, II.vii.1044, 1047; *Antony and Cleopatra* I.ii.246ff, III.xi.2100–1; *Troilus and Cressida* IV.ii.2367–72 and Q:H2ᵛ.

27 A. C. Bradley: 'Antony and Cleopatra', *Oxford Lectures on Poetry* (1941), p. 290; *Antony and Cleopatra* V.i.3140–2, and cf. Plutarch, Bullough V.310.

28 *Antony and Cleopatra* III.ii.1602ff.

29 Cut by Bullough, but see the Dent edition of *Plutarch's Lives* (1899), ix.61. Also quoted: *Antony and Cleopatra* IV.ii.2441–2.

30 *2 Henry IV* IV.v.Q:H4, I.

31 Title quotation from *3 Henry VI* II.i.741. Referred to *Much Ado* IV.i.Q:G2ᵛ; *2 Henry VI* II.iv.1265; *Henry VIII* V.i.2960; *Titus* III.i.Q:F3.

32 *Julius Caesar* IV.iii.2134 and see V.iii.2591–3; *Macbeth* II.iii.863–4, 845 –7, 886–91, 909–10. Holinshed suggests the contrast in reactions: Donwald's 'over earnest diligence in the severe inquisition and triall of the offendors heerein' aroused suspicion in the other lords, who 'doubted to utter what they thought, till time and place should better serve thereunto, and heereupon got them awaie everie man to his home' (Bullough VII.483).

33 Title quotation: *Timon* IV.iii.2140. Quoted: *3 Henry VI* I.iv.549; *Titus* V.i.Q:Iᵛ–J2. A significant elaboration of the source (Bullough VI.41):

Titus, 'laying his Hand on a Block, . . . gave the wicked Moor his Sword, who immediately struck it off, and inwardly laugh'd at the Villainy'.

34 *A Midsummer Night's Dream* V.i.Q:G3ᵛ.

35 *Richard II* V.ii.Q:H4; *King Lear* IV.iii.Q:H4ᵛ (not in F); *Richard II* III.ii.Q:E4ᵛ.

36 *Much Ado* I.i.Q:A2ᵛ.

37 *All's Well* IV.iii.2169–74.

38 *King Lear* V.iii.3159–62, II.ii.1242–3; *Measure for Measure* IV.iii.2196–7; *Tempest* I.ii.604–6.

39 *Cymbeline* V.iv.3137–8; *Tempest* III.i.1321–2; *Winter's Tale* V.ii.3024–5, 3059–61, 3081–4. Compare the unnatural confusion of Claudius's marriage celebrations 'With an auspitious, and a dropping eye, / With mirth in funerall, and with dirdge in marriage' (*Hamlet* I.ii.Q2:B3ᵛ).

Chapter 7: Silence and pause

1 Quoted: E. Wilson ed. *Shaw on Shakespeare* (Harmondsworth, 1969), p. 70. For a suggestive discussion of Shakespeare's introduction of pauses by half-lines and metrical gaps, see R. Flatter: *Shakespeare's Producing Hand* (1948), sections III and IV. His later discussion is largely undermined by its reliance on punctuation and line-division, which can be compositorial. Curiously, Shakespeare's widespread and pointed use of silence has otherwise been mostly ignored. A. Thaler: *Shakspere's Silences* (Cambridge, Mass., 1929) considers it predominantly in terms of characterisation. Later critics commit incidental errors; for Hasler (*Shakespeare's Theatrical Notation* (Bern, 1974) p. 11) complete silence cannot be directed through dialogue. I-S. Ewbank: *Shakespeare, Ibsen and the Unspeakable* (1976) passes quickly from some obvious Shakespearean examples to his use of rhetoric for the unspeakable.

2 *Richard III* I.iv.953–6; *Merchant of Venice* II.ix.Q:E.

3 *1 Henry VI* II.iv.928–30. Medwall's *Nature* also starts with a silence.

4 *1 Henry VI* II.v.1070ff, cf. Hall, Bullough III.47.

5 *Titus* III.ii.1456–9, 1477, 1487–8; not in Q. The scene is a non-narrative independent theatrical elaboration similar to the 1602 Additions to *The Spanish Tragedy*. Both conform to Webster's later description in his *Induction* to Marston's *Malcontent*: 'What are your additions?' 'Sooth not greatly needefull, only as your sallet to your greate feast . . .' (ll. 77–9).

6 Title quotation, *Richard III* IV.iv.2898; also quoted: Seneca: *Phaedra*, l. 607; *Spanish Tragedy* (1592), ll. 2050–70; Gascoigne's *Supposes*, Bullough I.157.

7 *Venus and Adonis* ll. 331ff; *Titus* II.iv.1109–10; *Two Gentlemen* I.ii.182–5, II.ii.584–6.

8 *2 Henry VI* I.iii.512–48, II.iv.1265 and Hall, Bullough III.102, III.ii.1725–9.

9 *Henry VIII* V.i.2957–60 (cf. Foxe's account, Bullough IV.487 – Shakespeare adds Cranmer's silence, but not his tears); *Richard II*

I.iii.540–7; *Cymbeline* III.iv.1673ff, V.iv.3063–4; Sonnet 23, l. 13.

10 See *SFF* p. 297 for transference of song in *Twelfth Night*, and p. 358 for cutting of Willow Song in Q *Othello*. For Cordelia, see H. Gardner; *Religion and Literature*, pp. 68–9; *Lear* V.iii.3236–7 (cf. I.i.163), and Tilley, S 447.

11 *Merchant of Venice* I.i.Q:A3ᵛ.

12 *Taming of the Shrew* I.i.372–4, II.i.885–6. My italics.

13 Tilley, S 446.

14 *Taming of the Shrew* IV.v.2318.

15 Quoted: *Winter's Tale* I.ii.83; *Merry Wives* V.v.2700ff; *Troilus and Cressida* III.ii.Q:F2–3; *Tempest* III.i.1331ff.

16 *Coriolanus* II.i.1081, IV.ii.2567, and V.iii.3386ff. For Plutarch, see Bullough V.538–9.

17 Title-quote: *Lear* I.i.67; *Hero and Leander* I.186; *1 Henry VI* V.iii.2502ff.

18 *Much Ado* II.i.Q:C2ᵛ–3 and Wilson, *op. cit.*, pp. 166, 169, III.ii.Q:Eᵛ; *As You Like It* I.ii.415.

19 *Measure for Measure* V.i.2891–2, 2936.

20 *Cymbeline* V.v.3713–6.

21 *Lear* I.i.275–6, 216, 95–6. For a series of analogues, culminating in Christ's silence at the interrogation of Pilate, Herod and Caiaphas (recurrent in mediaeval drama) see J. Levenson: 'What the Silence Said: Still Points in *King Lear*', *Shakespeare 1971*, ed. C. Leech and J. M. R. Margeson (Univ. of Toronto Press, 1972), pp. 215–29.

22 G. Grigson ed. *Poems of John Clare's Madness* (1949), p. 216.

23 Title-quote: *Winter's Tale* V.ii.3023–4; *Lear* I.iv.706–7; *Much Ado* II.i.Q:C2ᵛ; *As You Like It* I.ii.424; L. Tolstoy: 'Shakespeare and the Drama', *Recollections and Essays*, ed. Aylmer Maude (1961), pp. 352–3.

24 *Coriolanus* V.iii.3539 and Bullough V.540–1. For another interpretation, see C. M. Sicherman: '*Coriolanus*: The Failure of Words', *ELH* 39 (1972), pp. 189–207. 'Silence' (*Winter's Tale* III.ii.1185) is, according to Greg, a compositorial or scribal error, placing speech as SD (see *SFF* p. 416).

25 Quoted: *Coriolanus* III.i.1985–6, III.ii.2180–1, V.iii.3385, I.i.137. For the isolationism of Shakespeare's villains, cf. Richard at *3 Henry VI* V.vi.3156ff (quoted on p. 66); Proteus: 'I to my selfe am deerer then a friend' (*Two Gentlemen* II.vi.952); Iago: 'Vertue? A figge, 'tis in our selues that we are thus or thus' (*Othello* I.iii.Q:Dᵛ); Edmund: 'An admirable euasion of Whore-master-man, to lay his Goatish disposition on the charge of a Starre . . . I should haue bin that I am, had the maidenlest Starre in the Firmament twinkled on my bastardizing' (*Lear* I.ii.455ff); even Caliban: 'I am all the Subiects that you haue, / Which first was min owne King' (*Tempest* I.ii.480–1). Cf. also *Venus and Adonis* l. 166: 'Things growing to them selues, are growths abuse'.

26 Pliny: *Natural History* 35.73–4. Final quotation from Joseph Warton: *The Adventurer* no. 113 (Dec. 4, 1753), writing on Shakespeare.

Chapter 8: Costume

1 A. Dyce, ed. J. Ford: *The Lover's Melancholy* I.ii. p. 22: Gifford's note, from Steevens.

2 Quoted or referred to: *Julius Caesar* I.i.11; Sir W. Scott: *The Heart of Midlothian*, ch. xxii; *This England* (Harmondsworth 1969), p. 62; T. Lodge: *Rosalynde* (1590), Bullough II.248; Laneham's *Letter: Whearin, part of the entertainment untoo the Queenz Majesty, at Killingwoorth Castl . . . iz signified* (1575), quoted in D. M. Bergeron: *English Civic Pageantry, 1558–1642* (1971), p. 32; *Edward II* II.ii.11–46; *Pericles* II.ii.Q:C4–C4ᵛ; Nashe: *The Unfortunate Traveller, Works* II. 271–2; Holinshed, Bullough IV. 193. See also M. C. Linthicum: *Costume in the Drama of Shakespeare and his Contemporaries* (Oxford 1936), particularly on colour symbolism, and for an Oriental analogue, cf. Pound's note to 'The Jewel Stairs' Grievance', *Cathay, Collected Shorter Poems of Ezra Pound* (1973), p. 142.

3 *Henslowe's Diary*, ed. R. A. Foakes and R. T. Rickert (Cambridge, 1961), p. 73 (20/- each), and for *Henry VIII*, see pp. 171, 224, n. 1. For contemporary reference to the players' wearing of 'cast suites', see e.g. Nashe: *Summer's Last Will, Works* III.293, and H. Peacham: *The Compleat Gentleman* (1634), B2; for their richness, e.g. Nashe: *Pierce Penilesse, Works* I.215.

4 Quoted: *Winter's Tale* IV.iv.2033ff; *Taming of the Shrew* IV.iii.2073–4; *Much Ado* III.iv.Q:Fᵛ, II.i.Q:C3; *Pericles* IV.ii.Q:F4. For an explanation of some of the technical terms quoted, see Linthicum, *op. cit.*, pp. 173, 182 plate vi.

5 *2 Henry IV* Ind. Q:A2; *Winter's Tale* IV.i.1583, 1595, *Troilus and Cressida* Prol, l. 24, and for comparable parallel instances, see T. W. Craik: *The Tudor Interlude* (Leicester 1958), pp. 65–6 and D. M. Bergeron: 'The Emblematic Nature of English Civic Pageantry', *Ren.Dr.* (1968), pp. 167–198.

6 *Coriolanus* I.ix.746–7 (and, for his emphasised bloodiness, cf. *2 Tamburlaine* III.ii.116: 'Blood is the God of Wars rich livery'), II.i.1061–2, II.iii.1426, IV.iv.2621–2; *Julius Caesar* I.ii.84, 119–20; *All's Well* I.i.3, and see ch. 9 p. 176; *Richard II* II.ii.Q:D4.

7 *Henry V* IV.viii.2785ff; *Macbeth* V.iii.2277. Changes of dress for degeneration and regeneration in the Tudor Interlude analysed by Craik, *op. cit.*, p. 78ff.

8 *1 Tamburlaine* I.ii.8, 33, 41ff; see also *Edward II* IV.vii.97, V.vi.95; *Dido* II.i.80ff (Dido dresses Aeneas in the robes of Sichaeus). Most flamboyant are the white, scarlet and black banners and costume symbolising the stages of Tamburlaine's waning clemency at the Siege of Damascus, in *2 Tamburlaine*. He enters *al in scarlet* ('Now hang our bloody collours by Damascus, / Reflexing hewes of blood upon their heads' IV.iv.SD, ll. 1–2), then *all in blacke, and verie melancholy* ('now when furie and incensed hate / Flings slaughtering terrour from my coleblack tents', V.i.62SD, 71–2).

9 *Hamlet* II.i.Q2:E2, III.i.Q2:G3ᵛ, II.i.Q2:E2, I.v.Q2:D3, and cf. *As You Like It* III.ii.1558ff for the conventional lover's marks. The two-month

time gap separating the two scenes pointed out by Bradley:*Shakespearean Tragedy*, pp. 129–30, is immaterial in theatrical terms.

10 For similar readings of the Pyrrhus speech, see C. R. N. Routh: 'The Pyrrhus speech in Hamlet', *TLS* (Aug. 5, 1944), p. 379; A. Johnston: 'The Player's Speech in *Hamlet*', *SQ* (1962), pp. 21–30; C. Leech: 'The hesitation of Pyrrhus', *The Morality of Art*, ed. D. W. Jefferson (1969), pp. 41–9; and (in ignorance of Routh) M. C. Bradbrook: 'Shakespeare's Primitive Art', *Proceedings of the British Academy 1965* (1966), p. 226. The point struck Mr Routh forcibly when watching a performance of the play; it is wholly obscured in the learned and discursive essays of Clifford Leech and Arthur Johnston. For the Troy picture in *Rape of Lucrece*, see W. S. Heckscher: 'Shakespeare in His Relationship to the Visual Arts', *RORD* (1970–1), pp. 25–35.

11 *Macbeth* V.iii.2252, 2254, 2271, 2273, 2277, 2282, 2216–7. For a different reading, see M. Bluestone: *From Story to Stage* (The Hague, 1974), pp. 99–100: 'Macbeth truly cannot buckle his distempered cause within the belt of rule . . . stage action . . . perceptualizes a Macbeth who has for the moment outgrown his armor, his vaulting ambitions now so huge' [sic].

12 *King John* III.iv.1486–7, and cf. the entry of the distracted Queen *with her haire about her ears* (*Richard III* II.ii.1306, SD authorial); *Enter Ofelia playing on a Lute, and her haire downe singing* (*Hamlet* IV.v.Q1:G4ᵛ, *distracted* F:2766); *Enter Cassandra rauing* (*Troilus and Cressida* II.ii.Q:D2ᵛ; *with her haire about her eares*, F:1082–3).

13 *2 Henry IV* I.i.205–10, and see Craik, *op. cit.*, p. 77, for several interludes in which the sick wear kerchiefs; cf. also *2 Return from Parnassus*, ll. 442–3.

14 *Julius Caesar* II.i.966.

15 D. E. Jones: *The Plays of T. S. Eliot* (1969), pp. 19–20, and cf. Heywood's *A Woman Killed with Kindness*, where Wendoll runs *over the stage in a night gown*, and *the Maid in her smock* stops Frankford striking him; in later references Wendoll was 'like a spright' and the interceding maid 'like the angel's hand' (XIII.67 SD, XVI.122–3, XIII.68).

16 Imagery of war for love: e.g. *Spanish Tragedy* (1592), ll. 788–99, 901–10; Harington's translation of *Orlando Furioso*, V.47 (Bullough II.93); Brooke's *Romeus and Juliet*, ll. 897–8 (Bullough I.309). Particularly common is the woman's virginity as a besieged city and vice versa, e.g. in Nashe's *Unfortunate Traveller*, *Works* II.209 ('Turwin lost her maidenhead, and opened her gates to more than Iane Trosse did'); Jonson's *Alchemist*, where Doll Common is 'our Castle, our cinque-Port' (III.iii.18); *Romeus and Juliet*, ll. 921–2 (Bullough I.309); *All's Well* I.i.117–32; *Henry V* V.ii.3306–3313; *Rape of Lucrece* ll. 433ff. See further Heckscher, *op. cit.*, pp. 25–7, 61–2, n. 14; his examples extend from the classics to the punning title of Hemingway's *A Farewell to Arms*. For the last, cf. *Duchess of Malfi* V.ii.172–3: Bosola taking the pistol from Julia: 'Come, come, I'll disarme you, / And arme you thus'. Next quotation from *Antony and Cleopatra* I.iii.382–4, and cf. also IV.xii.2781–2.

17 Plutarch, Bullough V.307.

18 The addition was identified but not interpreted in Dover Wilson's Cambridge edition (1950), p. 209. If Fredson Bowers is correct that the Folio text was set up from scribal copy of author's MS, then the scribe has preserved the marginal addition exactly. See *On Editing Shakespeare* (Pennsylvania, 1955), p. 114, n. 9.

19 For the parallel image of the shackled hero, cf. *Antony and Cleopatra* IV.xiv.2909ff, and cf. *Venus and Adonis* ll. 98–9; for the specifically erotic connotations of 'pants' cf. *Othello* II.i.844. Note that in this image of their love-making Cleopatra takes the dominant position.

20 *Antony and Cleopatra* II.v.1046ff, IV.xii.2770–1, IV.xiv.2871–2.

21 *Troilus and Cressida* I.i.Q:A2. The point about Eros is also made by Quiller-Couch: *Studies in Literature, Second Series* (Cambridge 1922), p. 177. For a different discussion, see also R. B. Waddington: 'Antony and Cleopatra: "What Venus did with Mars"', *Shk. Studies* (1966), pp. 210–27.

22 See *Twelfth Night* IV.ii.2049–50; *Spanish Tragedy* (1592), ll. 2667ff; *Pericles* IV.vi.Q:G3ᵛ; *Much Ado* II.i.519ff; *Merry Wives* V.v.Q:G2 SD; *Richard III* III.v.2082–3 and cf. Hall, Bullough III.267; *Macbeth* II.ii.734 –5; *Othello* V.i.3138 (not in Cinthio, Bullough VII.249).

23 *Merry Wives* V.v.2530, 2578, cf. *Twelfth Night* I.i.26–8, and see J. M. Steadman: 'Falstaff as Actaeon: A Dramatic Emblem', *SQ* (1963), pp. 231–44.

24 *Romeo and Juliet* I.v.614–6.

25 *Troilus and Cressida* I.iii.Q:B4, III.ii.Q:F2, I.ii.418–9; *Twelfth Night* I.v.525–7.

26 *Measure for Measure* V.i.2921–3.

27 *Measure for Measure* IV.i.1834.

28 *Measure for Measure* V.i.2595–6, cf. III.i.1447–8; V.i.2542–3, 2578. My italics.

29 *Measure for Measure* V.i.2497, 2717–8; *King Lear* IV.vi.2597–8.

30 *Henry V* IV.iii.2270–1; Chaucer: *The Monk's Tale, Canterbury Tales* VII.2367–74; *King Lear* III.iv.1886. For the feathers and motley dress of vices, see Craik, *op. cit.*, p. 66ff; for dressing and undressing in the Tudor Interlude, see R. Southern: *The Staging of Plays before Shakespeare* (1973), pp. 66–7; for the nakedness of innocence, cf. naked Man, in *Nature*: 'I nede none other vesture, / / Nature hath clothed me / as yet suffysantly / / Gyltles of syn / and as a mayden pure / / I were on me / the garment of innocencye' (B2ᵛ), and, of course, unfallen Adam and Eve.

31 *2 Henry VI* I.iii.465, *Contention* Q:D2 SD (translating the implicit direction of the dialogue at II.iv.1206–10), and cf. Heywood's *2 Edward IV (Works* I, p. 165) where the same staging and point are made. M. H. Golden points out that Lady Macbeth appears as a penitent in her sleep-walking scene also ('stage imagery', *A Shakespeare Encyclopaedia*, ed. O. J. Campbell and E. G. Quinn (1974), p. 820).

32 *A Shrew* Q:C3ᵛ.

33 *Titus* II.i.Q:C3; *Richard III* I.ii.448–60; *King Lear* IV.vi.2606–8; for Falstaff, see *2 Henry IV* I.ii.303ff, 478ff, II.i.640ff, II.ii.852–4.

34 *All's Well* I.ii.308–10 (for Bertram's plumes and patches see also

III.v.1702–3, IV.v.2576ff); *As You Like It* IV.i.1949; *All's Well* IV.v.2482–3, 2487, III.v.1711, II.iii.1155ff, 1110ff, V.ii.2663–4, 2691–3, IV.iii.2431–2: *Tempest* V.i.2270–1.

35 *Antony and Cleopatra* I.i.46–7; earlier quotation from *Timon* IV.iii. 1933.

36 *King Lear* I.ii.359–60. My italics.

37 *Timon* IV.iii.2067, 2070–1.

38 *King Lear* III.iv.1891–2.

39 *King Lear* III.iv.1886–8 (my italics) and cf. France on Cordelia, whose apparent crime before her father caused her 'to dismantle / So many folds of fauour' (I.i.238–9).

40 *King Lear* IV.i.2216–8 (my italics), III.ii.1725–6 and cf. IV.i.2200–2. Johnson picked up the other moral aphorism shared by Gloucester and Lear (III.iv.1814–7, IV.i.2252–6) but missed the point of the parallel ('Lear has before uttered the same sentiment, which indeed cannot be too strongly impressed, though it may be too often repeated', *Johnson on Shakespeare* II.691).

41 *King Lear* IV.i.2226, 2240, 2231; J. Skelton: *Magnyfycence, Works* I.305, ll. 2425ff.

42 IV.vi.2442–3, II.iii.1272, IV.vi.2668–70, V.iii.3086–7, 3073ff.

43 *King Lear* I.iv.534.

44 L. Tolstoy: 'Shakespeare and the Drama', *Recollections and Essays* (1961), p. 334.

45 *King Lear* IV.i.2200; J. Florio trans. Montaigne: *Essays* (Everyman ed. 1965), II.192, 201.

46 *Love's Labour's Lost* V.ii.Q:H3. Other speech-costume correlations at *King Lear* I.i.306: 'Time shall vnfold what plighted [i.e. pleated] cunning hides', cf. Tarquin, 'Hiding base sin in pleats of Maiestie' (*Rape of Lucrece* l. 93), and Brutus, long disguised as a fool: 'now he throwes that shallow habit by' and 'Began to cloath his wit in state and pride' (*Rape of Lucrece* ll. 1814, 1809); insides-outsides theme in parallel metaphors of speech and dress at *Cymbeline* V.iv.3170–4. Jonson translates a pertinent extract from Seneca, *Epist.* cxiv. 3.11: 'Whersoever manners, and fashions are corrupted, Language is. It imitates the publicke riot. The excesse of Feasts, and apparell, are the notes of a sick State; and the wantonnesse of language, of a sick mind' *Timber, Works* VIII.593.

47 *Pericles* II.i.Q:C2ᵛ; *King Lear* IV.vi.2551–2; *Pericles* II.ii.Q:C4ᵛ (a probable echo of *1 Tamburlaine* I.ii.162–3), V.i.Q:I,Iᵛ.

48 *King John* I.i.199–203; cf. also *Thomas of Woodstock* ll. 1492ff, Bullough III.474.

49 *Winter's Tale* V.ii.3133–4, 3137–41, 3160–1, IV.iv.1949–50.

50 J. Dryden: *Preface to Troilus and Cressida* (1679), D. Nichol Smith ed. *Shakespeare Criticism, 1623–1840* (1964), p. 21 (an ironic theft of *Macbeth* V.ii.2198–2200). Cloten's ostentatious dress is noted at *Cymbeline* II.iii.1049–50.

51 *Cymbeline* II.iii.1099, 1111–3; *Johnson on Shakespeare* II.908, and see E. Wilson ed. *Shaw on Shakespeare* (Harmondsworth, 1969), pp. 42–3.

52 *Cymbeline* IV.ii.2396–7, and for the common image of loud words as

money in a purse, cf. Nashe: *Unfortunate Traveller, Works* II.255; *Hamlet* V.ii.Q2:N2ᵛ (not in F); *Timon* IV.ii.1558–9.

53 *Cymbeline* V.i.2889–90.

54 *Tempest* IV.i.1805, I.ii.453–4, III.iii.1583, 1535–6; *Henslowe's Diary*, p. 325.

55 *Measure for Measure* II.ii.874–5; *Tempest* IV.i.1868, 1900–1. I have omitted the clothes imagery (not obviously staged) in *Macbeth* since it is well known. For the decoying of Stephano and Trinculo, cf. *Troilus and Cressida* V.vi.3462–8, V.viii, in which Hector fatally pursues a soldier for his golden armour (an incident taken from Lydgate, Bullough VI.177–9). Shakespeare re-cycling again?

56 *Tempest* I.ii.109–11, 173, 183, 203. The difficulties of producing this long scene (which takes 'a full half hour to perform') after I.i. are noted by N. Shrimpton: 'Directing the Romances: 1. Directing *The Tempest*', *SS* 29 (1976), pp. 64–5.

57 *Troilus and Cressida* II.ii.Q:D2; *Antony and Cleopatra* I.ii.223; *Measure for Measure* III.i.1224–6, and for the last, cf. also *Much Ado* IV.i.1881–6; *All's Well* V.iii.2764–2773; *Timon* III.vi.1453–4; *2 Henry IV* I.iii.603ff; *Antony and Cleopatra* I.iv.474–8.

Chapter 9: Properties

1 Letter of Sir Henry Wotton, 2 July 1613, from *W. Shk.*, II.344; for Kean's *Dream*, see A. Nicoll: *A History of Late Nineteenth Century Drama, 1850–1900* (Cambridge 1946), I.41; for Tree's *Antony and Cleopatra*, see *The Times*, January 4, 1907.

2 *Revenger's Tragedy* I.i and III.v. Although Tourneur's authorship is debated, I subscribe to it here.

3 Squirrels for quickness, cats for liberty. See his *Part of the King's Entertainment*, ll. 156, 478.

4 Nashe: *Summer's Last Will*, ll. 360ff (*Works* III.244); *Arden of Feversham*, l. 2316 (and see ll. 2133–4), ll. 1384ff, and cf. a verbal image to the same effect, in *Cymbeline* III.iv.1754ff.

5 *1 Henry VI* II.iv (and for this scene's possible origins, see Bullough III.28, 346ff); *Two Gentlemen* II.iii.609ff; *Hamlet* III.ii.2215ff, *Othello* V.ii.3246ff.

6 *Pericles* IV.vi.Q:H; *Sons and Lovers* ch. viii (Harmondsworth, 1960), pp. 245–6; G. Eliot: 'The Natural History of German Life: Riehl', *Essays and Leaves from a Note-Book* (1885), p. 207.

7 *1 Henry IV* V.iii.Q:Kᵛ (SD probably authorial); Osborne's remark was given in a television interview, 6 May 1974. For visualised puns, cf. the ending of *The Italian Job* – a literalised cliff-hanger, with a coach poised, end-on, half-way over a cliff, thieves at one end of the coach, stolen gold at the end over the abyss. Every move to the gold tipped the coach further over; any attempt for the thieves to get out would also have made it drop.

8 See M. Jourdain: *English Decoration and Furniture of the Early Renaissance*

(1924), pp. 241–2: A 'Scarcity of chairs is due to their rarity during the early Renaissance. Stools and forms outnumbered the chairs in hall and parlour till the Restoration . . . In domestic use the chair was the rightful seat of the master of the house, only given up by courtesy . . .' My conclusions corroborate those of T. J. King: *Shakespearean Staging* (Cambridge, Mass. 1971), pp. 18–9, 38–9, 57–8, 76–7, 86–7, 94–5, and G. F. Reynolds: 'Some Principles of Elizabethan Staging, II', *M.Phil.* (1905), p. 92.

9 Tables for council-chambers: *Richard III* III.iv.1966 SD; *Othello* I.iii.Q:C (SD probably authorial); *Henry VIII* V.iii.3035 SD; for banquets e.g. *Titus* V.iii.2524 SD, *Timon* I.ii.490; for more detailed SDs see e.g. *Hamlet* V.ii.Q2:N3ᵛ (SD probably authorial) and F:3675–6; *Romeo and Juliet* I.v.Q2:C2ᵛ, IV.iv.Q2:Kᵛ (both SDs probably authorial). Cushions: *Hamlet* V.ii.Q2:N3ᵛ (SD probably authorial); *Coriolanus* II.ii.1203 (SD probably authorial). Quoted: *The Shrew* Ind.II.151–2.

10 *Merry Wives* III.iii.Q:Eᵛ, V.v.Q:Gᵛ SDs; *2 Henry VI* II.i.894, II.iii.1117ff, SDs probably authorial; standard army hardware not worth illustration.

11 *Merchant of Venice* II.ii.Q:Cᵛ (SD probably authorial); *Coriolanus* I.i.2–3 (SD probably authorial). For petitioners, see *The Merchant* as above, and *Titus* IV.iii.Q:Hᵛ (SD probably authorial); for rebels, *Contention* IV.ii.Q:F3 SD; *Romeo and Juliet* I.i.Q2:A3, A4 (SDs probably authorial).

12 *A Shrew* Ind.I.Q:A3, IV.iii.Q:D4ᵛ (cf. *1 Tamburlaine* IV.iv.40–1); *Timon* IV.iii.1825; *Henry V* I.ii.404ff; *Titus* IV.iii.Q:G4ᵛ; J. M. Steadman: 'Falstaff as Actaeon: A Dramatic Emblem', *SQ* (1963), p. 244, n. 52.

13 *Henslowe's Diary*, ed. R. A. Foakes and R. T. Rickert (Cambridge, 1961) p. 319.

14 *2 Henry VI* II.i.716 and *Contention* Q:Cᵛ; *Pericles* II.i.Q:C2, C3; *Twelfth Night* III.i.1304, III.ii.1388, III.iv.1694; *Cymbeline* II.iv.1255–6. I do not think these descriptions require a precedent stage reality, as in *Julius Caesar* (see ch. 1, p. 25 above). a) They require an unprecedented number of elaborate props, and b) there is no premium on historical accuracy here. A bed, candle, book and chest will suffice.

15 *1 Henry VI* I.i.9, 25, and see E. K. Chambers: *The Elizabethan Stage* (Oxford 1923), III.79, n. 3, where he suggests black hangings were hung from the tiring-house walls. *All's Well* I.i.2–3; *Lucrece* l. 766; *Macbeth* V.v.2321.

16 *Henry VIII* II.i.890 (SD probably authorial), and Holinshed, Bullough IV.462; *Merchant of Venice* IV.i.Q:G4ᵛ, H2ᵛ (cf. *2 Henry IV* V.ii.2987–8). S. Chew takes the knife as a 'stock symbol of perfidy' rather than justice – *The Virtues Reconciled* (Toronto 1947), p. 48. J. Doebler goes well beyond Shakespeare's clear directions when he fancifully suggests that Shylock should leave in the white shirt and with the candle of the penitent (*Shakespeare's Speaking Pictures* (Albuquerque, 1974), p. 62).

17 *2 Henry VI* II.iii.1076–93, III.i.1489–90 (and cf. *Thomas of Woodstock*, ll. 953ff, Bullough III.467).

18 Variants on the image: *Measure for Measure* III.i.1228ff, 'If thou art rich, thou'rt poore, / For like an Asse, whose backe with Ingots bowes, / Thou bearst thy heauie riches but a iournie, / And death vnloads thee';

Lear intends to 'Vnburthen'd crawle toward death' (*King Lear* I.i.46); see also *Richard II* V.v.2695–6. For another example of *The Tempest*'s recapitulatory techniques, see chapter 8, p. 168.

19 Functional letters in *King Lear* at I.ii.382, I.iv.853, I.v.875, II.ii.1242, III.iii.1761, III.v.1980, III.vii.2060, IV.v.2408, IV.vi.2715, V.i.2884, V.iii.2970, 3113; camouflage letters at IV.ii.2328, IV.v.2416, V.i.2898. Functional letters twice at *Measure for Measure* IV.ii.2058, IV.iii.2228, and camouflage at IV.v.2308. Letters and papers nine times in *All's Well* also (I.ii.238, II.ii.883–4, III.ii.1420, 1460, IV.iii.2326, V.i.2615, V.ii.2655, V.iii.2855, 3049).

20 T. Rymer: *A Short View of Tragedy, Critical Works*, ed. C. A. Zimansky (New Haven, 1956), pp. 163–4.

21 *Coriolanus* V.iv.3615ff; *Julius Caesar* I.ii.143, II.i.665 (my italics), and cf. Bullough V.82; *Richard II* V.ii.Q:H4ᵛ, cf. Bullough III.412, and see M. Black: 'Repeated Situations in Shakespeare's Plays', *Essays on Shakespeare and Elizabethan Drama in honour of Hardin Craig*, ed. R. Hosley (1963), pp. 254–6 (Black does not note the significant thematic additions).

22 *Antony and Cleopatra* I.v.552; *Hamlet* V.i.Q2:M3ᵛ, V.ii.Q2:N3ᵛ, and see A. C. Bradley: *Shakespearean Tragedy*, pp. 61–2. For a different reading, see B. Gellert: 'The Iconography of Melancholy in the Graveyard Scene of Hamlet', *S.Phil.* (1970), pp. 57–66. In her article on 'stage imagery', M. H. Golden says of Cleopatra, somewhat categorically, 'a woman with vipers at her breast is the sign of Luxuria' as well as suggesting 'a Madonna or Charity' (*A Shakespeare Encyclopaedia*, p. 820).

23 *Romeo and Juliet* III.ii.Q2:Gᵛ SD, V.iii.Q2:M, IV.v.Q2:K3, III.iii.Q2:Hᵛ, III.iv.Q2: H2ᵛ, III.v.Q2:H3ᵛ, last SD from IV.iii.Q1:I. Johnson's *Preface*, *Johnson on Shakespeare* I.66; S. T. Coleridge: *Shakespearean Criticism*, ed. T. M. Raysor (1964), I.7.

24 Benedict Nightingale in the *New Statesman*, 20 April 1973; *As You Like It* II.i.622–3.

25 *Richard II* IV.i.2107–8, contrasting with III.iv.Q:G3ᵛ; and III.ii.Q:F2 contrasting with IV.i.2119–20. Richard's handing Bolingbroke the crown is not from Holinshed (Bullough III.406); it may have been suggested by Daniel's *Civil Wars* (*ibid.* 453), or, if he read it, Berners' translation of Froissart (*ibid.* III.431). Bucket and scales images are Shakespeare's own.

26 *Richard II* IV.i.2122ff, 2176ff, 2215–6; M. Mahood: *Shakespeare's Word-play* (1957), p. 87; *Hamlet* I.ii.Q2:B4ᵛ ('I haue that within which passes showe / These but the trappings and the suites of woe'); *King Lear* I.i.144.

Chapter 10: Sources, sub-plots and conclusions

1 *Julius Caesar* I.iii.466–7.

2 Bullough III.54; *1 Henry VI* II.i.720, SD probably authorial.

3 Bullough III.54, 52 (and, for the effectiveness of Talbot's name, see also III.74); *1 Henry VI* II.i.765–70.

4 Bullough III.73–4, cf. *1 Henry VI* IV.iii–iv.2010ff. The Auvergne scene may have been suggested by Talbot's capture at Bullough III.59.

5 *Richard III* III.ii–iv, cf. Bullough III.262–7 (Shakespeare cuts the violence in the Tower); Bullough V.120–4, 128–32, much condensed in *Julius Caesar* V.ii–v; Bullough V.511–3 and *Coriolanus* I.iv.523ff (the encounter between Coriolanus and Aufidius is fictional); Bullough V.316 and *Antony and Cleopatra* V.ii.3531–87.

6 Bullough IV.466–7, 478 and *Henry VIII* II.iv.1332–9, 1363–5; Bullough IV.483–4 and *Henry VIII* IV.i.2420–2445; Bullough IV.484 and *Henry VIII* V.v.3354–63. Foxe at Bullough IV.488 and *Henry VIII* V.iii.3181. For the dramatisation of *Julius Caesar*, see chapter 1, pp. 23–7.

7 Bullough IV.396 and *Henry V* IV.iv.2435. Quoted: *Henry V* Prologue ll. 25, 18.

8 Bullough III.183 and *3 Henry VI* II.v.1189ff (SD probably authorial); Bullough III.250 and *Richard III* II.i.1222ff (see chapter 4, p. 73); Bullough IV.186 and *1 Henry IV* II.iii.849ff.

9 Bullough III.291, 338–9 and *Richard III* V.iii.3561ff; Bullough V.96 and *Julius Caesar* II.i.953–82 and see chapter 8, p. 144.

10 Bullough IV.467–8 and *Henry VIII* II.iv.1366–1410; Bullough IV.399 –400 and *Henry V* IV.viii.2795–2825; Bullough V.296 and *Antony and Cleopatra* III.vi.1825–1833; Bullough V.539–40 and *Coriolanus* V.iii.3449–3538.

11 Bullough III.280 and *Richard III* IV.ii.2590–4; *Measure for Measure* V.i.2361ff cf. Bullough II.485–6; *Antony and Cleopatra* II.iii.963, III.xi.2048 (SDs probably authorial); *Troilus and Cressida* V.iii.Q:L^v, cf. Bullough VI.205.

12 *Two Gentlemen* IV.ii.1752–3, V.iv.2126–30, cf. Bullough I.244–5. *Richard II* IV.i.2198ff, cf. Bullough III.407.

13 Bullough I.513–4.

14 *Antony and Cleopatra* II.vii.1464ff; quotation from *Promos and Cassandra*, Bullough II.500 (Whetstone's main theme is bribery).

15 *Macbeth* V.iii.2252ff (not in Holinshed, Bullough VII.504–5), III.iv.1299 (SD: *Enter the Ghost of Banquo, and sits in Macbeths place*). Forman's account of the performance he saw is untrustworthy, dovetailing non-Shakespearean details from the sources with the play (see L. Scragg: 'Macbeth on Horseback', *SS* 26 (1973), pp. 81–8), but this can only be remembered from the play: 'The next night, being at supper . . . he began to speake of Noble Banco, and to wish that he wer there. And as he thus did, standing vp to drincke a Carouse to him, the ghoste of Banco came and sate down in his cheier be-hind him. *And he turninge About to sit down Again sawe the goste of banco, which fronted him so* . . .' (My italics. See new Arden ed. *Macbeth* (1969), p. xv).

16 *Winter's Tale* IV.iv.1890–1916, cf. Bullough VIII.181. For Lear, cf. Bullough VII.393, for Gloucester, cf. Bullough VII.405–6. Hermione's death, cf. Bellaria's swoon, Bullough VIII.171. Last quotation: *Winter's Tale* III.ii.1432 (my italics). For *Cymbeline*, see n. 17. *Tempest* has no known narrative source.

17 In *Frederyke of Jennen* Ambrose's wife has no father; her husband's

reaction to her reapperance is not described (Bullough VIII.76). There is no source for Imogen's two deaths, discovered by her brothers, and here.

18 *1 Henry IV* II.ii.Q:C3ᵛ. For some different examples, on the same principle, see J. Shaw: 'The Staging of Parody and Parallels in *1 Henry IV*', *SS* 20 (1967), pp. 61–73.

19 *All's Well* IV.ii.2068ff; not in Painter (who has a ring with no symbolic significance), Bullough II.395.

20 *Hamlet* III.ii.Q2:H2ᵛ (and Q1:F4), IV.iv.Q2:K3 (not in F), V.ii.3581–2 (not in Q2), II.ii.1409ff.

21 On delay: Claudius at *Hamlet* IV.vii.Q2:L4ᵛ (not in F), Player King at III.ii.2054ff (the speech Hamlet wrote?). For the Ophelia-prototype, see Belleforest, Bullough VII.91–2, and the Polonius-prototype *ibid.* 93 –101. Since the manner of Hamlet's death differs from Saxo and Belleforest, the Laertes figure could originate in either the Ur-Hamlet or Shakespeare's play. The girl does not go mad in Saxo or Belleforest.

22 The blinding, Bullough VII.405; the cut murder attempt on Leir and Perillus, *ibid.* 373–80. Lear's madness is most closely related to the Annesley scandal (*ibid.*, 309–11).

23 Divine thunder in *Leir*, Bullough VII.377, 379; the Arcadian story also begins with a storm (*ibid.* 403). For prosaic use of costume in *Leir*, see Bullough VII.352, 386, 391. In *King Lear* II.iv.1584 the first thunder roll suggests the rending of Lear's heart.

24 *Julius Caesar* I.ii.143–6; *Timon* IV.iii.1824–5; *Henry V* IV.vii.2557–8. The same technique is prefigured in the illustrative insets of the mating horses and hunted hare in *Venus and Adonis*, ll. 259ff, 679ff, and Troy picture in the *Rape of Lucrece*, ll. 1366ff. For different recent discussions of the Elizabethan use of subplots, see I-S. Ekeblad: 'The "Impure Art" of John Webster', *RES* (1958), pp. 253–67; R. Levin: 'Elizabethan "Clown" Subplots', *Essays in Criticism* (1966), pp. 84–90, 'The Unity of Elizabethan Multiple-Plot Drama', *ELH* (1967), pp. 425–446, and 'The Elizabethan "Three-Level" Play', *Ren. Dr.* (1969), pp. 23–38; H. Levin: 'The Shakespearean Overplot', *Ren. Dr.* (1965), pp. 63–71; N. Rabkin: 'The Double Plot: Notes on the History of a Convention', *Ren. Dr.* (1964), pp. 55–69. Only in 'Emblems in English Renaissance Drama', *Ren. Dr.* (1969), p. 49, does D. Mehl note that 'sometimes the subplot seems to be a literal application of themes and images suggested in the main plot', but he takes it no further.

25 'Perils of death crept into his secret chamber, and laie lurking in the bed of downe where his bodie was to . . . take rest. Oh what a suspected state therefore is that of a king . . .' (Bullough IV.181).

26 Bullough VII.483–4; *Macbeth* I.v.415–6, I.vii.484.

27 Suggested by the editor, Bullough III.307, 311, notes 2, 3; *Richard III* I.ii.366ff.

28 Quoted: Bullough VI.251 and *Timon* III.vi.1452, 1472, Bullough VI. 265, cf. Boiardo's *Timone*, *ibid.* 280; *Timon* I.ii.381–2. There is no such banquet in any of *Timon*'s clear sources, except the comedy of *Timon*, where his parasites are feasted with '*Stones painted like to*' artichokes (ll. 2065–6). This play is now dated c.1602–3 (see Malone ed. (1980), p.

xiv). The assumption that the masque is an afterthought is based on the contradictions in its presentation (an anticipatory direction ushering in *Maskers of Amazons* is left abandoned, and the real masque that enters several lines later is of *Cupid with the Maske of Ladies* whom he introduces as the 'fiue best Sences' – SDs most probably authorial. I.ii.455ff).

29 Bullough V.86 and *Julius Caesar* III.i.1429–30; Bullough VII.498 and *Macbeth* V.v.2330, 2334, III.vi.1506–8, and see *Hamlet* III.iii.2290ff. For further parallels, see e.g. Macbeth: 'To know my deed, / 'Twere best not know my selfe', and Ross of Scotland: 'Alas poore Countrey, / Almost affraid to know it selfe' (II.ii.737–8, IV.iii.2000–1).

30 Bullough III.403 and *Richard II* III.iii.1766ff; for Froissart see Bullough III.431 (but Shakespeare's source was more probably Daniel's *Civil Wars*, II.119, Bullough III.453–4); *Antony and Cleopatra* IV.iv.2503–22 and IV.xiv.2867ff.

31 Othello's fit may come from Fenton's Bandello (Bullough VII.259), to which the play's last act has greater affinities than to Cinthio's *Hecatommithi*. I cannot understand why Max Bluestone should say: 'In addition to the source, Othello wounds Iago, receives tactile proof that Iago is no devil, and thus takes on a greater measure of responsibility for the catastrophe, since Iago has no special diabolic advantage over Othello' (*From Story to Stage* (The Hague, 1974), pp. 123–4). S. L. Bethell: 'The Diabolic Images in *Othello*', *SS* 5 (1952), pp. 77–8, does not go so far as to see this as a staged corroboration of the play's linguistic suggestions.

32 *Antony and Cleopatra* I.i.13–6.

33 *Venus and Adonis* ll. 527–8 and 'Ripeness is all', l. 567 and *All's Well*, ll. 1021–4 and *Othello; Rape of Lucrece* ll. 31–2 and Posthumus of Imogen in *Cymbeline*, ll. 148–53 and *Macbeth*, l. 279 and *Troilus and Cressida* II.ii.1049–50, ll. 537–9 and *Hamlet* I.iv.Q2:D (not in F), etc.

34 E. A. Armstrong: *Shakespeare's Imagination*, (Lincoln, USA, 1965), p. 158, and *Love's Labour's Lost* III.i.Q:D; G. Wilson Knight: *The Crown of Life* (1947), p. 98 and *King Lear* III.iv.1789–91. Fawnia is set adrift in a storm, but washed ashore and found in a calm, and *Pandosto* has no bear and no Antigonus.

35 *Richard II* III.iv.1839ff; *Henry V* V.ii.3023–49 (and Epilogue 3374); *Hamlet* I.ii.Q2:C, and for some street tableaux on the same principles, see D. M. Bergeron: *English Civic Pageantry* (1971), p. 19.

36 *Richard II* IV.i.2210–2 and *Measure for Measure* II.iv.1135–7.

37 *Hamlet* III.ii.1996, 2131, *Othello* II.iii.Q:F3ᵛ; *Hamlet* V.ii.Q2:O and *Macbeth* I.vi.484–6; *Othello* V.ii.3239ff and *Macbeth* V.v.2344.

38 *More* (D) ll. 207–10 and *Pericles* II.i.Q:C2. Donne elaborates exactly the same emblem in *Progresse of the Soul*, st. xxxiii, and F. P. Wilson says the image is one of common life, comparing *The Pride of Life*, where men 'farit as fiscis in a pol / The gret eteit the smal' ('Shakespeare's Reading', *Shakespearian and other Studies* (Oxford, 1969), p. 141).

39 *Hamlet* III.iii.Q2:I and *Macbeth* V.i.2120ff; *King John* III.iv.1420–3; *King Lear* I.i.46.

40 *2 Henry IV* Induction Q:A2; *As You Like It* IV.iii.2216–8; *Hamlet* III.ii.Q2:G4ᵛ, Q2:H4; *Othello* II.i.Q:Eᵛ and III.i.

41 *As You Like It* II.vii.1156–7; *King Lear* III.ii.1671; *Timon* III.iv.1225, 1227.
42 T. S. Eliot: 'John Ford', *Selected Essays* (1966), p. 203.
43 *Edward II* IV.vii.29ff.
44 *Bartholomew Fair* IV.i.34; *Volpone* I.ii.6–23, V.iv, I.ii.97, V.v.1, and cf. *King Lear* III.iv.1873.
45 *Every Man In his Humour* (1616) III.i.103–5, V.v.31–5, Jonson's italics.
46 *A Woman Killed with Kindness* IV.21–3, XVII.78, XIII.124, XVI.30, and see also XIII.62. For Webster, see my brief essay, 'Moral Ambiguities', *TES* (21.9.73), p. 55.
47 Bullough II.486–7, and for several instances of the normal practice, see Bergeron: *op. cit.* pp. 15, 19, 25, etc.
48 *A Short View of Tragedy, Works*, p. 86. Last quotation from *Venus and Adonis*, l. 359.

Bibliography

Adams, J. C.	*The Globe Playhouse* (Cambridge, Mass. 1943)
Anon.	*Arden of Feversham* (Malone Society Reprint, 1940)
Anon.	*Edward III* (Tudor Facsimile Texts, 1910)
Anon.	*Tarltons Jests* (1638)
Anon.	*The First Part of Richard II*, or *Thomas of Woodstock* (Malone Society Reprint, 1929)
Anon.	*The Three Parnassus Plays (1598–1601)*, ed. J. B. Leishman (1949)
Anon.	*The World and the Child* (Tudor Facsimile Texts, 1909)
Anon.	*A Yorkshire Tragedy* (Tudor Facsimile Texts, 1910)
Armstrong, E. A.	*Shakespeare's Imagination* (Lincoln, USA 1965)
Bayne, Rev. R.	'Religion', *Shakespeare's England*, 2 vols (Oxford 1916), I. 48–78
Bergeron, D. M.	'The Emblematic Nature of English Civic Pageantry', *Ren. Dr.* (1968), pp. 167–98.
Bergeron, D. M.	*English Civic Pageantry, 1558–1642* (1971)
Berry, R.	*Shakespeare's Comedies, Explorations in Form* (Princeton 1972)
Berry, R.	*On Directing Shakespeare* (1977)
Berry, R.	*The Shakespearean Metaphor* (1978)
Bethell, S. L.	'Shakespeare's Actors', *RES* (1950), pp. 193–205
Bethell, S. L.	'Shakespeare's Imagery: The Diabolic Images in *Othello*', *SS* 5 (1952), pp. 62–80
Bluestone, M.	*From Story to Stage* (The Hague, 1974)
[Boswell, J.]	*Boswell's Life of Johnson*, ed. G. B. Hill and L. F. Powell, 6 vols (Oxford 1934–50)
Bowers, F.	*On Editing Shakespeare and the Elizabethan Dramatists* (Pennsylvania 1955)
Bradbrook, M. C.	*Elizabethan Stage Conditions* (repr. Hamden, Connecticut 1962)

Bradbrook, M. C.   *Shakespeare and Elizabethan Poetry* (1951)

Bradbrook, M. C.   *Shakespeare the Craftsman* (1969)

Bradbrook, M. C.   'Shakespeare's Primitive Art', *Proceedings of the British Academy 1965* (1966), pp. 215–34.

Bradbrook, M. C.   *Themes and Conventions of Elizabethan Tragedy* (Cambridge 1935)

Bradley, A. C.   *Oxford Lectures on Poetry* (repr. 1941)

Bradley, A. C.   *Shakespearean Tragedy* (repr. 1952)

Brown, J. R.   *Shakespeare's Plays in Performance* (Harmondsworth 1969)

Brown, J. R.   'The Study and Practice of Shakespeare Production', *SS* 18 (1965), pp. 58–69

Bullough, G. ed.   *Narrative and Dramatic Sources of Shakespeare*, 8 vols (1957–75)

Carlisle, C. J.   *Shakespeare from the Greenroom* (Chapel Hill 1969)

Castiglione, B.   *The Book of the Courtier*, trans. Sir T. Hoby (Everyman 1959)

Chambers, E. K.   *The Elizabethan Stage*, 4 vols (Oxford 1923)

Chambers, E. K.   *William Shakespeare, A Study of Facts and Problems*, 2 vols (Oxford 1930)

Charney, M.   'Hamlet without Words', *ELH* 32 (1965), pp. 457–77

Charney, M.   *Shakespeare's Roman Plays* (1960)

Charney, M.   'Shakespeare's Unpoetic Poetry', *Studies in English Literature* (1973), pp. 199–207

Coghill, N.   'The Basis of Shakespearian Comedy', *E & S* (1950), pp. 1–28

Coghill, N.   'Comic Form in *Measure for Measure*', *SS* 8 (1955), pp. 14–27

Coghill, N.   'Shakespeare as a Dramatist', *Talking of Shakespeare*, ed. J. Garrett (1954), pp. 23–47

Coghill, N.   *Shakespeare's Professional Skills* (Cambridge 1964)

Coleridge, S. T.   *Biographia Literaria*, ed. G. Watson (Everyman 1962)

Coleridge, S. T.   *Shakespearean Criticism*, ed. T. M Raysor, 2 vols (Everyman 1964)

Copley, A.   *Wits fittes and fancies* (1595)

Craik, T. W.   *The Tudor Interlude* (Leicester 1958)

Dekker, T.   *Dramatic Works*, ed. F. Bowers, 4 vols (Cambridge 1953–61)

Dekker, T.   *Non-Dramatic Works*, ed. A. B. Grosart, 5 vols (New York 1963)

Dessen, A. C. — 'Hamlet's Poisoned Sword: A Study in Dramatic Imagery', *Shk. Studies* (1969), pp. 53–69

Doebler, J. — *Shakespeare's Speaking Pictures, Studies in Iconic Imagery* (Albuquerque 1974)

Donne, J. — *Poems*, ed. H. J. C. Grierson, 2 vols (Oxford, repr. 1953)

Ekeblad, I-S. — 'The "Impure Art" of John Webster', *RES* (1958), pp. 253–67

Eliot, T. S. — *Selected Essays* (repr. 1966)

Elyot, Sir T. — *The Boke named The Gouernour*, ed. H. H. S. Croft, 2 vols (1880)

Ewbank, I-S. — 'More Pregnantly than Words', *SS* 24 (1971), pp. 13–18

Ewbank, I-S. — *Shakespeare, Ibsen and the Unspeakable* (1976)

Flatter, R. — *Shakespeare's Producing Hand* (1948)

Fletcher, J. — *Bonduca* (Malone Society Reprint, 1951)

Foakes, R. A. — 'The Player's Passion', *E & S* (1954), pp. 62–77

Foakes, R. A. — 'Suggestions for a New Approach to Shakespeare's Imagery', *SS* 5 (1952), p. 81–92

Ford, J. — *Works*, ed. W. Gifford, re-issued with additions by Rev. A. Dyce, 3 vols (1895)

Freeman, R. — *English Emblem Books* (1948)

Gardner, H. — *Religion and Literature* (1971)

[Gawdy, P.] — *Letters of Philip Gawdy*, ed. I. H. Jeayes (1906)

Gellert, B. — 'The Iconography of Melancholy in the Graveyard Scene of Hamlet', *S. Phil.* (1970), pp. 57–66

Golden, M. H. — 'stage imagery', *A Shakespeare Encyclopaedia*, ed. O. J. Campbell and E. G. Quinn (1974), pp. 819–20

Golden, M. H. — 'Stage Imagery in Shakespearean Studies', *SRO* (1965), pp. 10–20.

Granville-Barker, H. — *Prefaces to Shakespeare*, collected into 1 vol (1972)

Green, Rev. H. — *Shakespeare and the Emblem Writers* (1870)

Greg, W. W. — *Dramatic Documents from the Elizabethan Playhouses*, 2 vols (Oxford 1931)

Greg, W. W. — *The Shakespeare First Folio* (Oxford, repr. 1969)

Gurr, A. J.   'Elizabethan Action', *S. Phil.* (1966), pp. 144–56

Gurr, A.   *The Shakespearean Stage, 1574–1642* (Cambridge 1970)

Gurr, A. J.   'Who Strutted and Bellowed?', *SS* 16 (1963), pp. 95–102

Haaker, A.   'Non Sine Causa: The Use of Emblematic Method and Iconology in the Thematic Structure of *Titus Andronicus*', *RORD* (1970–1), pp. 143–68

Harbage, A.   'Elizabethan Acting', *PMLA* (1939), pp. 685–708

Hasler, J.   *Shakespeare's Theatrical Notation* (Bern 1957)

Heckscher, W. S.   'Shakespeare in His Relationship to the Visual Arts', *RORD* (1970–1), pp. 5–71

[Henslowe, P.]   *Henslowe's Diary*, ed. R. A. Foakes and R. T. Rickert (Cambridge 1961)

Heywood, T.   *Apology for Actors*, ed. J. P. Collier (Shakespeare Society 1841)

Heywood, T.   *A Woman Killed with Kindness*, ed. R. W. van Fossen (1961)

Heywood, T.   *The Dramatic Works*, 6 vols (1874)

Hosley, R.   'The Discovery-space in Shakespeare's Globe', *SS* 12 (1959), pp. 35–46

Hosley, R.   'The Gallery over the Stage in the Public Playhouse of Shakespeare's Time', *SQ* (1957), pp. 15–31

Hosley, R.   'Shakespeare's Use of a Gallery over the Stage', *SS* 10 (1957), pp. 77–89

Hosley, R.   'The Staging of Desdemona's Bed', *SQ* (1963), pp. 57–65

Hosley, R.   'The playhouses and the stage', *A New Companion to Shakespeare Studies*, ed. K. Muir and S. Schoenbaum (Cambridge 1971), pp. 15–34

Hosley, R.   'The Use of the Upper Stage in *Romeo and Juliet*', *SQ* (1954), pp. 371–9

Hosley, R.   'Was there a Music-room in Shakespeare's Globe?', *SS* 13 (1960) pp. 113–23

Ingram, W.   'Enter Macduffe; with Macbeth's Head', *Theatre Notebook* (Oct. 1971), pp. 75–7

[Johnson, S.]   *Johnson on Shakespeare*, ed. A. Sherbo, 2 vols (Yale 1968. Vols VII and VIII in *The Yale Edition of the Works of Samuel Johnson*, 1958–)

Jones, D. E.   *The Plays of T. S. Eliot* (1969)
[Jonson, B.]   *Ben Jonson*, ed. C. H. Herford and P. and E.
                           Simpson, 11 vols (Oxford 1925–52)
Joseph, B. L.   *Elizabethan Acting* (2nd ed. Oxford 1964)
King, T. J.   *Shakespearean Staging, 1599–1642* (Cam-
                           bridge, Mass. 1971)
Klein, D.   'Did Shakespeare Produce His Own Plays?',
                           MLR (1962), pp. 556–60
Klein, D.   'Elizabethan Acting', *PMLA* (1956), pp.
                           280–2
Knight, G. W.   *Shakespearean Production* (1964)
Knight, G. W.   *The Wheel of Fire* (repr. 1965)
Kyd, T.   *The Spanish Tragedy (1592)* (Malone Society
                           Reprint, 1948)
Kyd, T.   *The Spanish Tragedy (1602)* (Malone Society
                           Reprint, 1925)
Levenson, J.   'What the Silence Said: Still Points in *King
                           Lear*', *Shakespeare 1971*, ed. C. Leech and
                           J. M. R. Margeson (University of Toronto
                           Press, 1972), pp. 215–229
Levin, H.   'The Shakespearean Overplot', *Ren. Dr.*
                           (1965), pp. 63–71
Levin, R.   'Elizabethan "Clown" Subplots', *Essays in
                           Criticism* (1966), pp. 84–90
Levin, R.   'The Unity of Elizabethan Multiple-Plot
                           Drama', *ELH* (1967), pp. 425–46
Levin, R.   'The Elizabethan "Three-level" Play', *Ren.
                           Dr.* (1969), pp. 23–38
Linthicum, M. C.   *Costume in the Drama of Shakespeare and his
                           Contemporaries* (Oxford 1936)
Lyons, B. G.   'The Iconography of Ophelia', *ELH* (1977),
                           pp. 60–74
Lyons, C.   'Stage Imagery in Shakespeare's Plays',
                           *Essays on Shakespeare and Elizabethan Drama
                           in Honour of Hardin Craig*, ed. R. Hosley
                           (1963), pp. 261–74
Mahood, M. M.   *Shakespeare's Wordplay* (1957)
Marlowe, C.   *Complete Works*, ed. F. Bowers, 2 vols
                           (Cambridge 1973)
Matchett, W. H.   'Some Dramatic Techniques in *The Winter's
                           Tale*', *SS* 22 (1969), pp. 93–107
Medwall, H.   *Nature* (Tudor Facsimile Texts, 1908)
Mehl, D.   *The Elizabethan Dumb Show* (1965)
Mehl, D.   'Visual   and   Rhetorical   Imagery   in

	Shakespeare's Plays', *E&S* (1972), pp. 83–100
Mehl, D.	'Emblematic Theatre', *Anglia* (1977), pp. 130–138
Mehl, D.	'Emblematik im englischen Drama der Shakespearezeit', *Anglia* (1969), pp. 126–46
Mehl, D.	'Emblems in English Renaissance Drama', *Ren. Dr.* (1969), pp. 39–57
Middleton, T. and Rowley, W.	*The Changeling*, ed. N. W. Bawcutt (1961)
Montaigne, M. E. de	*Essays*, trans. J. Florio, ed. L. C. Harmer, 3 vols (Everyman 1965)
Muir, K.	*Shakespeare the Professional* (1973)
Nashe, T.	*Works*, ed. R. B. McKerrow, repr. with corrections by F. P. Wilson, 5 vols (Oxford 1958)
Nichol Smith, D. ed.	*Eighteenth Century Essays on Shakespeare* (Oxford 1963)
Nichol Smith, D.	*Shakespeare Criticism, A Selection 1623–1840* (1964)
Noble, R.	*Shakespeare's Biblical Knowledge* (1935)
North, Sir T.	trans. *Plutarch's Lives*, 10 vols (1899)
Peacham, H.	*The Compleat Gentleman* (Tudor and Stuart Library, Oxford 1906)
Poel, W.	*Shakespeare in the Theatre* (1913)
Poel, W.	*Some Notes on Shakespeare's Stage and Players* (Manchester 1916)
Rabkin, N.	'The Double Plot: Notes on the History of a Convention', *Ren. Dr.* (1964), pp. 55–69
Reynolds, G. F.	'Some Principles of Elizabethan Staging, I', *M.Phil.* II (1904–5), pp. 581–614
Reynolds, G. F.	'Some Principles of Elizabethan Staging, II', *M.Phil.* III (1905–6), pp. 69–97.
Reynolds, G. F.	*The Staging of Elizabethan Plays at the Red Bull Theater* (New York 1940)
Rosenberg, M.	'Elizabethan Actors: Men or Marionettes?' *PMLA* (1954), pp. 915–27
Ross, L. J.	'The Meaning of Strawberries in Shakespeare', *Studies in the Renaissance* (1960), pp. 225–40
Ross, L. J.	'Shakespeare's "Dull Clown" and Symbolic Music', *SQ* (1966), pp. 107–28
Routh, C. R. N.	'The Pyrrhus Speech in *Hamlet*', *TLS* (Aug 5 1944), p. 379

Rymer, T. *The Critical Works of Thomas Rymer*, ed. C. A. Zimansky (New Haven 1956)

Schuman, S. 'Emblems and the English Renaissance Drama: A Checklist', *RORD* (1969), pp. 43–56

Seltzer, D. 'The Actors and Staging', *A New Companion to Shakespeare Studies*, ed. K. Muir and S. Schoenbaum (Cambridge 1971), pp. 35–54

[Shaw, G. B.] *Shaw on Shakespeare*, ed. E. Wilson (Harmondsworth 1969)

Sicherman, C. M. '*Coriolanus*: The Failure of Words', *ELH* (1972), pp. 189–207

Sidney, Sir P. *Poems*, ed. W. A. Ringler (Oxford 1962)

Skelton, J *Poetical Works*, ed. Rev. A. Dyce, 2 vols (1843)

Smith, W. D. 'Stage Business in Shakespeare's Dialogue', *SQ* (1953), pp. 311–16

Southern, R. *The Staging of Plays before Shakespeare* (1973)

Spencer, T. J. B. 'Shakespeare and the Elizabethan Romans', *SS* 10 (1957), pp. 27–38

Spurgeon, C. F. E. *Shakespeare's Imagery* (Cambridge, repr. 1965)

Stamm, R. *Shakespeare's Word Scenery* (Zurich and St Galen, 1954)

Stamm, R. *The Shaping Powers at Work* (Heidelberg 1967)

Stamm, R. 'Elizabethan Stage Practice and the Transmutation of Source Material', *SS* 12 (1959), pp. 64–70

Steadman, J. M. 'Falstaff as Actaeon: A Dramatic Emblem', *SQ* (1963), pp. 231–44

Steadman, J. M. 'Iconography and Renaissance Drama: Ethical and Mythological Themes', *RORD* (1970–1), pp. 73–122

Steadman, J. M. 'Iconography and Methodology in Renaissance and Dramatic Study: Some Caveats', *SRO* (1972–4), pp. 38–52

Stoppard, T. *The Real Inspector Hound* (2nd ed, 1970)

Styan, J. L. *Shakespeare's Stagecraft* (Cambridge 1967)

Thaler, A. *Shakespeare's Silences* (Cambridge, Mass. 1929)

Thorp, M. F.	'Shakespeare and the Fine Arts', *PMLA* (1931), pp. 672–93
Tilley, M. P.	*A Dictionary of Proverbs in England in the Sixteenth and Seventeenth Centuries* (Michigan 1950)
Tolstoy, L.	'Shakespeare and the Drama', *Recollections and Essays*, ed. A. Maude (1961)
Tourneur, C.	*The Revenger's Tragedy*, ed. R. A. Foakes (1966)
Underhill, A.	'Law', *Shakespeare's England*, 2 vols (Oxford 1916), I.381–412
Venezky, A. S.	*Pageantry on the Shakespearean Stage* (New York 1951)
Waddington, R. B.	'Antony and Cleopatra: "What Venus did with Mars"', *Shk. Studies* (1966), pp. 210–27
Watkins, R.	*On Producing Shakespeare* (1950)
Watkins, R. and Lemmon, J.	*The Poet's Method* (1974)
Webster, J.	*The Complete Works*, ed. F. L. Lucas, 4 vols (1927)
Wells, S.	*Literature and Drama* (1970)
Wickham, G.	*Early English Stages*, 2 vols, the second published in two parts (1959–72)
Wilson, F. P. (reviser)	*The Oxford Dictionary of English Proverbs* (Oxford 1970)
Wilson, F. P.	*Shakespearian and Other Studies*, ed. H. Gardner (Oxford 1969)

Index

II
Topics

III
Authors